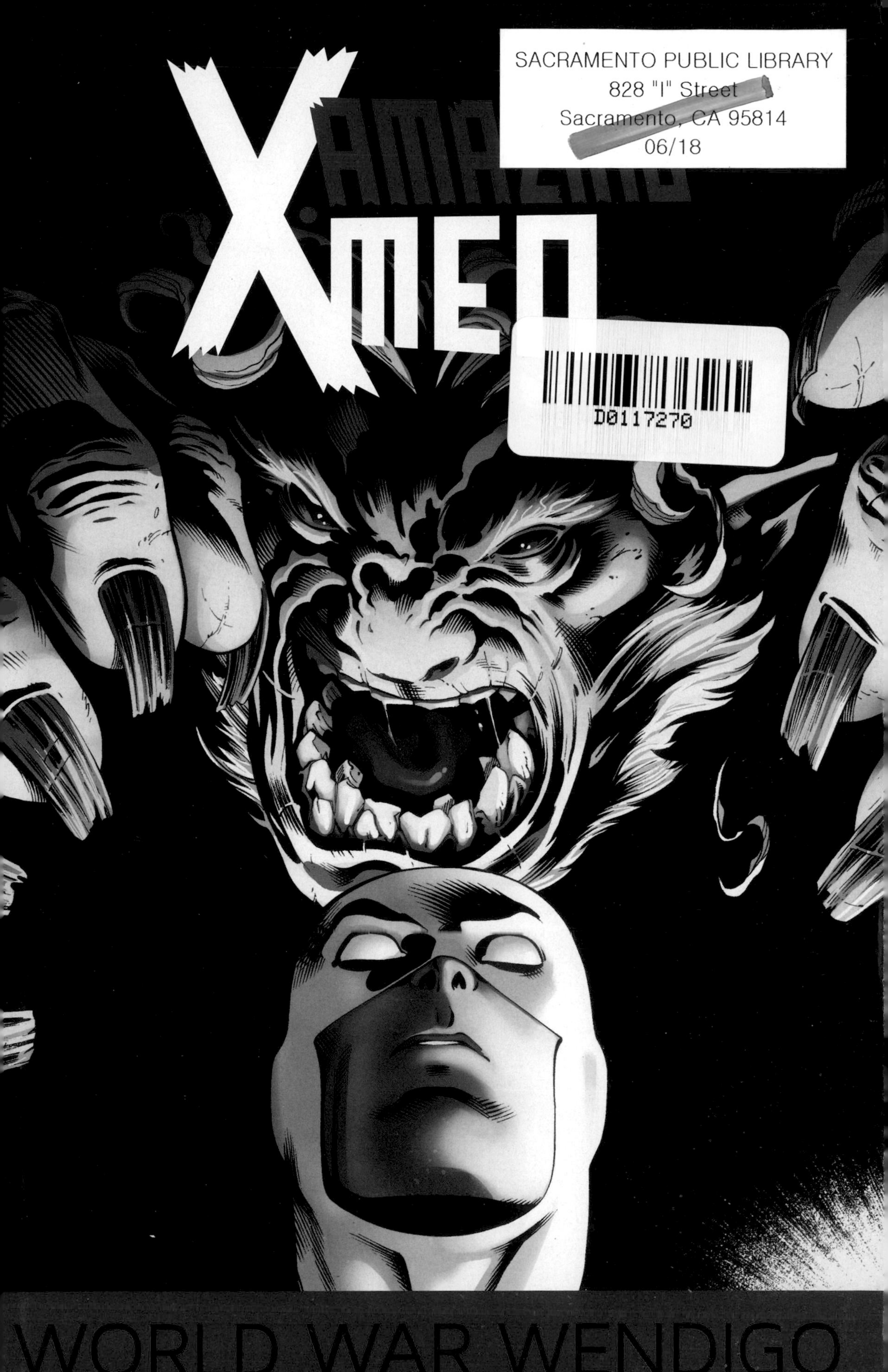

Amazing X-Men

WORLD WAR WENDIGO

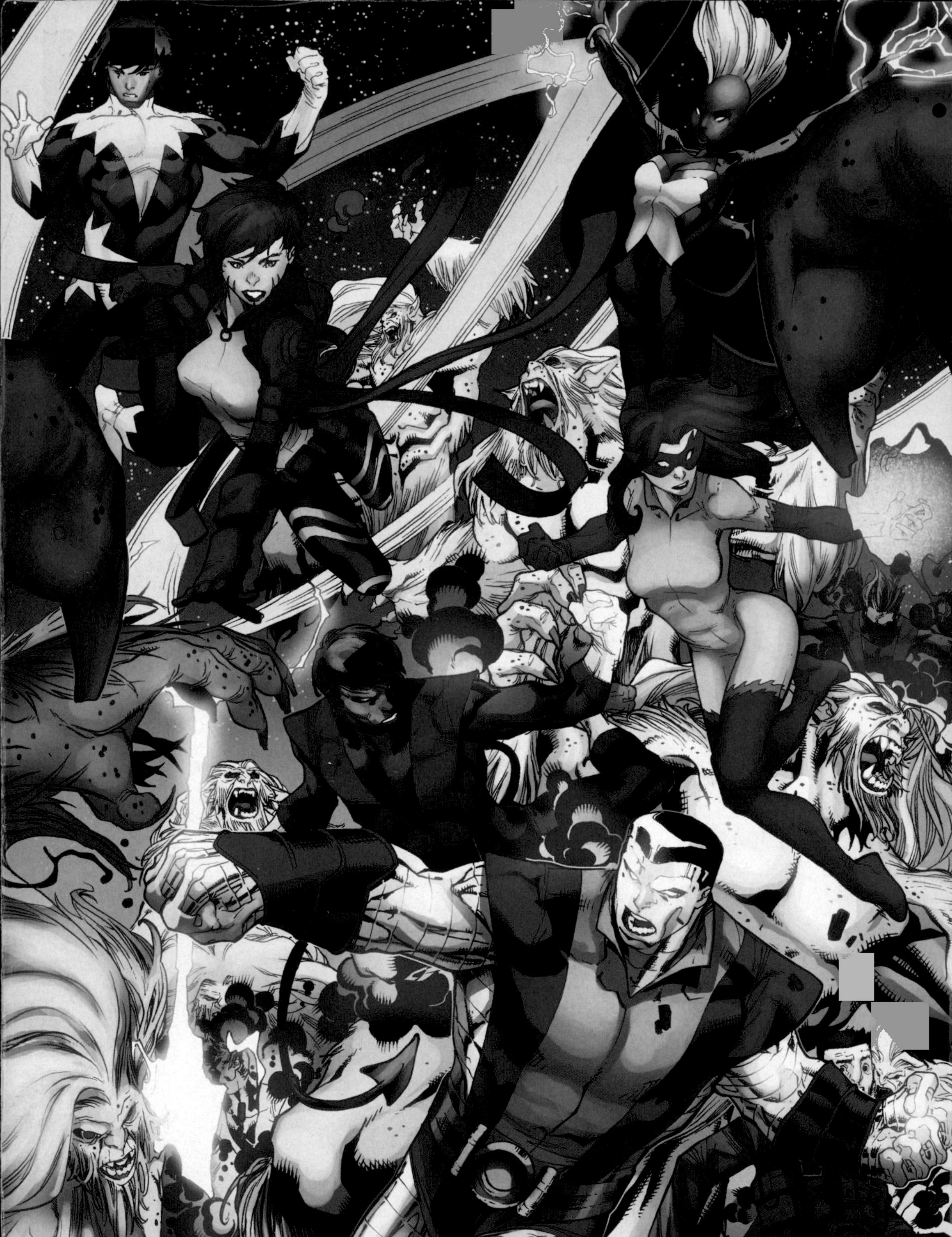

WORLD WAR WENDIGO

AMAZING X-MEN

ISSUE #7

KATHRYN **IMMONEN** — **WRITER**
PACO **MEDINA** — **PENCILER**
JUAN **VLASCO** — **INKER**
RACHELLE **ROSENBERG** — **COLORIST**

ISSUES #8-12

CRAIG **KYLE** & CHRIS **YOST**
WRITERS

ED **McGUINNESS**
PENCILER, #8

MARK **FARMER**
INKER, #8

CARLO **BARBERI**
WITH IBAN COELLO (#10 & #12)
PENCILERS, #9-12

WALDEN **WONG**
WITH DAVID MEIKIS (#9), CARLO BARBERI (#9),
IBAN COELLO (#10 & #12), MARC DEERING (#11-12),
JUAN VLASCO (#11) & LIVESAY (#12)
INKERS, #9-12

RACHELLE **ROSENBERG**
COLORIST

LETTERER: JOE CARAMAGNA
COVER ART: KRIS ANKA & CHRIS SOTOMAYOR (#7),
ED McGUINNESS & MARTE GRACIA (#8-9)
AND CARLO BARBERI & RACHELLE ROSENBERG (#10-12)
ASSISTANT EDITORS: XANDER JAROWEY & FRANKIE JOHNSON
EDITORS: NICK LOWE & MIKE MARTS

X-MEN CREATED BY STAN LEE & JACK KIRBY

COLLECTION EDITOR: JENNIFER GRÜNWALD ASSISTANT EDITOR: SARAH BRUNSTAD
ASSOCIATE MANAGING EDITOR: ALEX STARBUCK EDITOR, SPECIAL PROJECTS: MARK D. BEAZLEY
SENIOR EDITOR, SPECIAL PROJECTS: JEFF YOUNGQUIST SVP PRINT, SALES & MARKETING: DAVID GABRIEL

EDITOR IN CHIEF: AXEL ALONSO CHIEF CREATIVE OFFICER: JOE QUESADA
PUBLISHER: DAN BUCKLEY EXECUTIVE PRODUCER: ALAN FINE

AMAZING X-MEN VOL. 2: WORLD WAR WENDIGO. Contains material originally published in magazine form as AMAZING X-MEN #7-12. First printing 2014. ISBN# 978-0-7851-8822-3. Published by MARVEL WORLDWIDE, INC., a subsidiary of MARVEL ENTERTAINMENT, LLC. OFFICE OF PUBLICATION: 135 West 50th Street, New York, NY 10020. Copyright © 2014 Marvel Characters, Inc. All rights reserved. All characters featured in this issue and the distinctive names and likenesses thereof, and all related indicia are trademarks of Marvel Characters, Inc. No similarity between any of the names, characters, persons, and/or institutions in this magazine with those of any living or dead person or institution is intended, and any such similarity which may exist is purely coincidental. **Printed in Canada.** ALAN FINE, EVP - Office of the President, Marvel Worldwide, Inc. and EVP & CMO Marvel Characters B.V.; DAN BUCKLEY, Publisher & President - Print, Animation & Digital Divisions; JOE QUESADA, Chief Creative Officer; TOM BREVOORT, SVP of Publishing; DAVID BOGART, SVP of Operations & Procurement, Publishing; C.B. CEBULSKI, SVP of Creator & Content Development; DAVID GABRIEL, SVP Print, Sales & Marketing; JIM O'KEEFE, VP of Operations & Logistics; DAN CARR, Executive Director of Publishing Technology; SUSAN CRESPI, Editorial Operations Manager; ALEX MORALES, Publishing Operations Manager; STAN LEE, Chairman Emeritus. For information regarding advertising in Marvel Comics or on Marvel.com, please contact Niza Disla, Director of Marvel Partnerships, at ndisla@marvel.com. For Marvel subscription inquiries, please call 800-217-9158. **Manufactured between 10/31/2014 and 12/8/2014 by SOLISCO PRINTERS, SCOTT, QC, CANADA.**

10 9 8 7 6 5 4 3 2 1

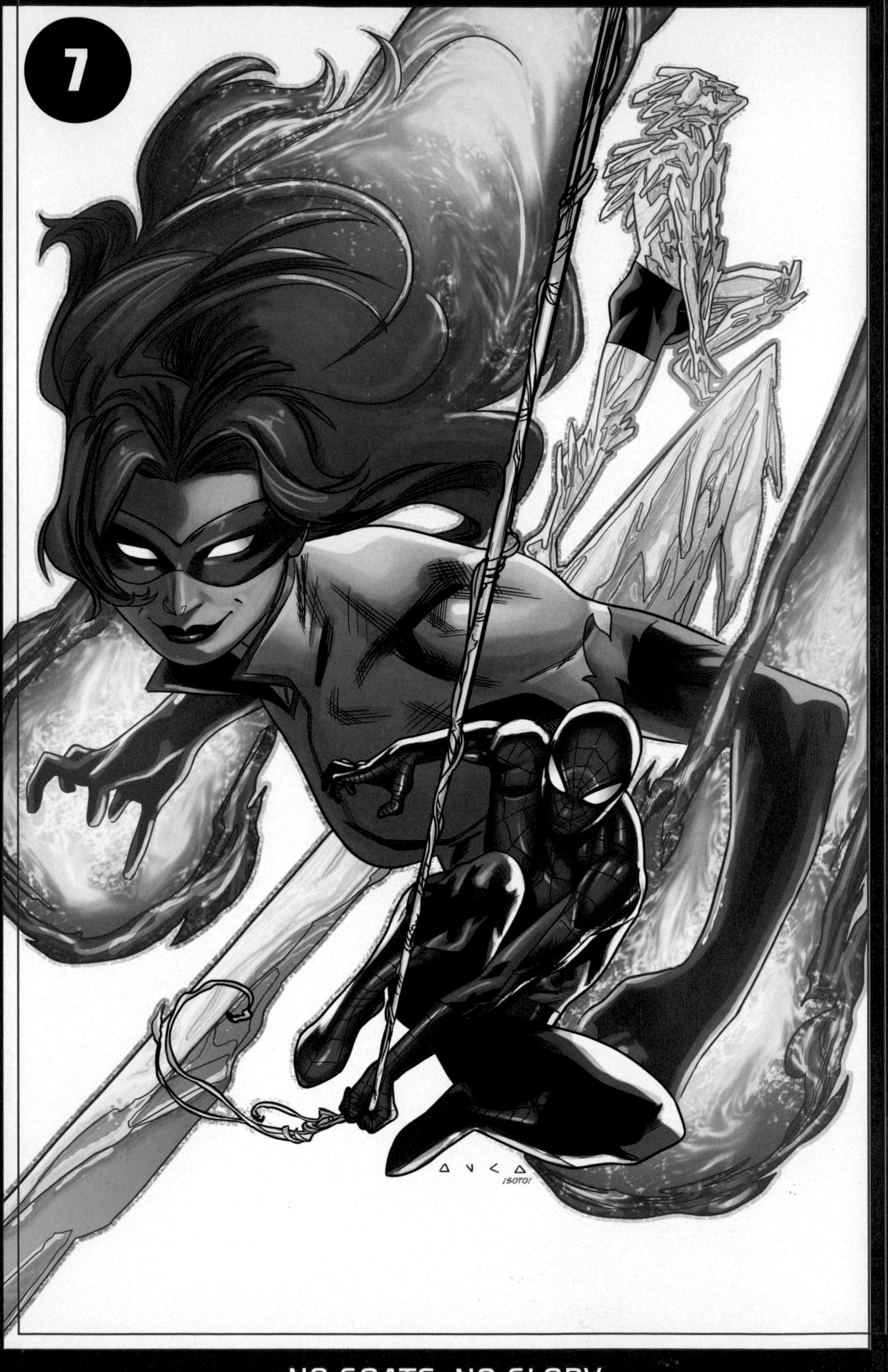
7
¡SOTO!

NO GOATS, NO GLORY

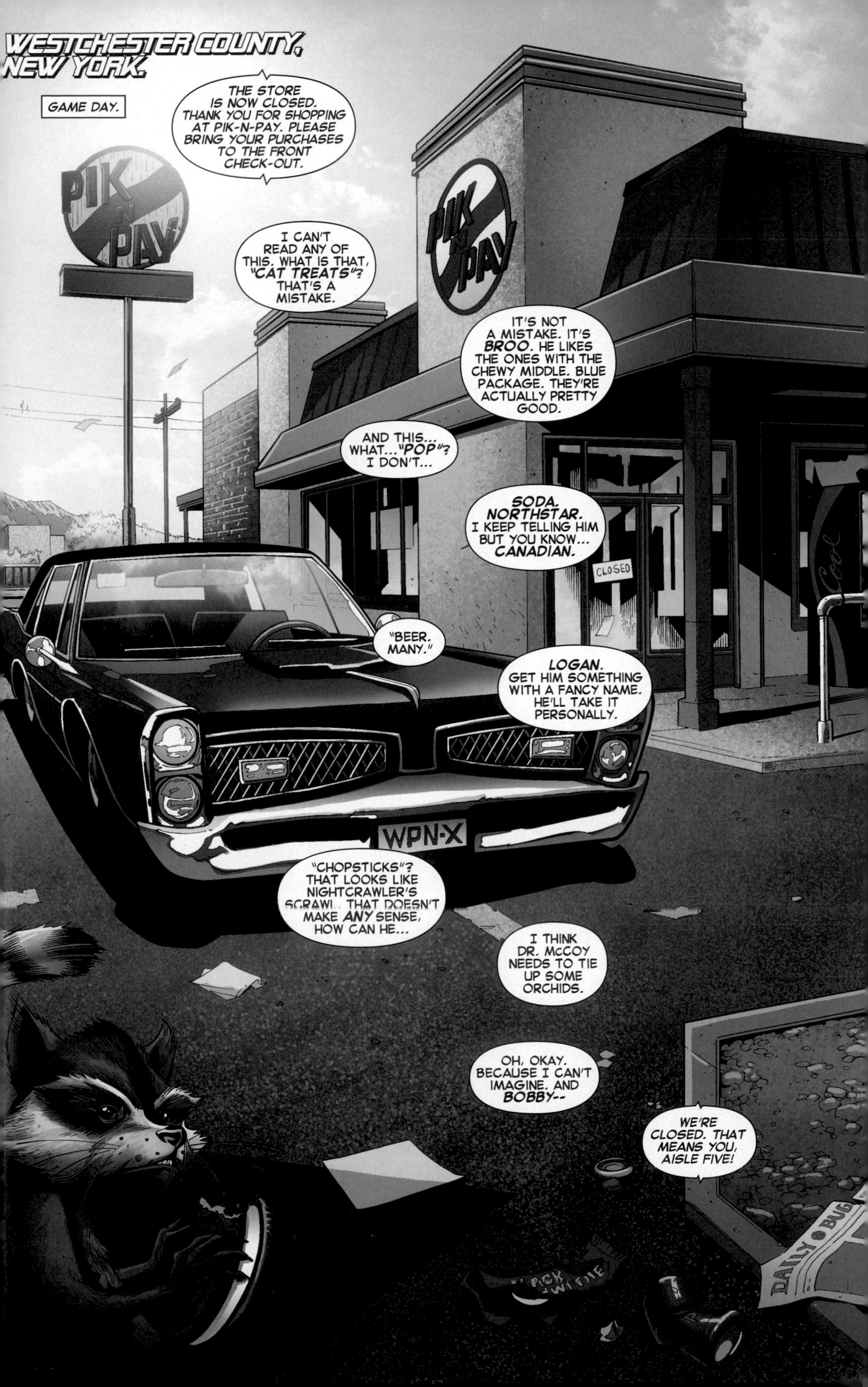
WESTCHESTER COUNTY, NEW YORK.
GAME DAY.
THE STORE IS NOW CLOSED. THANK YOU FOR SHOPPING AT PIK-N-PAY. PLEASE BRING YOUR PURCHASES TO THE FRONT CHECK-OUT.
PIK N PAY
I CAN'T READ ANY OF THIS. WHAT IS THAT, "CAT TREATS"? THAT'S A MISTAKE.
IT'S NOT A MISTAKE. IT'S BROO. HE LIKES THE ONES WITH THE CHEWY MIDDLE. BLUE PACKAGE. THEY'RE ACTUALLY PRETTY GOOD.
AND THIS... WHAT... "POP"? I DON'T...
SODA. NORTHSTAR. I KEEP TELLING HIM BUT YOU KNOW... CANADIAN.
CLOSED
"BEER. MANY."
LOGAN. GET HIM SOMETHING WITH A FANCY NAME. HE'LL TAKE IT PERSONALLY.
WPN-X
"CHOPSTICKS"? THAT LOOKS LIKE NIGHTCRAWLER'S SCRAWL. THAT DOESN'T MAKE ANY SENSE. HOW CAN HE...
I THINK DR. McCOY NEEDS TO TIE UP SOME ORCHIDS.
OH, OKAY. BECAUSE I CAN'T IMAGINE. AND BOBBY--
WE'RE CLOSED. THAT MEANS YOU, AISLE FIVE!

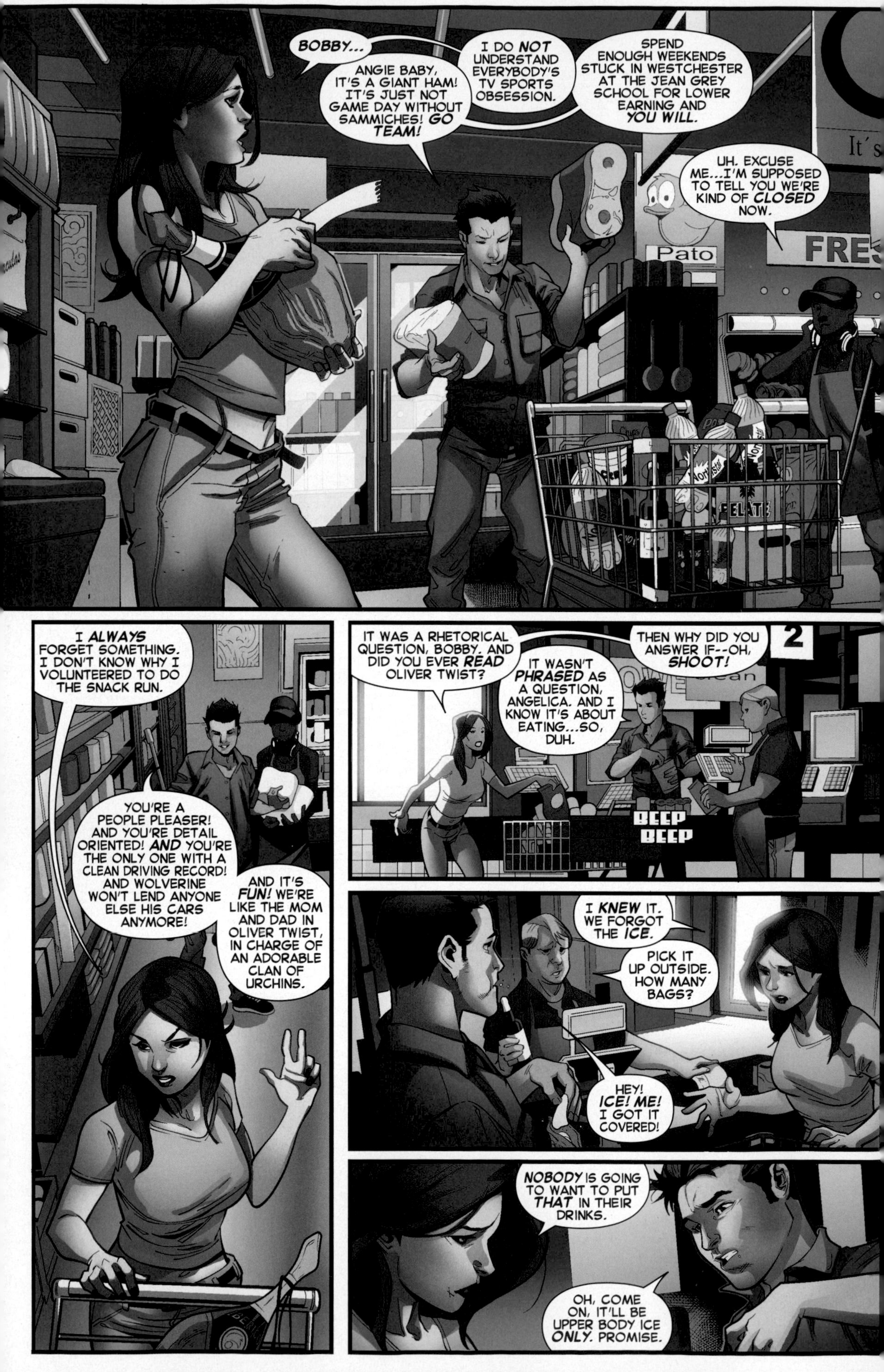
BOBBY...
ANGIE BABY, IT'S A GIANT HAM! IT'S JUST NOT GAME DAY WITHOUT SAMMICHES! GO TEAM!
I DO NOT UNDERSTAND EVERYBODY'S TV SPORTS OBSESSION.
SPEND ENOUGH WEEKENDS STUCK IN WESTCHESTER AT THE JEAN GREY SCHOOL FOR LOWER EARNING AND YOU WILL.
UH. EXCUSE ME...I'M SUPPOSED TO TELL YOU WE'RE KIND OF CLOSED NOW.
Pato
FRES
I ALWAYS FORGET SOMETHING. I DON'T KNOW WHY I VOLUNTEERED TO DO THE SNACK RUN.
YOU'RE A PEOPLE PLEASER! AND YOU'RE DETAIL ORIENTED! AND YOU'RE THE ONLY ONE WITH A CLEAN DRIVING RECORD! AND WOLVERINE WON'T LEND ANYONE ELSE HIS CARS ANYMORE!
AND IT'S FUN! WE'RE LIKE THE MOM AND DAD IN OLIVER TWIST, IN CHARGE OF AN ADORABLE CLAN OF URCHINS.
IT WAS A RHETORICAL QUESTION, BOBBY. AND DID YOU EVER READ OLIVER TWIST?
IT WASN'T PHRASED AS A QUESTION, ANGELICA. AND I KNOW IT'S ABOUT EATING...SO, DUH.
THEN WHY DID YOU ANSWER IF--OH, SHOOT!
2
BEEP BEEP
I KNEW IT. WE FORGOT THE ICE.
PICK IT UP OUTSIDE. HOW MANY BAGS?
HEY! ICE! ME! I GOT IT COVERED!
NOBODY IS GOING TO WANT TO PUT THAT IN THEIR DRINKS.
OH, COME ON, IT'LL BE UPPER BODY ICE ONLY. PROMISE.

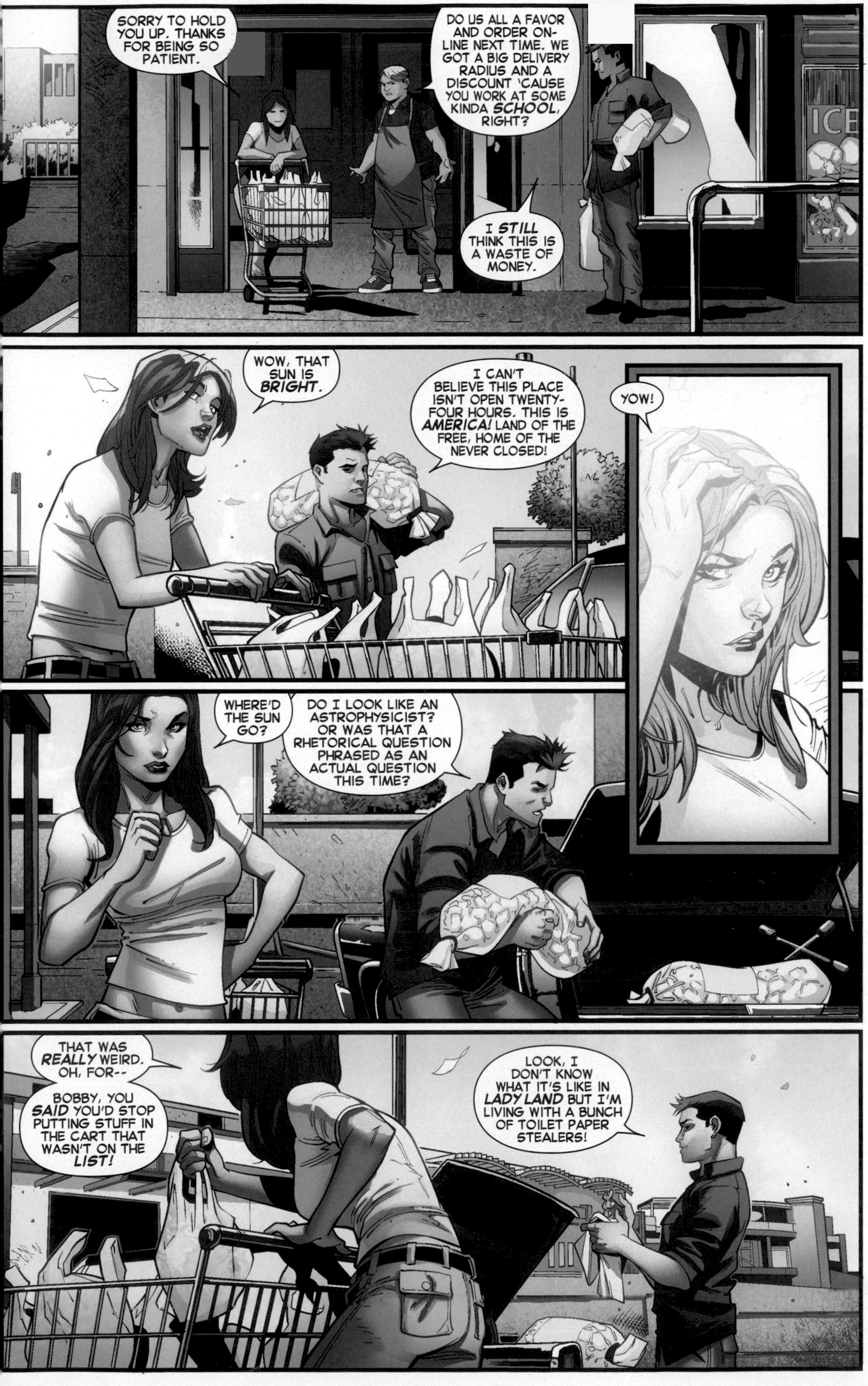
SORRY TO HOLD YOU UP. THANKS FOR BEING SO PATIENT.
DO US ALL A FAVOR AND ORDER ON-LINE NEXT TIME. WE GOT A BIG DELIVERY RADIUS AND A DISCOUNT 'CAUSE YOU WORK AT SOME KINDA SCHOOL, RIGHT?
I STILL THINK THIS IS A WASTE OF MONEY.
ICE
WOW, THAT SUN IS BRIGHT.
I CAN'T BELIEVE THIS PLACE ISN'T OPEN TWENTY-FOUR HOURS. THIS IS AMERICA! LAND OF THE FREE, HOME OF THE NEVER CLOSED!
YOW!
WHERE'D THE SUN GO?
DO I LOOK LIKE AN ASTROPHYSICIST? OR WAS THAT A RHETORICAL QUESTION PHRASED AS AN ACTUAL QUESTION THIS TIME?
THAT WAS REALLY WEIRD. OH, FOR--
BOBBY, YOU SAID YOU'D STOP PUTTING STUFF IN THE CART THAT WASN'T ON THE LIST!
LOOK, I DON'T KNOW WHAT IT'S LIKE IN LADY LAND BUT I'M LIVING WITH A BUNCH OF TOILET PAPER STEALERS!

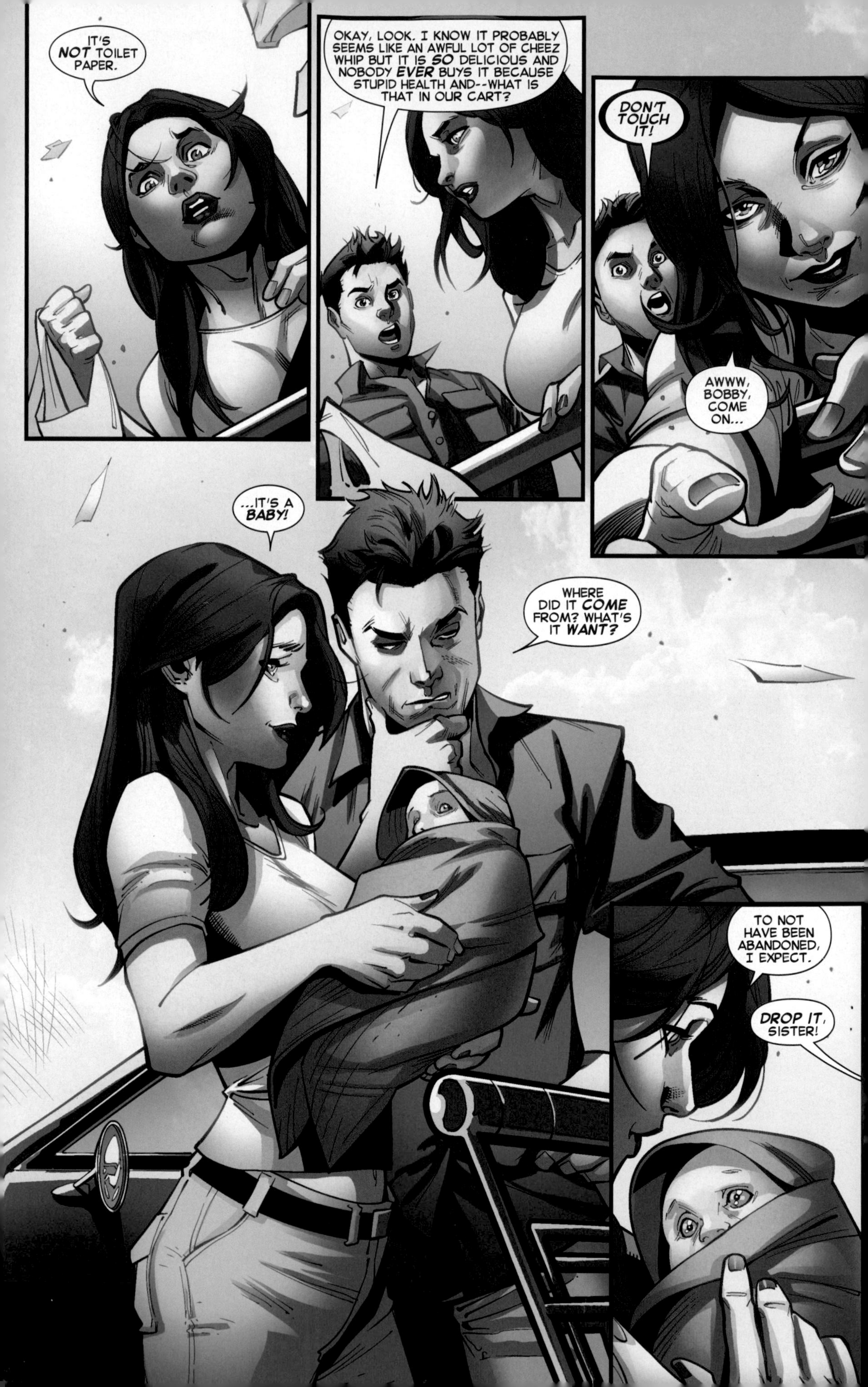
IT'S NOT TOILET PAPER.
OKAY, LOOK. I KNOW IT PROBABLY SEEMS LIKE AN AWFUL LOT OF CHEEZ WHIP BUT IT IS SO DELICIOUS AND NOBODY EVER BUYS IT BECAUSE STUPID HEALTH AND--WHAT IS THAT IN OUR CART?
DON'T TOUCH IT!
AWWW, BOBBY, COME ON...
...IT'S A BABY!
WHERE DID IT COME FROM? WHAT'S IT WANT?
TO NOT HAVE BEEN ABANDONED, I EXPECT.
DROP IT, SISTER!

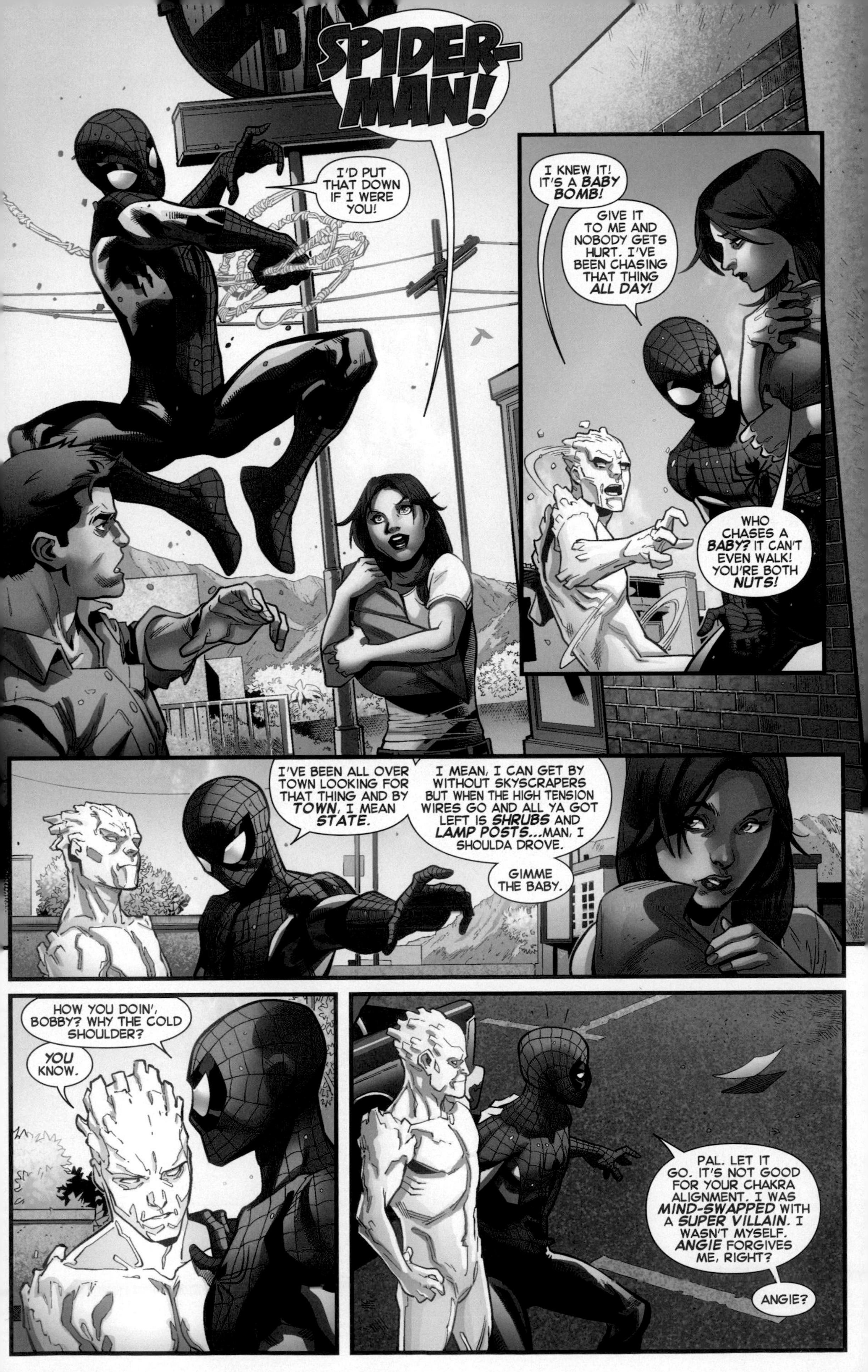
SPIDER-MAN!
I'D PUT THAT DOWN IF I WERE YOU!
I KNEW IT! IT'S A BABY BOMB!
GIVE IT TO ME AND NOBODY GETS HURT. I'VE BEEN CHASING THAT THING ALL DAY!
WHO CHASES A BABY? IT CAN'T EVEN WALK! YOU'RE BOTH NUTS!
I'VE BEEN ALL OVER TOWN LOOKING FOR THAT THING AND BY TOWN, I MEAN STATE.
I MEAN, I CAN GET BY WITHOUT SKYSCRAPERS BUT WHEN THE HIGH TENSION WIRES GO AND ALL YA GOT LEFT IS SHRUBS AND LAMP POSTS...MAN, I SHOULDA DROVE.
GIMME THE BABY.
HOW YOU DOIN', BOBBY? WHY THE COLD SHOULDER?
YOU KNOW.
PAL. LET IT GO. IT'S NOT GOOD FOR YOUR CHAKRA ALIGNMENT. I WAS MIND-SWAPPED WITH A SUPER VILLAIN. I WASN'T MYSELF. ANGIE FORGIVES ME, RIGHT?
ANGIE?

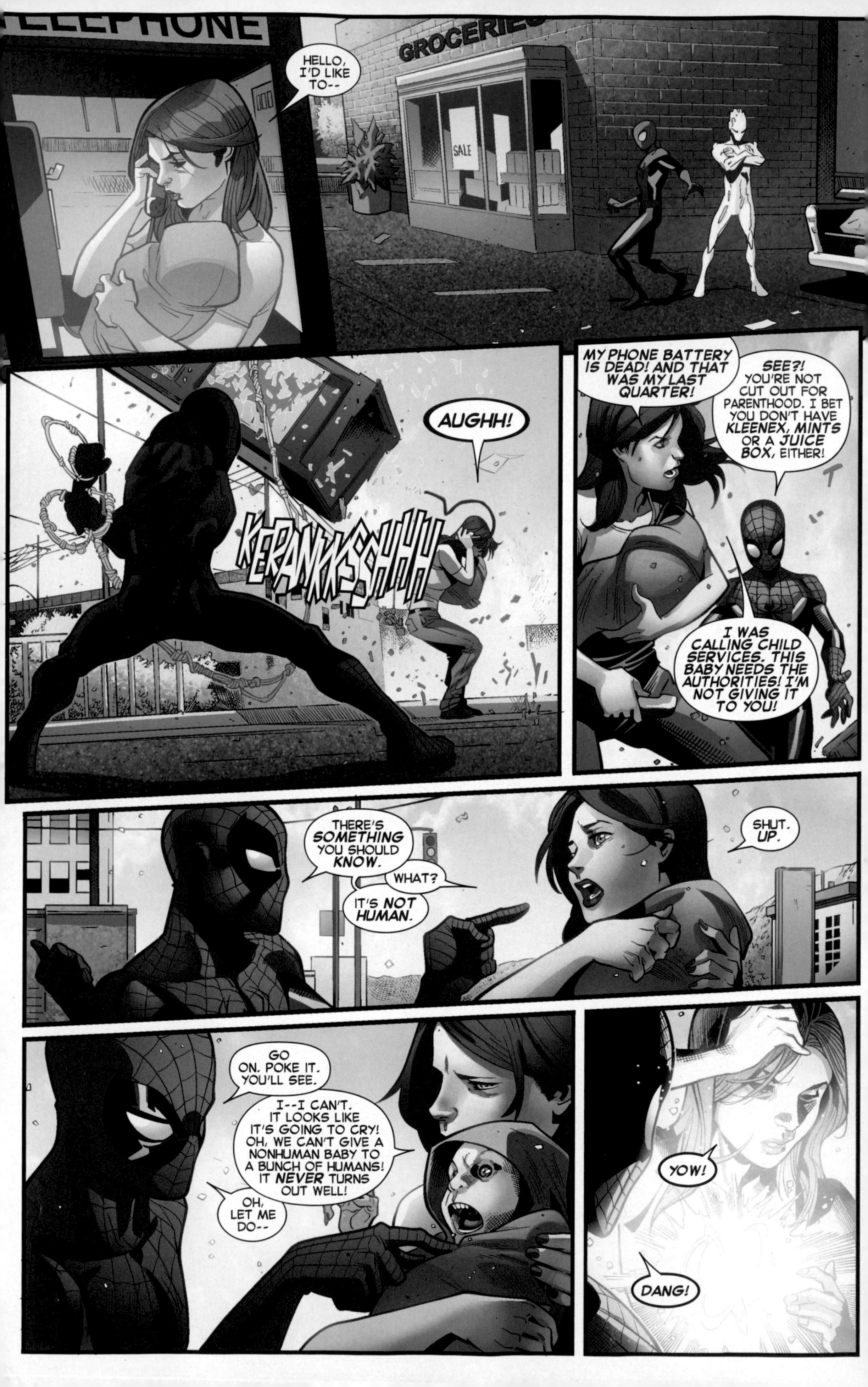
TELEPHONE
GROCERIES
HELLO, I'D LIKE TO--
SALE
AUGHH!
KERANKKSSHHH
MY PHONE BATTERY IS DEAD! AND THAT WAS MY LAST QUARTER!
SEE?! YOU'RE NOT CUT OUT FOR PARENTHOOD. I BET YOU DON'T HAVE KLEENEX, MINTS OR A JUICE BOX, EITHER!
I WAS CALLING CHILD SERVICES. THIS BABY NEEDS THE AUTHORITIES! I'M NOT GIVING IT TO YOU!
THERE'S SOMETHING YOU SHOULD KNOW.
WHAT?
IT'S NOT HUMAN.
SHUT. UP.
GO ON. POKE IT. YOU'LL SEE.
I--I CAN'T. IT LOOKS LIKE IT'S GOING TO CRY! OH, WE CAN'T GIVE A NONHUMAN BABY TO A BUNCH OF HUMANS! IT NEVER TURNS OUT WELL!
OH, LET ME DO--
YOW!
DANG!

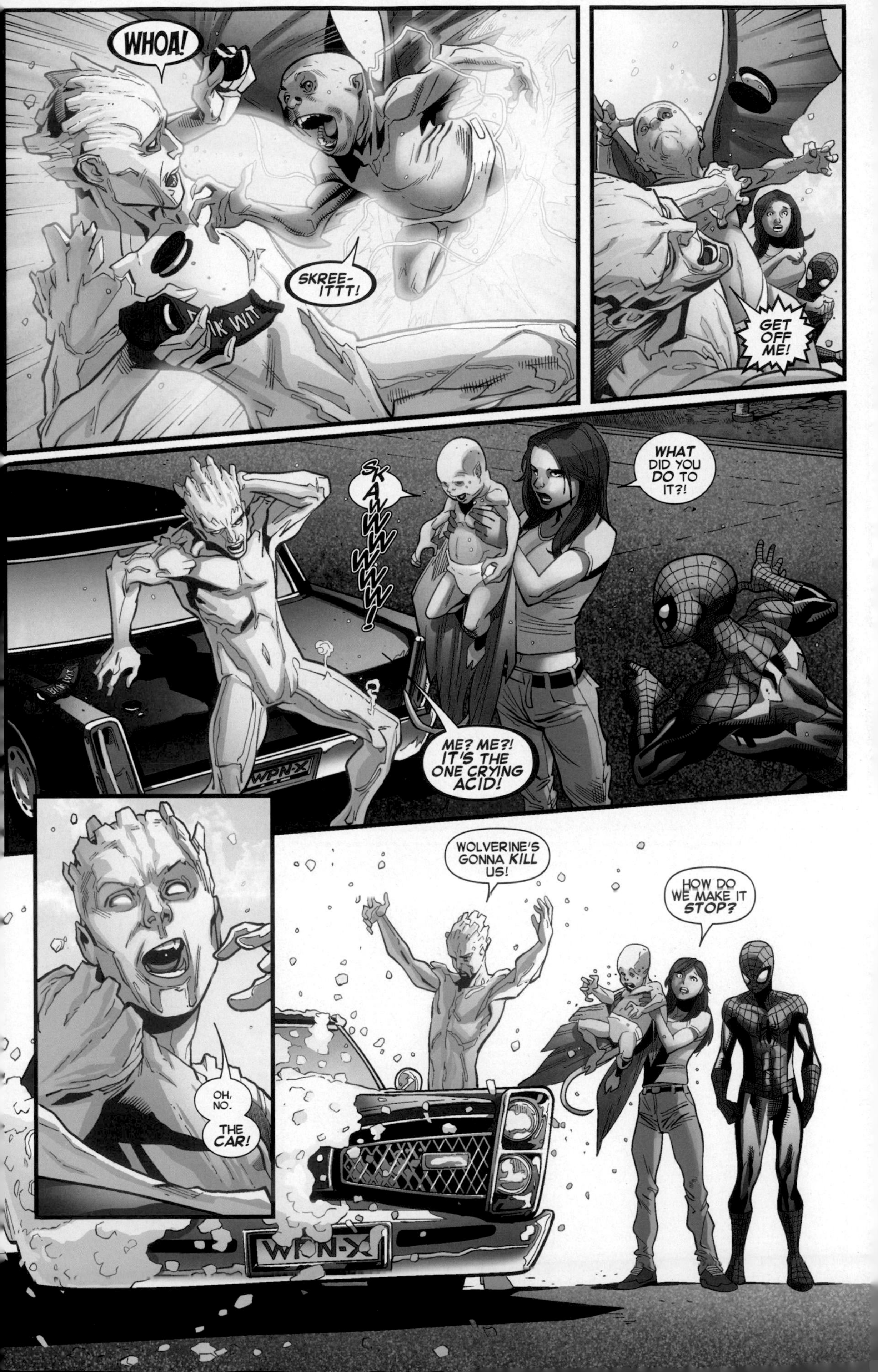
WHOA!
SKREE-ITTTT!
DIK WIT
GET OFF ME!
WHAT DID YOU DO TO IT?!
SKAWWWWWWW!
ME? ME?! IT'S THE ONE CRYING ACID!
OH, NO.
THE CAR!
WOLVERINE'S GONNA KILL US!
HOW DO WE MAKE IT STOP?
WPN-X

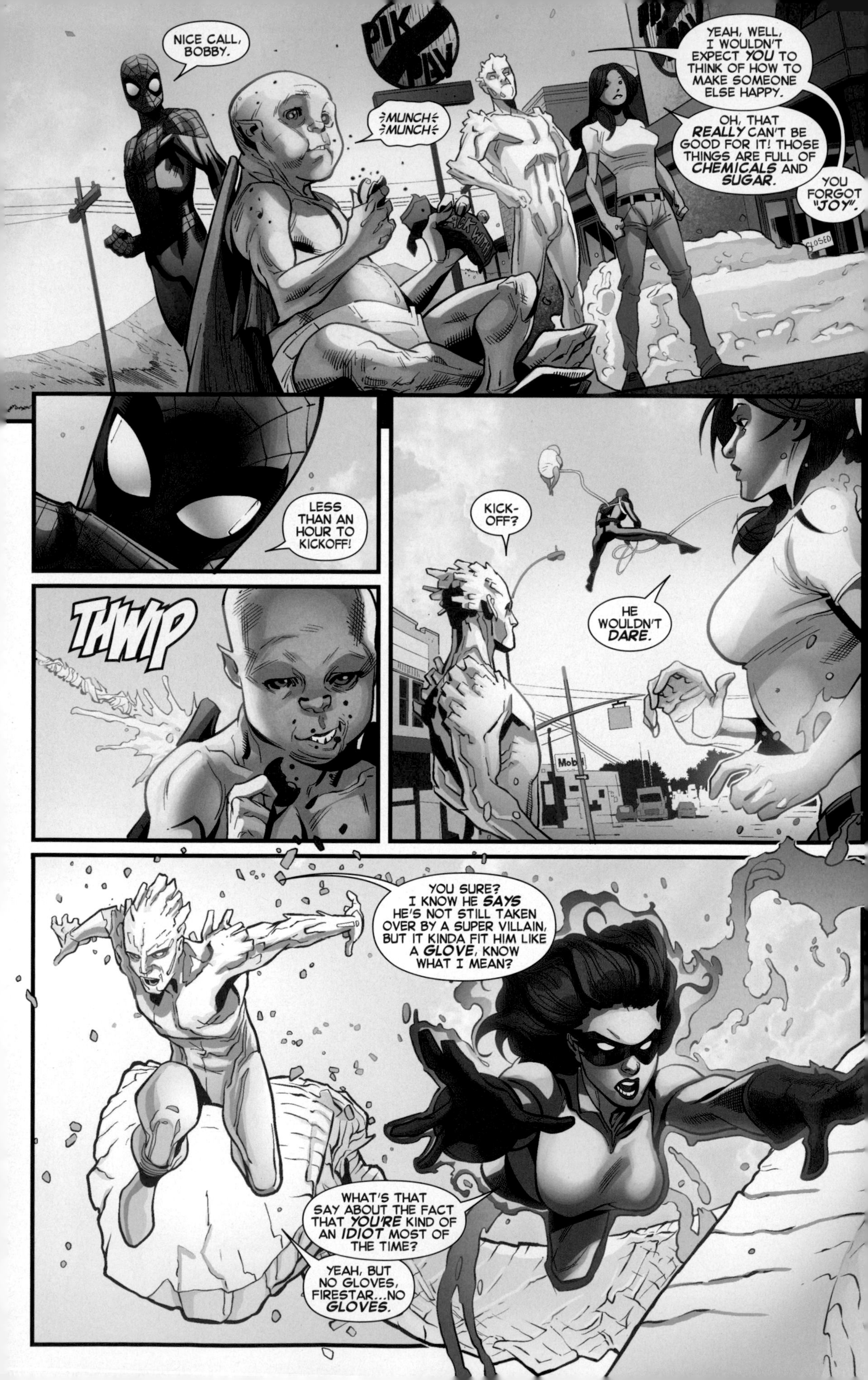
NICE CALL, BOBBY.
MUNCH MUNCH
YEAH, WELL, I WOULDN'T EXPECT YOU TO THINK OF HOW TO MAKE SOMEONE ELSE HAPPY.
OH, THAT REALLY CAN'T BE GOOD FOR IT! THOSE THINGS ARE FULL OF CHEMICALS AND SUGAR.
YOU FORGOT "JOY".
CLOSED
LESS THAN AN HOUR TO KICKOFF!
THWIP
KICK-OFF?
HE WOULDN'T DARE.
YOU SURE? I KNOW HE SAYS HE'S NOT STILL TAKEN OVER BY A SUPER VILLAIN, BUT IT KINDA FIT HIM LIKE A GLOVE, KNOW WHAT I MEAN?
WHAT'S THAT SAY ABOUT THE FACT THAT YOU'RE KIND OF AN IDIOT MOST OF THE TIME?
YEAH, BUT NO GLOVES, FIRESTAR...NO GLOVES.

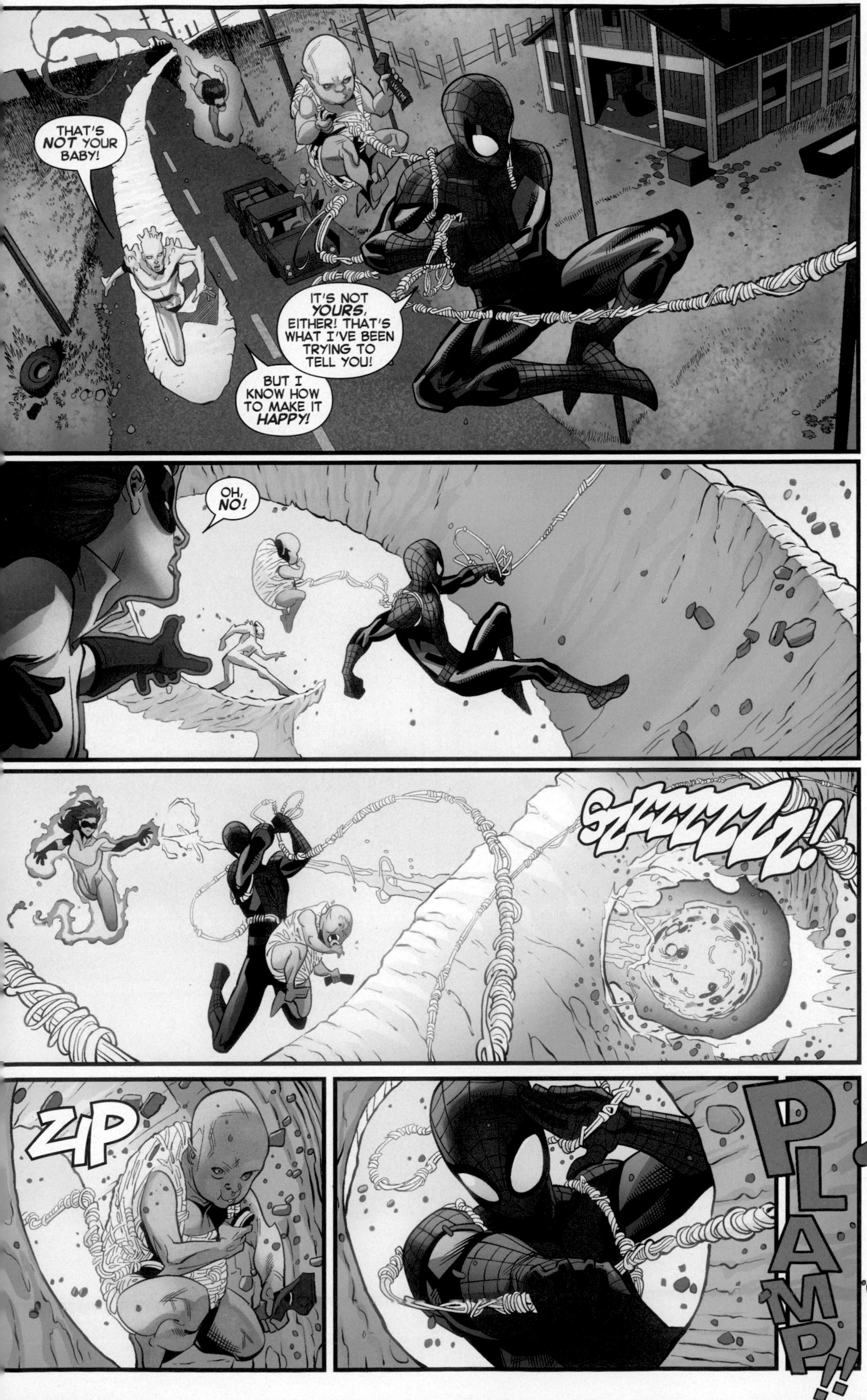

THAT'S NOT YOUR BABY!
IT'S NOT YOURS, EITHER! THAT'S WHAT I'VE BEEN TRYING TO TELL YOU!
BUT I KNOW HOW TO MAKE IT HAPPY!
OH, NO!
SZZZZZZ!
ZIP
PLAMP!!

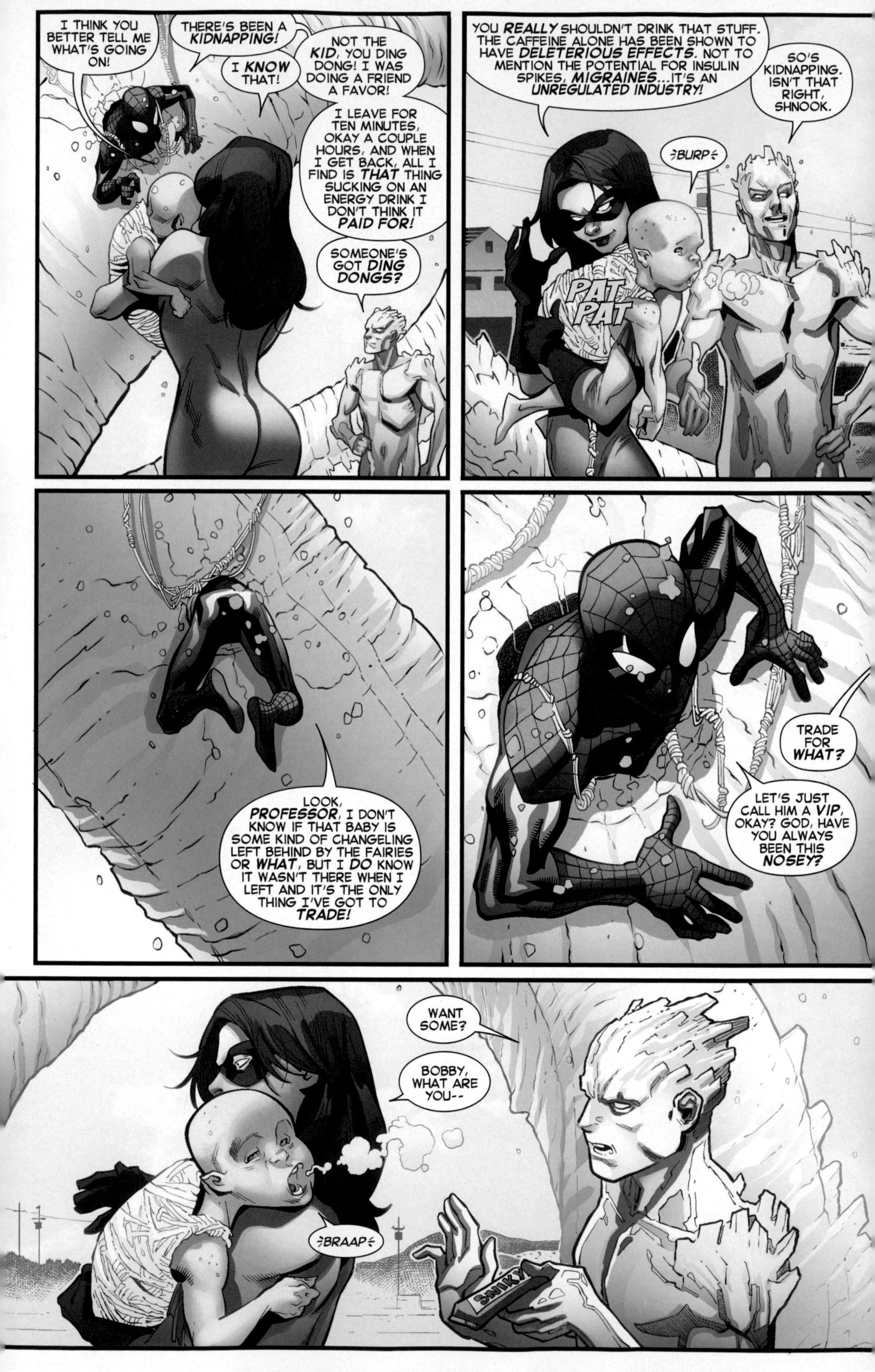
I THINK YOU BETTER TELL ME WHAT'S GOING ON!
THERE'S BEEN A KIDNAPPING!
I KNOW THAT!
NOT THE KID, YOU DING DONG! I WAS DOING A FRIEND A FAVOR!
I LEAVE FOR TEN MINUTES, OKAY A COUPLE HOURS, AND WHEN I GET BACK, ALL I FIND IS THAT THING SUCKING ON AN ENERGY DRINK I DON'T THINK IT PAID FOR!
SOMEONE'S GOT DING DONGS?
YOU REALLY SHOULDN'T DRINK THAT STUFF. THE CAFFEINE ALONE HAS BEEN SHOWN TO HAVE DELETERIOUS EFFECTS. NOT TO MENTION THE POTENTIAL FOR INSULIN SPIKES, MIGRAINES...IT'S AN UNREGULATED INDUSTRY!
SO'S KIDNAPPING. ISN'T THAT RIGHT, SHNOOK.
BURP
PAT PAT
LOOK, PROFESSOR, I DON'T KNOW IF THAT BABY IS SOME KIND OF CHANGELING LEFT BEHIND BY THE FAIRIES OR WHAT, BUT I DO KNOW IT WASN'T THERE WHEN I LEFT AND IT'S THE ONLY THING I'VE GOT TO TRADE!
TRADE FOR WHAT?
LET'S JUST CALL HIM A VIP, OKAY? GOD, HAVE YOU ALWAYS BEEN THIS NOSEY?
WANT SOME?
BOBBY, WHAT ARE YOU--
BRAAP
SNIKY

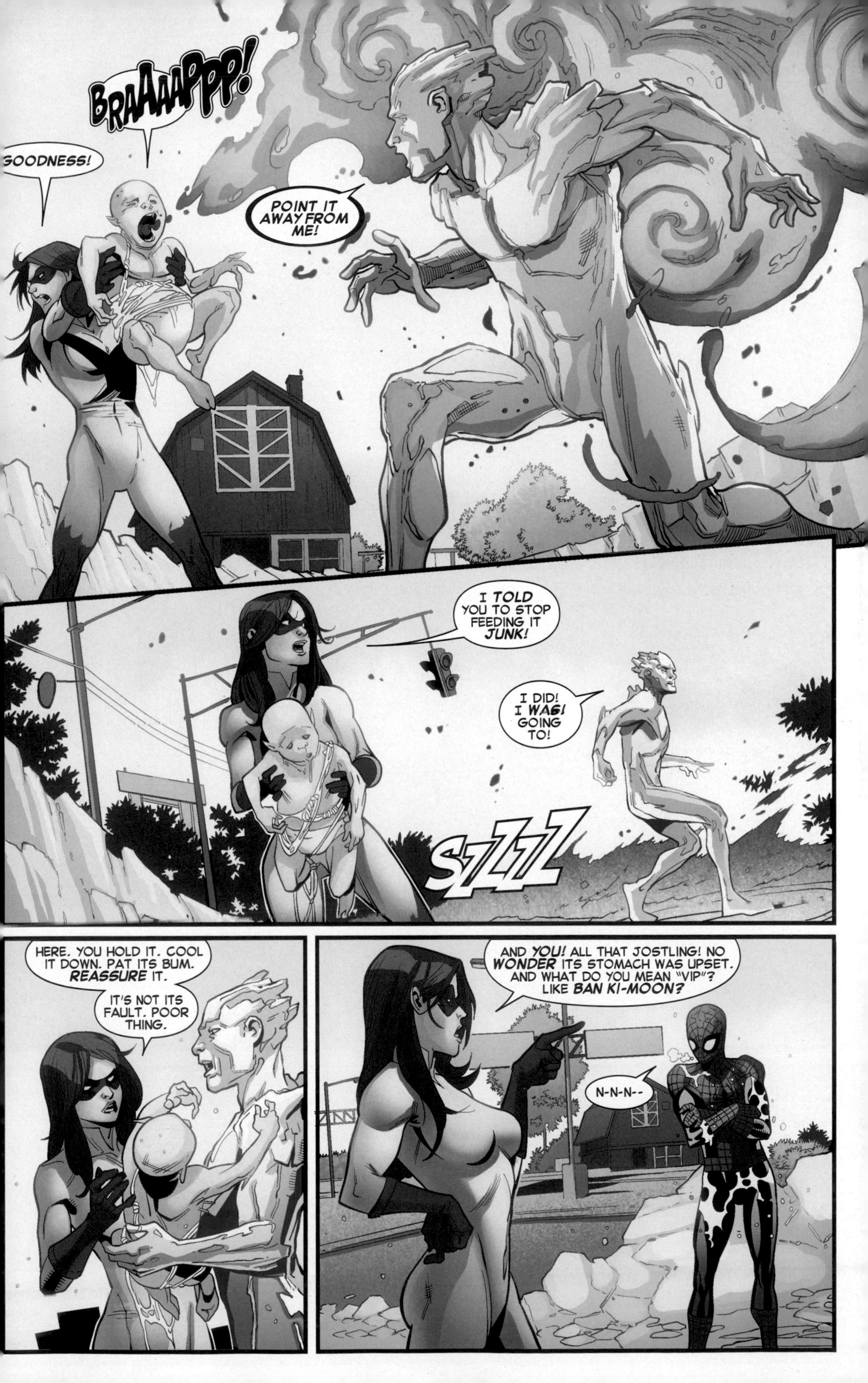

BRAAAAPPP!
GOODNESS!
POINT IT AWAY FROM ME!
I TOLD YOU TO STOP FEEDING IT JUNK!
I DID! I WAS! GOING TO!
SZZZ
HERE. YOU HOLD IT. COOL IT DOWN. PAT ITS BUM. REASSURE IT.
IT'S NOT ITS FAULT. POOR THING.
AND YOU! ALL THAT JOSTLING! NO WONDER ITS STOMACH WAS UPSET. AND WHAT DO YOU MEAN "VIP"? LIKE BAN KI-MOON?
N-N-N--

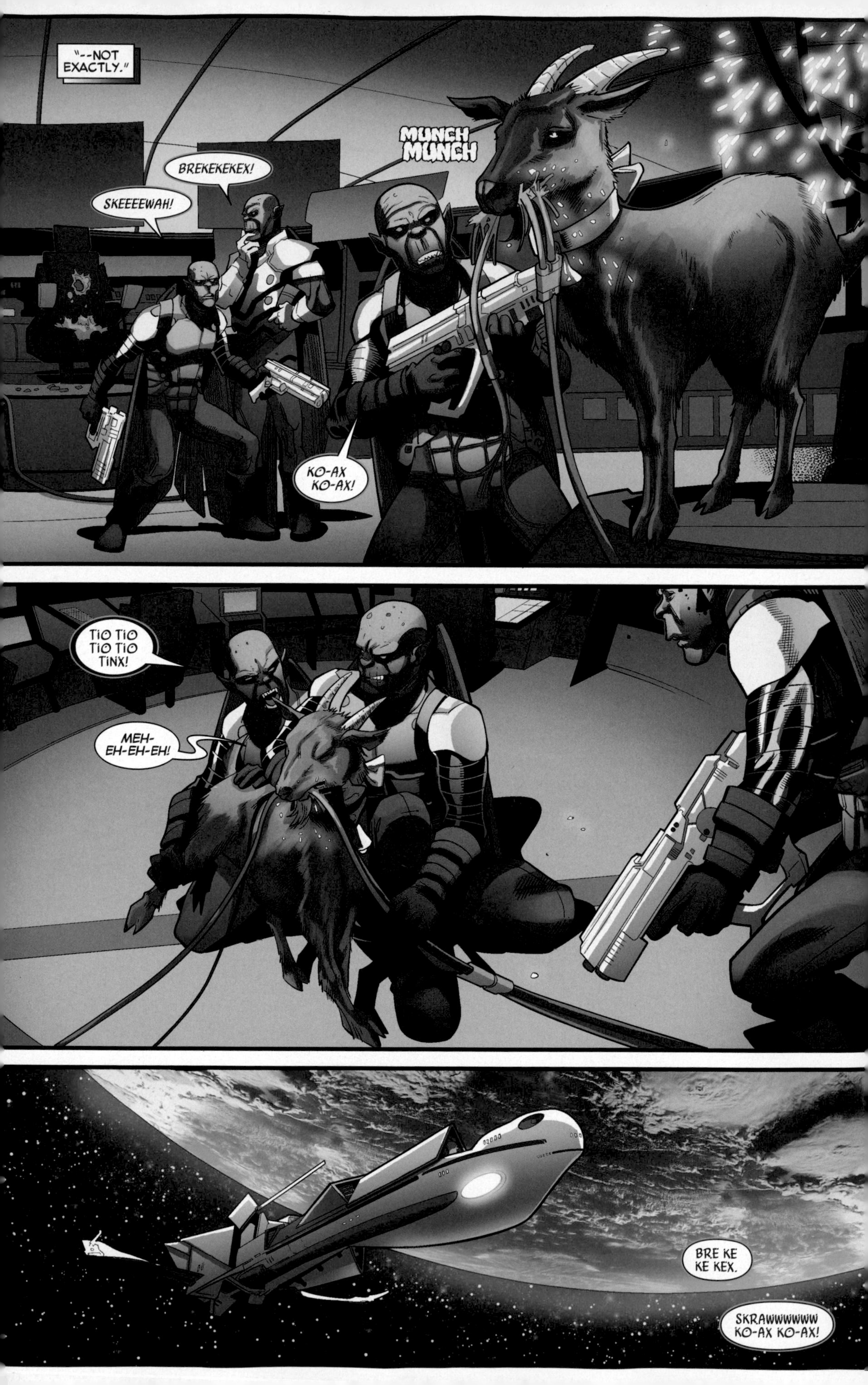
"--NOT EXACTLY."
MUNCH MUNCH
BREKEKEKEX!
SKEEEEWAH!
KO-AX KO-AX!
TIO TIO TIO TIO TINX!
MEH-EH-EH-EH!
BRE KE KE KEX.
SKRAWWWWWW KO-AX KO-AX!

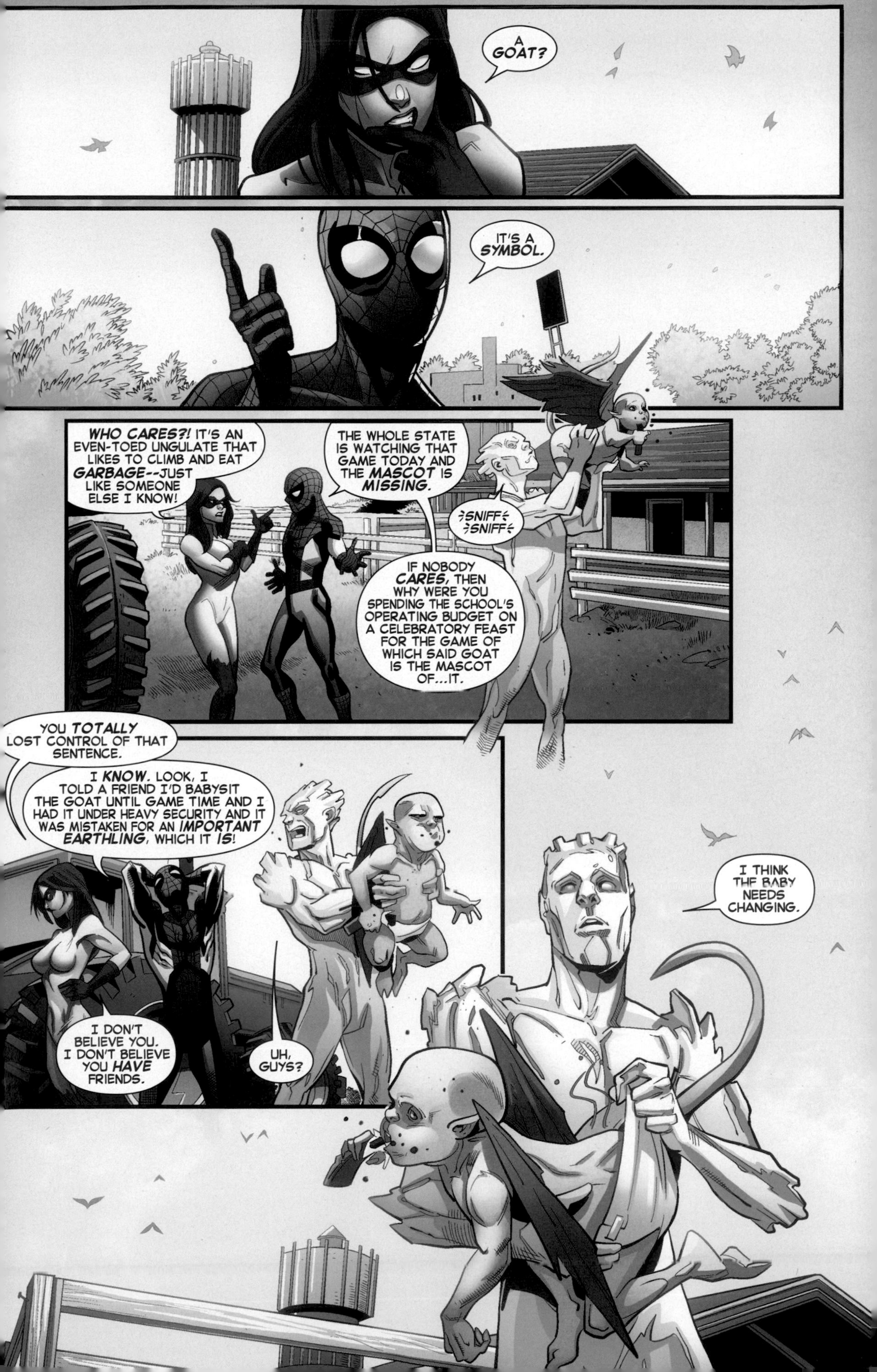
A GOAT?
IT'S A SYMBOL.
WHO CARES?! IT'S AN EVEN-TOED UNGULATE THAT LIKES TO CLIMB AND EAT GARBAGE--JUST LIKE SOMEONE ELSE I KNOW!
THE WHOLE STATE IS WATCHING THAT GAME TODAY AND THE MASCOT IS MISSING.
SNIFF SNIFF
IF NOBODY CARES, THEN WHY WERE YOU SPENDING THE SCHOOL'S OPERATING BUDGET ON A CELEBRATORY FEAST FOR THE GAME OF WHICH SAID GOAT IS THE MASCOT OF...IT.
YOU TOTALLY LOST CONTROL OF THAT SENTENCE.
I KNOW. LOOK, I TOLD A FRIEND I'D BABYSIT THE GOAT UNTIL GAME TIME AND I HAD IT UNDER HEAVY SECURITY AND IT WAS MISTAKEN FOR AN IMPORTANT EARTHLING, WHICH IT IS!
I DON'T BELIEVE YOU. I DON'T BELIEVE YOU HAVE FRIENDS.
UH, GUYS?
I THINK THE BABY NEEDS CHANGING.

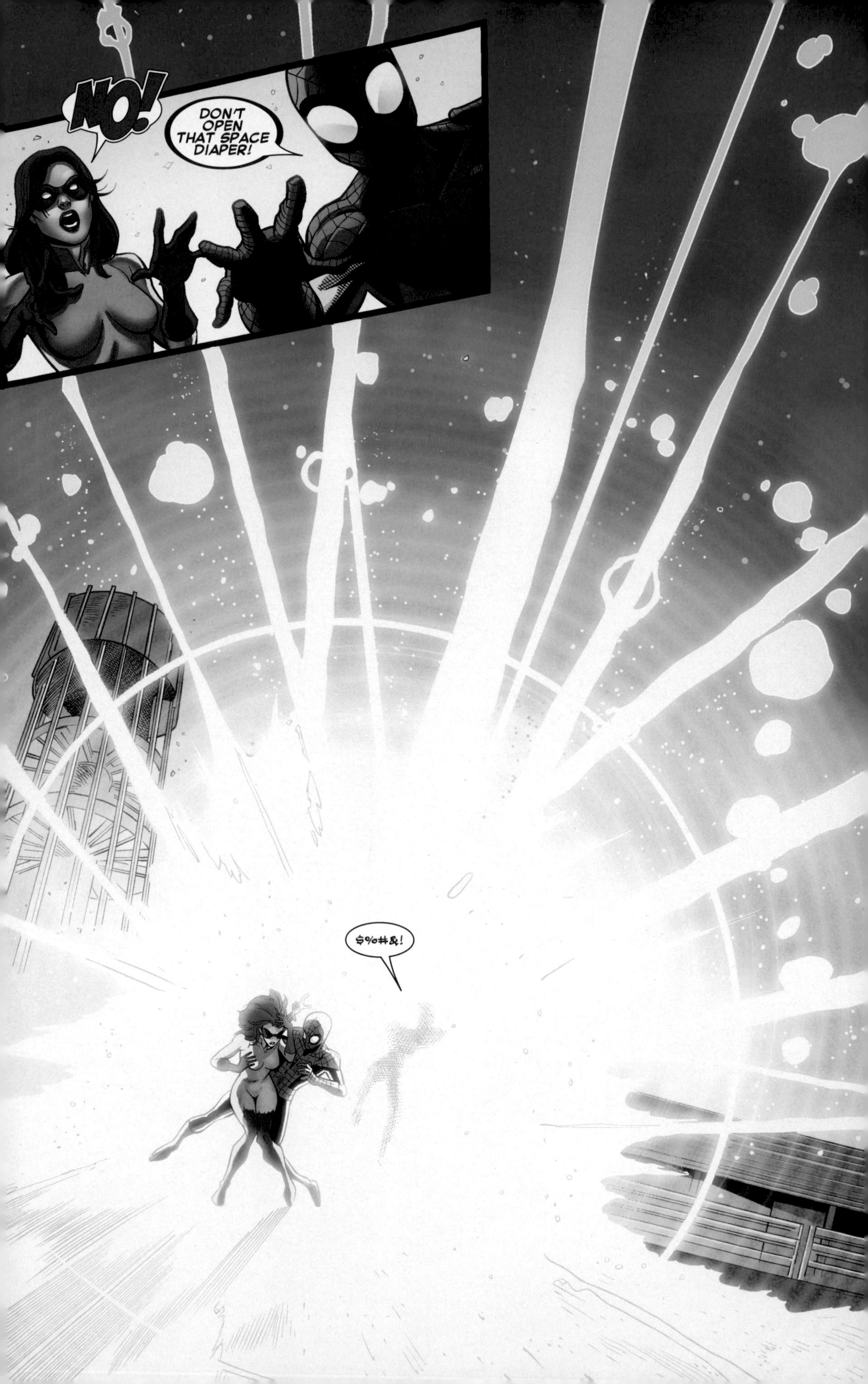
NO!
DON'T OPEN THAT SPACE DIAPER!
$%#&!

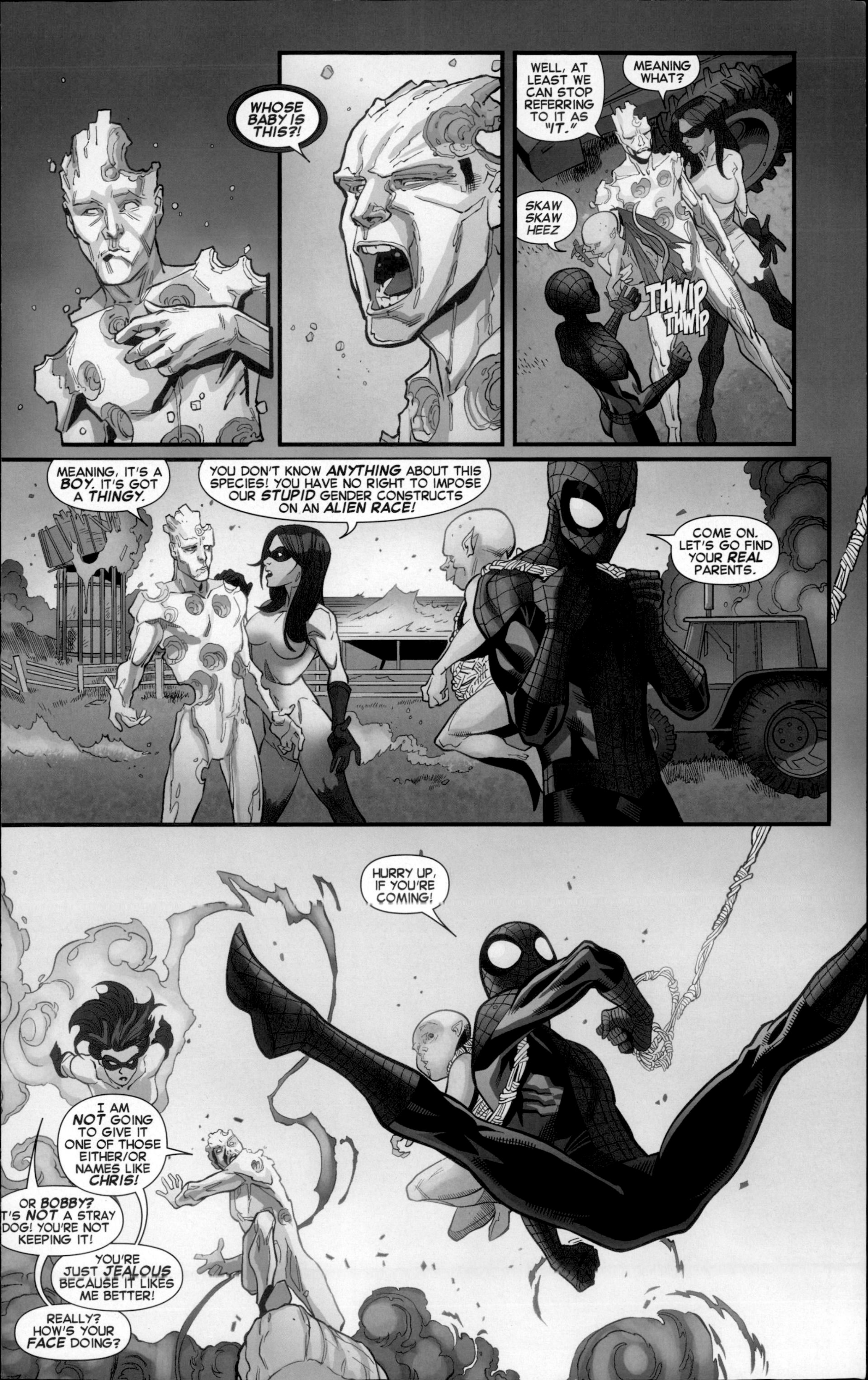
WHOSE BABY IS THIS?!
WELL, AT LEAST WE CAN STOP REFERRING TO IT AS "IT."
MEANING WHAT?
SKAW SKAW HEEZ
THWIP THWIP
MEANING, IT'S A BOY. IT'S GOT A THINGY.
YOU DON'T KNOW ANYTHING ABOUT THIS SPECIES! YOU HAVE NO RIGHT TO IMPOSE OUR STUPID GENDER CONSTRUCTS ON AN ALIEN RACE!
COME ON. LET'S GO FIND YOUR REAL PARENTS.
HURRY UP, IF YOU'RE COMING!
I AM NOT GOING TO GIVE IT ONE OF THOSE EITHER/OR NAMES LIKE CHRIS!
OR BOBBY? IT'S NOT A STRAY DOG! YOU'RE NOT KEEPING IT!
YOU'RE JUST JEALOUS BECAUSE IT LIKES ME BETTER!
REALLY? HOW'S YOUR FACE DOING?

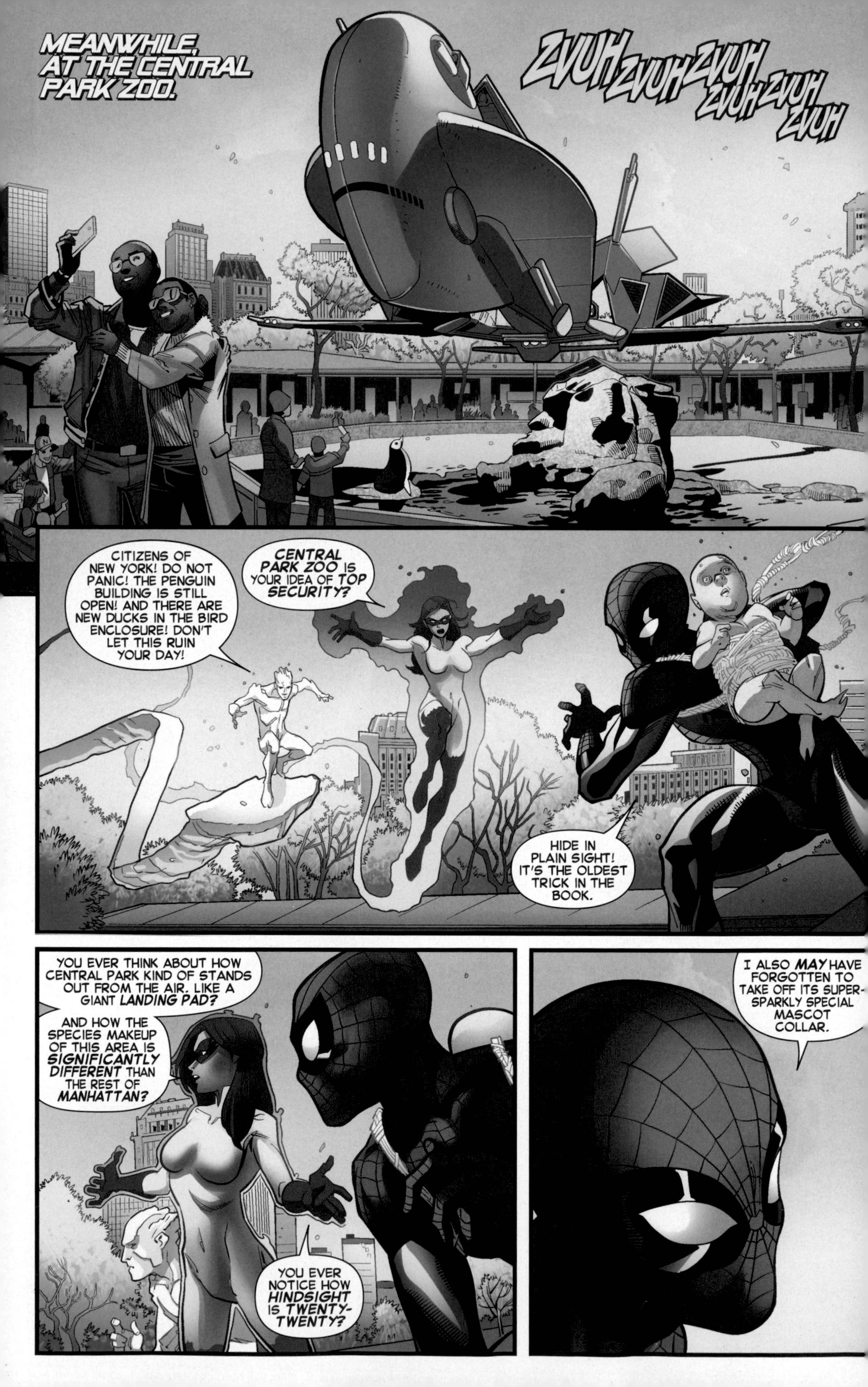
MEANWHILE, AT THE CENTRAL PARK ZOO.
ZVUH ZVUH ZVUH ZVUH ZVUH ZVUH
CITIZENS OF NEW YORK! DO NOT PANIC! THE PENGUIN BUILDING IS STILL OPEN! AND THERE ARE NEW DUCKS IN THE BIRD ENCLOSURE! DON'T LET THIS RUIN YOUR DAY!
CENTRAL PARK ZOO IS YOUR IDEA OF TOP SECURITY?
HIDE IN PLAIN SIGHT! IT'S THE OLDEST TRICK IN THE BOOK.
YOU EVER THINK ABOUT HOW CENTRAL PARK KIND OF STANDS OUT FROM THE AIR. LIKE A GIANT LANDING PAD?
AND HOW THE SPECIES MAKEUP OF THIS AREA IS SIGNIFICANTLY DIFFERENT THAN THE REST OF MANHATTAN?
YOU EVER NOTICE HOW HINDSIGHT IS TWENTY-TWENTY?
I ALSO MAY HAVE FORGOTTEN TO TAKE OFF ITS SUPER-SPARKLY SPECIAL MASCOT COLLAR.

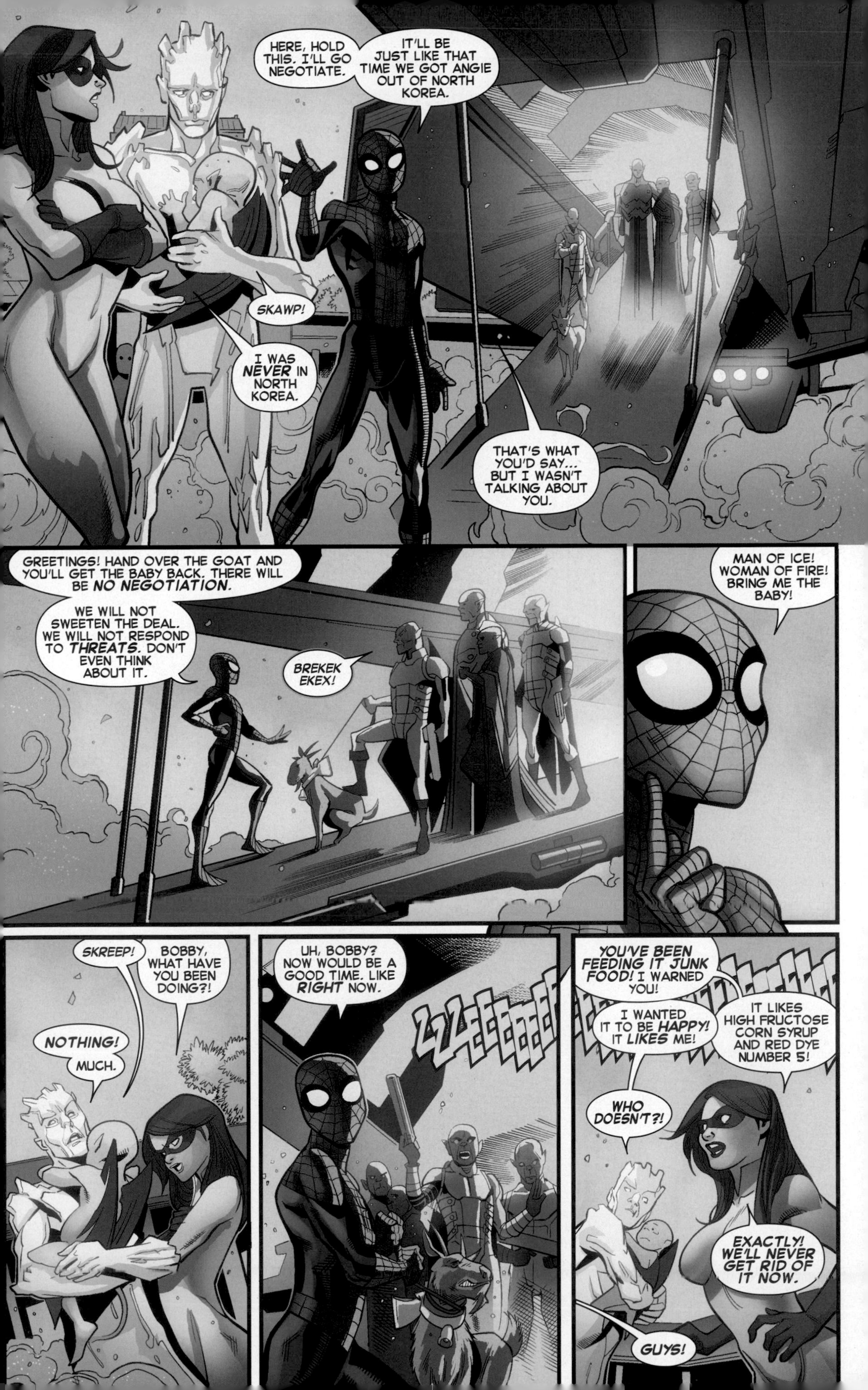
HERE, HOLD THIS. I'LL GO NEGOTIATE.
IT'LL BE JUST LIKE THAT TIME WE GOT ANGIE OUT OF NORTH KOREA.
SKAWP!
I WAS NEVER IN NORTH KOREA.
THAT'S WHAT YOU'D SAY... BUT I WASN'T TALKING ABOUT YOU.
GREETINGS! HAND OVER THE GOAT AND YOU'LL GET THE BABY BACK. THERE WILL BE NO NEGOTIATION.
WE WILL NOT SWEETEN THE DEAL. WE WILL NOT RESPOND TO THREATS. DON'T EVEN THINK ABOUT IT.
BREKEK EKEX!
MAN OF ICE! WOMAN OF FIRE! BRING ME THE BABY!
SKREEP!
BOBBY, WHAT HAVE YOU BEEN DOING?!
NOTHING!
MUCH.
UH, BOBBY? NOW WOULD BE A GOOD TIME. LIKE RIGHT NOW.
ZZZEEEEEEE
YOU'VE BEEN FEEDING IT JUNK FOOD! I WARNED YOU!
I WANTED IT TO BE HAPPY! IT LIKES ME!
IT LIKES HIGH FRUCTOSE CORN SYRUP AND RED DYE NUMBER 5!
WHO DOESN'T?!
EXACTLY! WE'LL NEVER GET RID OF IT NOW.
GUYS!

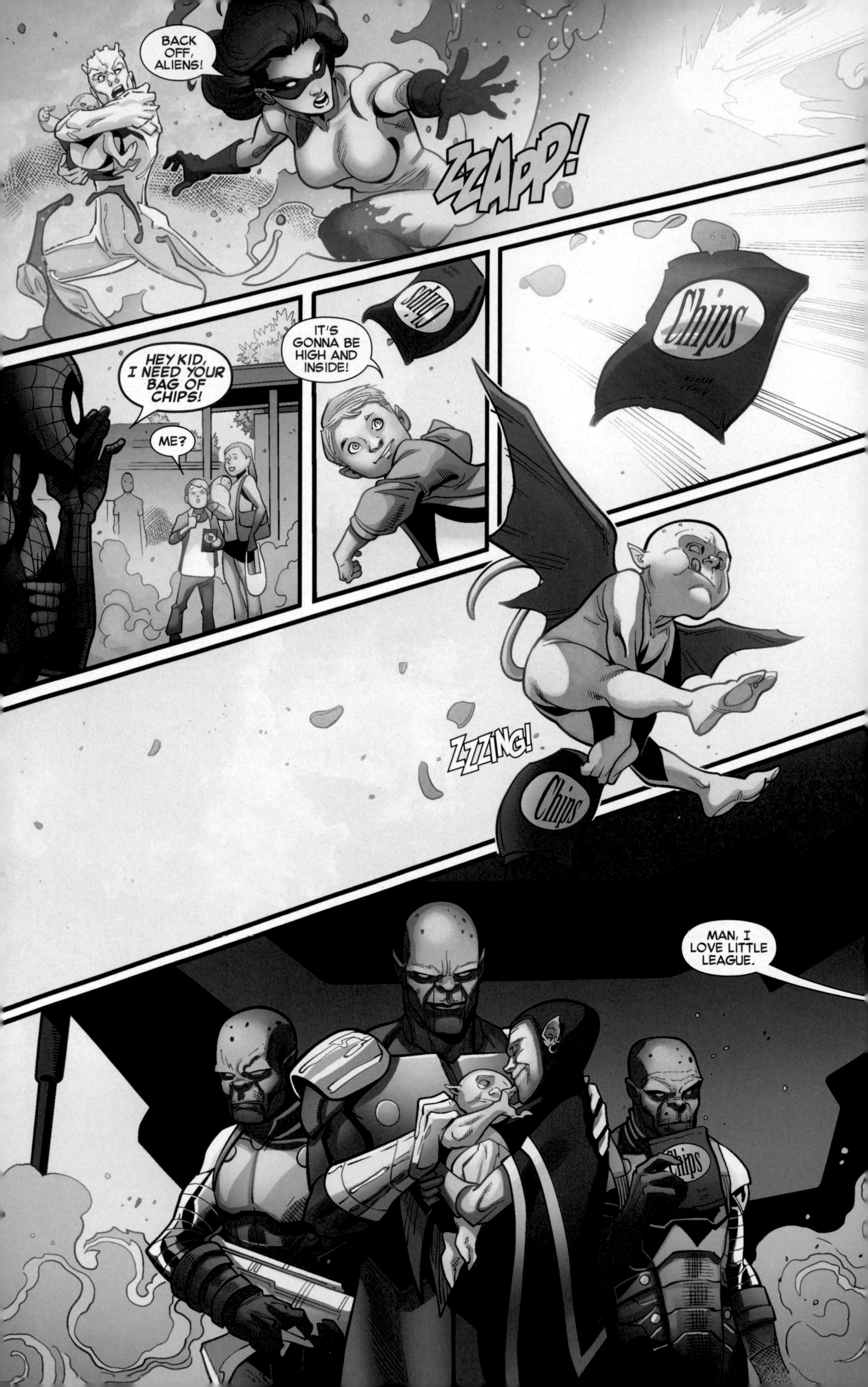
BACK OFF, ALIENS!
ZZAPP!
HEY KID, I NEED YOUR BAG OF CHIPS!
ME?
IT'S GONNA BE HIGH AND INSIDE!
Chips
ZZZING!
MAN, I LOVE LITTLE LEAGUE.

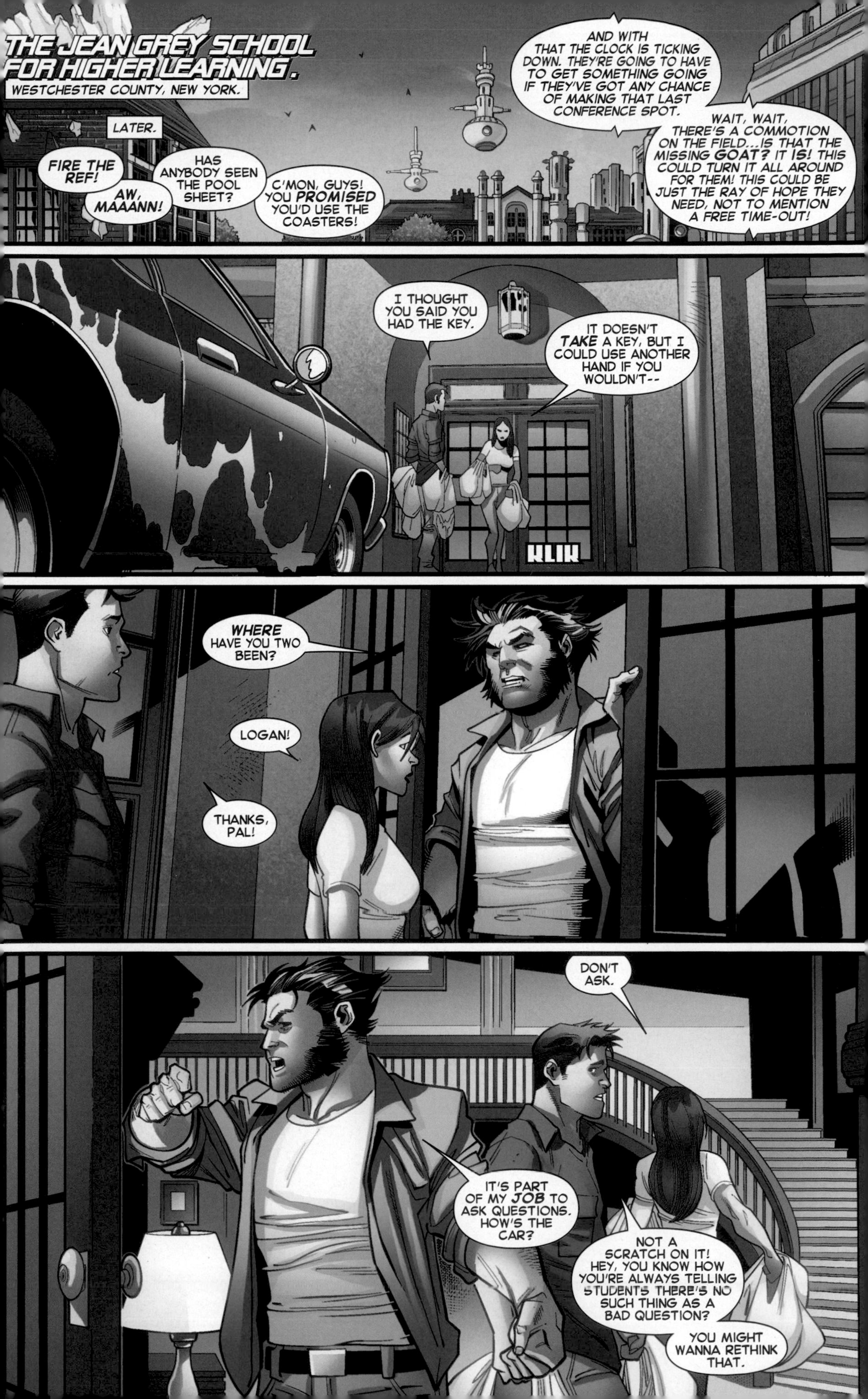
THE JEAN GREY SCHOOL FOR HIGHER LEARNING.
WESTCHESTER COUNTY, NEW YORK.
LATER.
FIRE THE REF!
AW, MAAANN!
HAS ANYBODY SEEN THE POOL SHEET?
C'MON, GUYS! YOU PROMISED YOU'D USE THE COASTERS!
AND WITH THAT THE CLOCK IS TICKING DOWN. THEY'RE GOING TO HAVE TO GET SOMETHING GOING IF THEY'VE GOT ANY CHANCE OF MAKING THAT LAST CONFERENCE SPOT.
WAIT, WAIT, THERE'S A COMMOTION ON THE FIELD... IS THAT THE MISSING GOAT? IT IS! THIS COULD TURN IT ALL AROUND FOR THEM! THIS COULD BE JUST THE RAY OF HOPE THEY NEED, NOT TO MENTION A FREE TIME-OUT!
I THOUGHT YOU SAID YOU HAD THE KEY.
IT DOESN'T TAKE A KEY, BUT I COULD USE ANOTHER HAND IF YOU WOULDN'T--
KLIK
WHERE HAVE YOU TWO BEEN?
LOGAN!
THANKS, PAL!
DON'T ASK.
IT'S PART OF MY JOB TO ASK QUESTIONS. HOW'S THE CAR?
NOT A SCRATCH ON IT! HEY, YOU KNOW HOW YOU'RE ALWAYS TELLING STUDENTS THERE'S NO SUCH THING AS A BAD QUESTION?
YOU MIGHT WANNA RETHINK THAT.

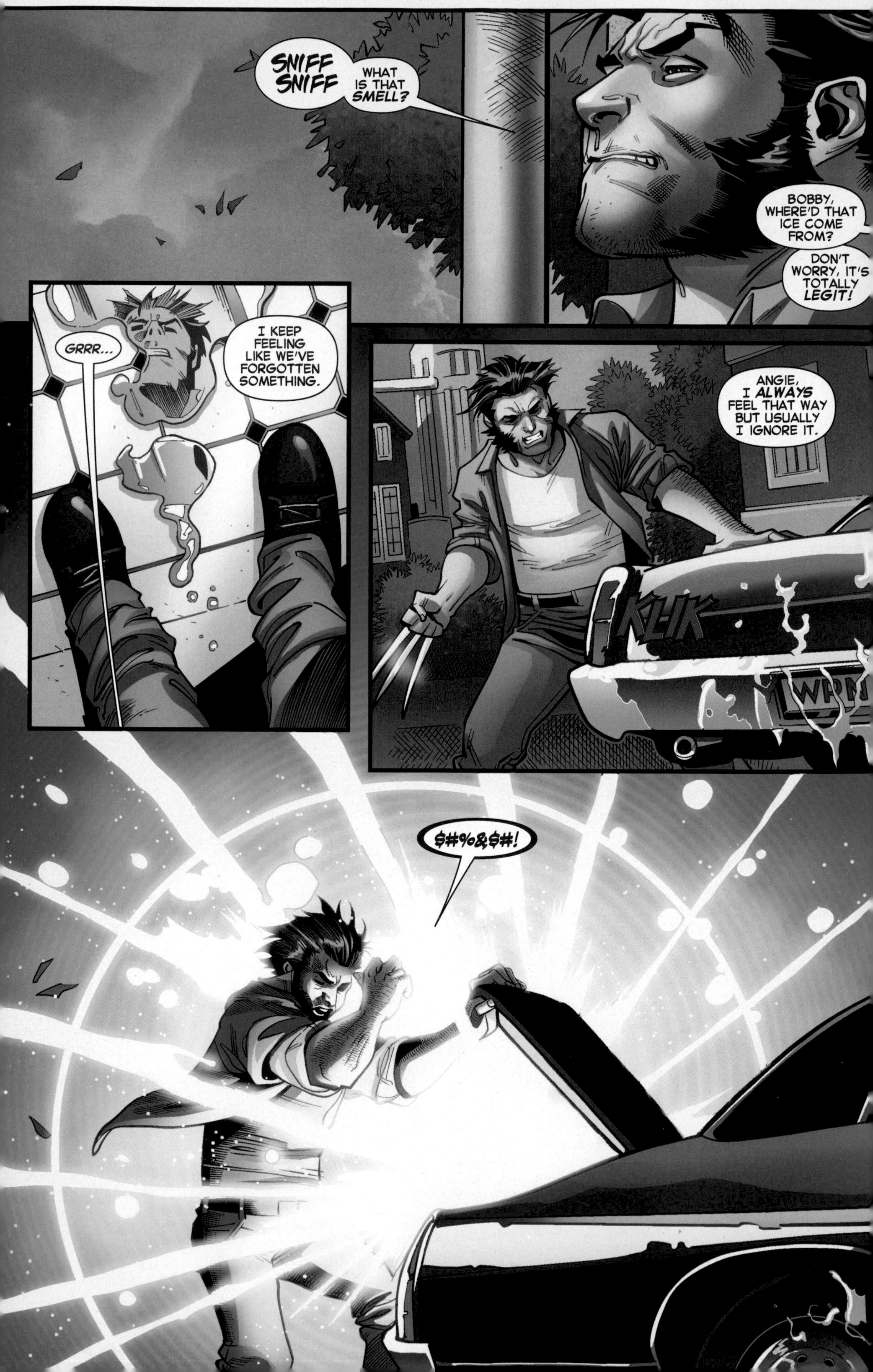
SNIFF SNIFF
WHAT IS THAT SMELL?
BOBBY, WHERE'D THAT ICE COME FROM?
DON'T WORRY, IT'S TOTALLY LEGIT!
GRRR...
I KEEP FEELING LIKE WE'VE FORGOTTEN SOMETHING.
ANGIE, I ALWAYS FEEL THAT WAY BUT USUALLY I IGNORE IT.
KLIK
WRN
$#%&$#!

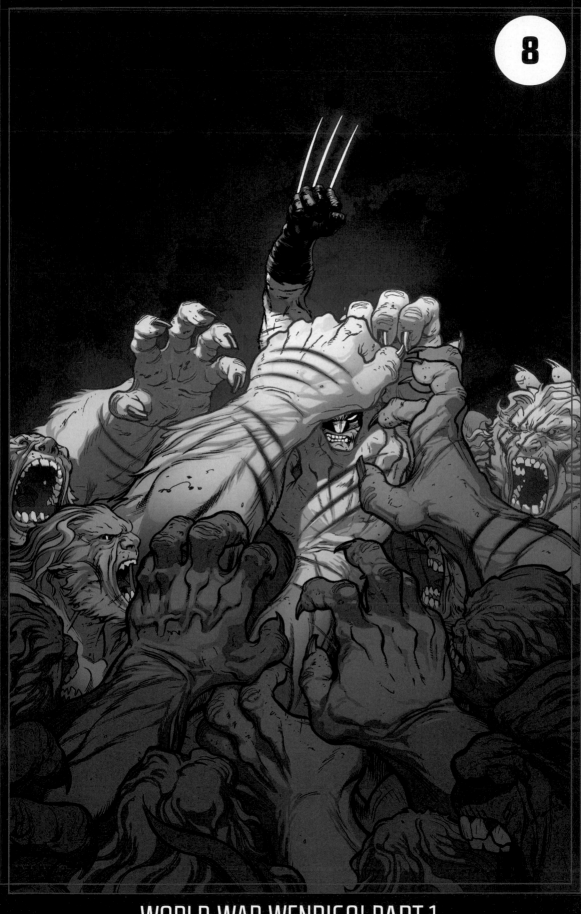

WORLD WAR WENDIGO! PART 1

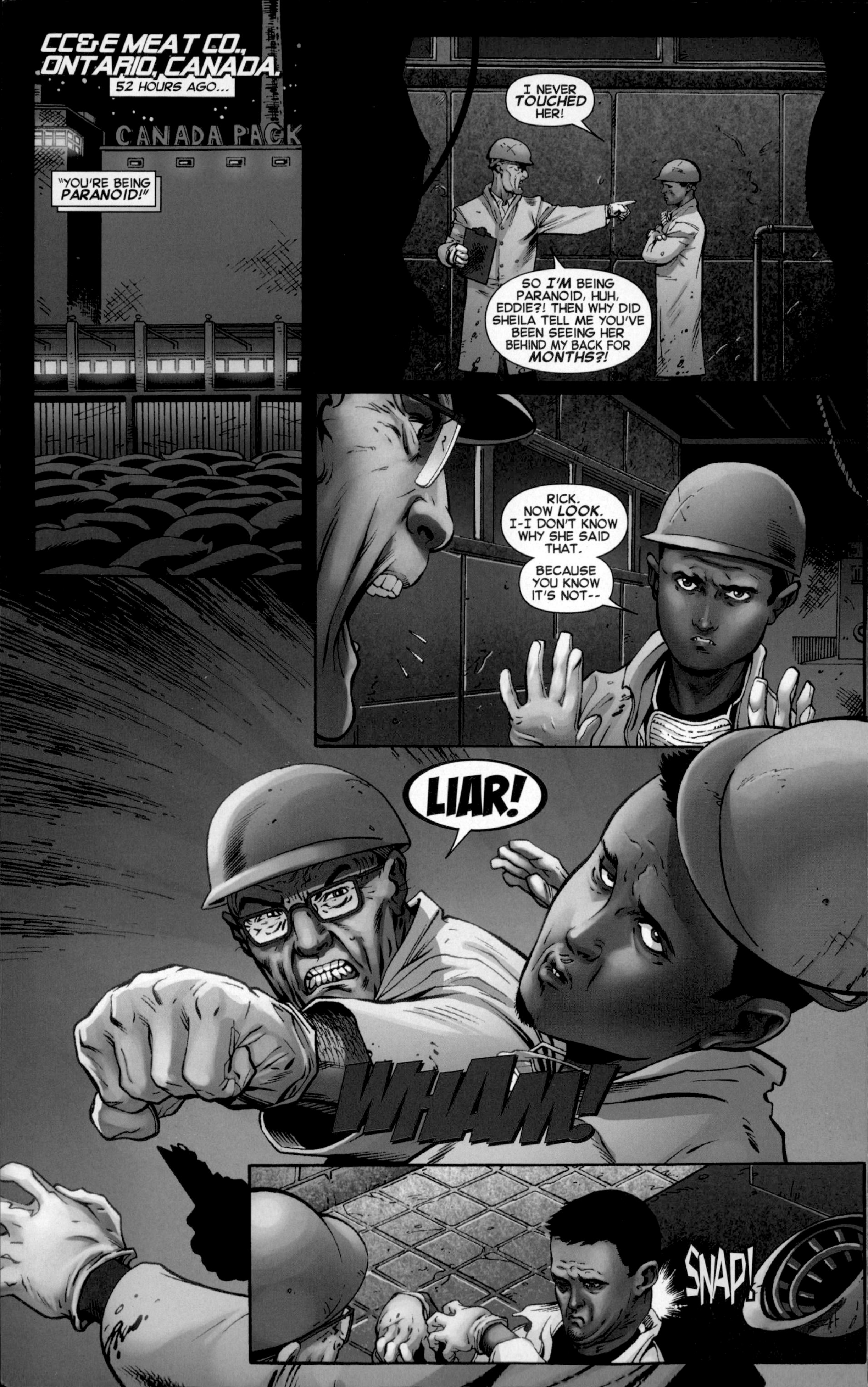
CC&E MEAT CO., ONTARIO, CANADA.
52 HOURS AGO...
CANADA PACK
"YOU'RE BEING PARANOID!"
I NEVER TOUCHED HER!
SO I'M BEING PARANOID, HUH, EDDIE?! THEN WHY DID SHEILA TELL ME YOU'VE BEEN SEEING HER BEHIND MY BACK FOR MONTHS?!
RICK. NOW LOOK. I-I DON'T KNOW WHY SHE SAID THAT.
BECAUSE YOU KNOW IT'S NOT--
LIAR!
WHAM!
SNAP!

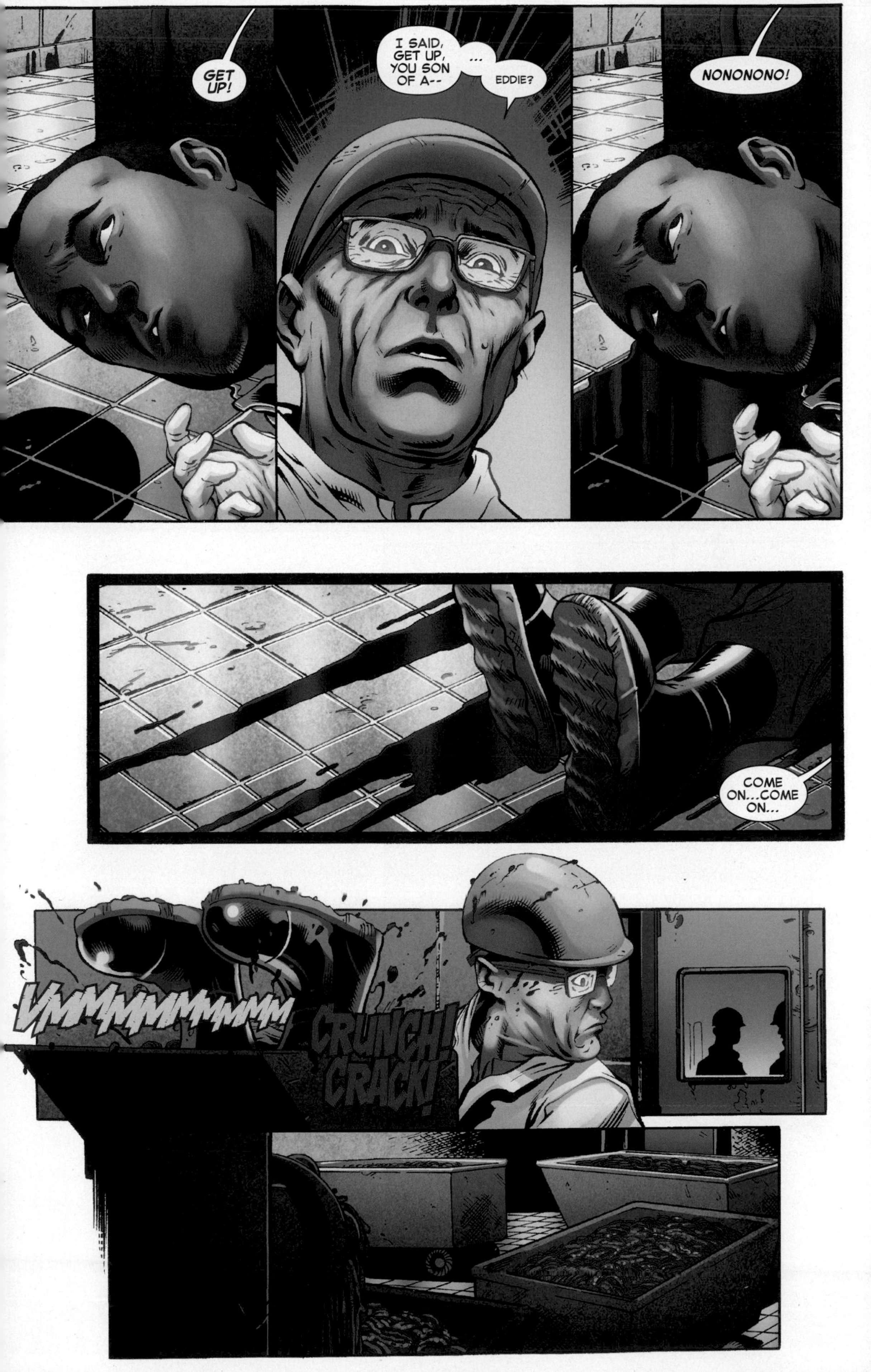

GET UP!
I SAID, GET UP, YOU SON OF A--
...
EDDIE?
NONONONO!
COME ON...COME ON...
VMMMMMMMMMMM
CRUNCH! CRACK!

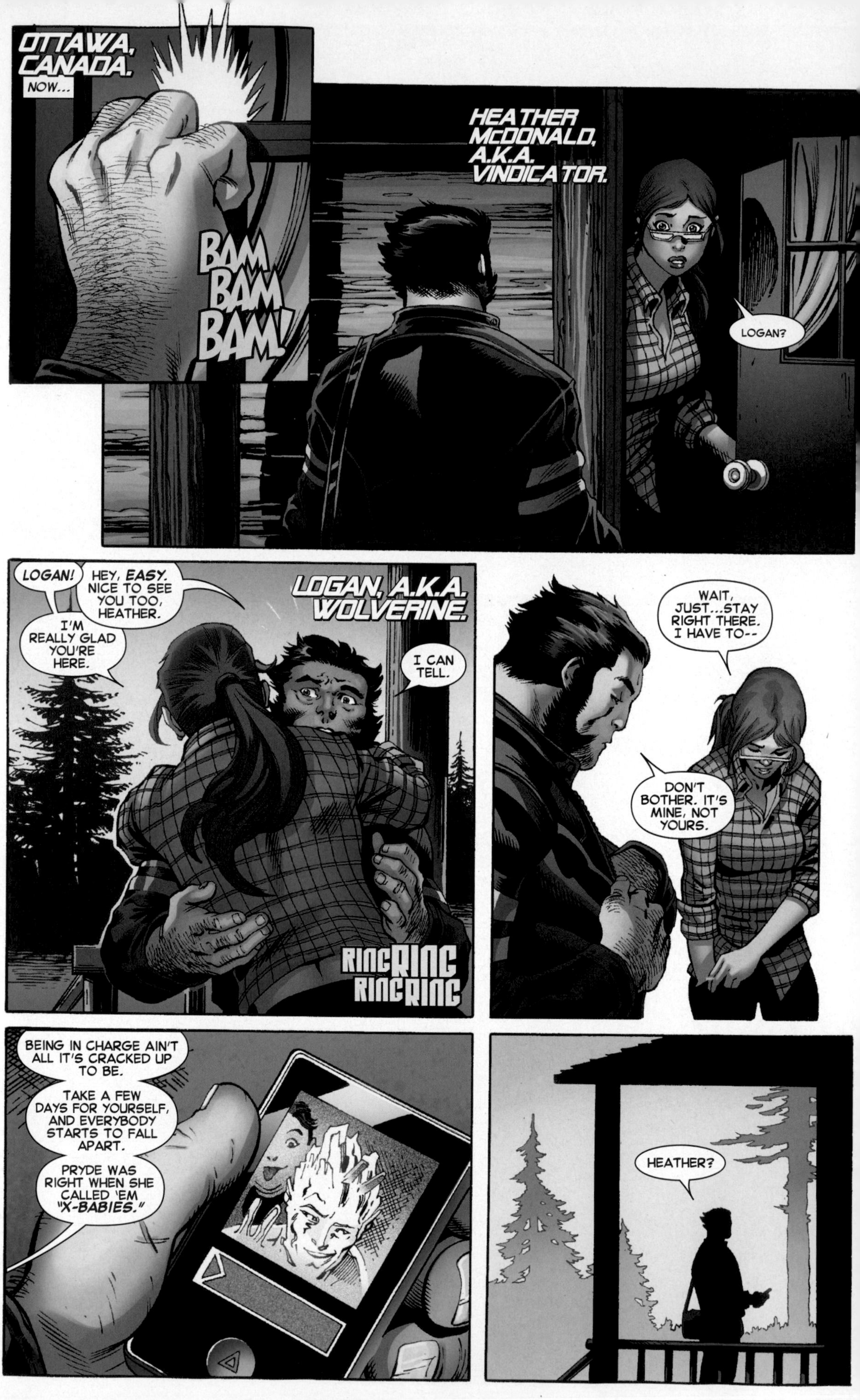
OTTAWA, CANADA.
NOW...
BAM BAM BAM!
HEATHER McDONALD, A.K.A. VINDICATOR.
LOGAN?
LOGAN!
HEY, EASY. NICE TO SEE YOU TOO, HEATHER.
I'M REALLY GLAD YOU'RE HERE.
LOGAN, A.K.A. WOLVERINE.
I CAN TELL.
RINGRING RINGRING
WAIT, JUST...STAY RIGHT THERE. I HAVE TO--
DON'T BOTHER. IT'S MINE, NOT YOURS.
BEING IN CHARGE AIN'T ALL IT'S CRACKED UP TO BE.
TAKE A FEW DAYS FOR YOURSELF, AND EVERYBODY STARTS TO FALL APART.
PRYDE WAS RIGHT WHEN SHE CALLED 'EM "X-BABIES."
HEATHER?

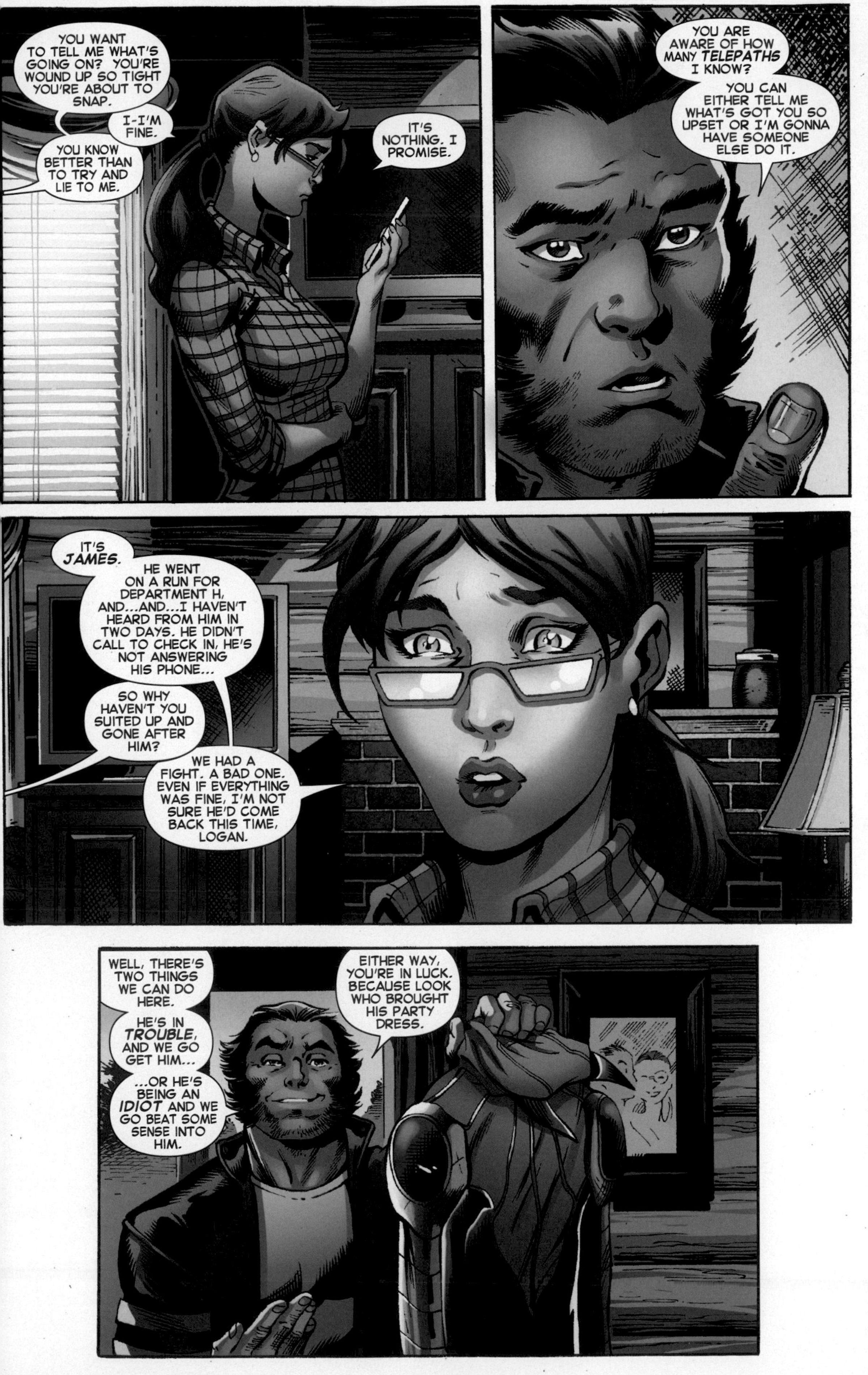
YOU WANT TO TELL ME WHAT'S GOING ON? YOU'RE WOUND UP SO TIGHT YOU'RE ABOUT TO SNAP.
I-I'M FINE.
YOU KNOW BETTER THAN TO TRY AND LIE TO ME.
IT'S NOTHING. I PROMISE.
YOU ARE AWARE OF HOW MANY *TELEPATHS* I KNOW?
YOU CAN EITHER TELL ME WHAT'S GOT YOU SO UPSET OR I'M GONNA HAVE SOMEONE ELSE DO IT.
IT'S *JAMES*.
HE WENT ON A RUN FOR DEPARTMENT H, AND...AND...I HAVEN'T HEARD FROM HIM IN TWO DAYS. HE DIDN'T CALL TO CHECK IN, HE'S NOT ANSWERING HIS PHONE...
SO WHY HAVEN'T YOU SUITED UP AND GONE AFTER HIM?
WE HAD A FIGHT. A BAD ONE. EVEN IF EVERYTHING WAS FINE, I'M NOT SURE HE'D COME BACK THIS TIME, LOGAN.
WELL, THERE'S TWO THINGS WE CAN DO HERE.
HE'S IN *TROUBLE*, AND WE GO GET HIM...
...OR HE'S BEING AN *IDIOT* AND WE GO BEAT SOME SENSE INTO HIM.
EITHER WAY, YOU'RE IN LUCK. BECAUSE LOOK WHO BROUGHT HIS PARTY DRESS.

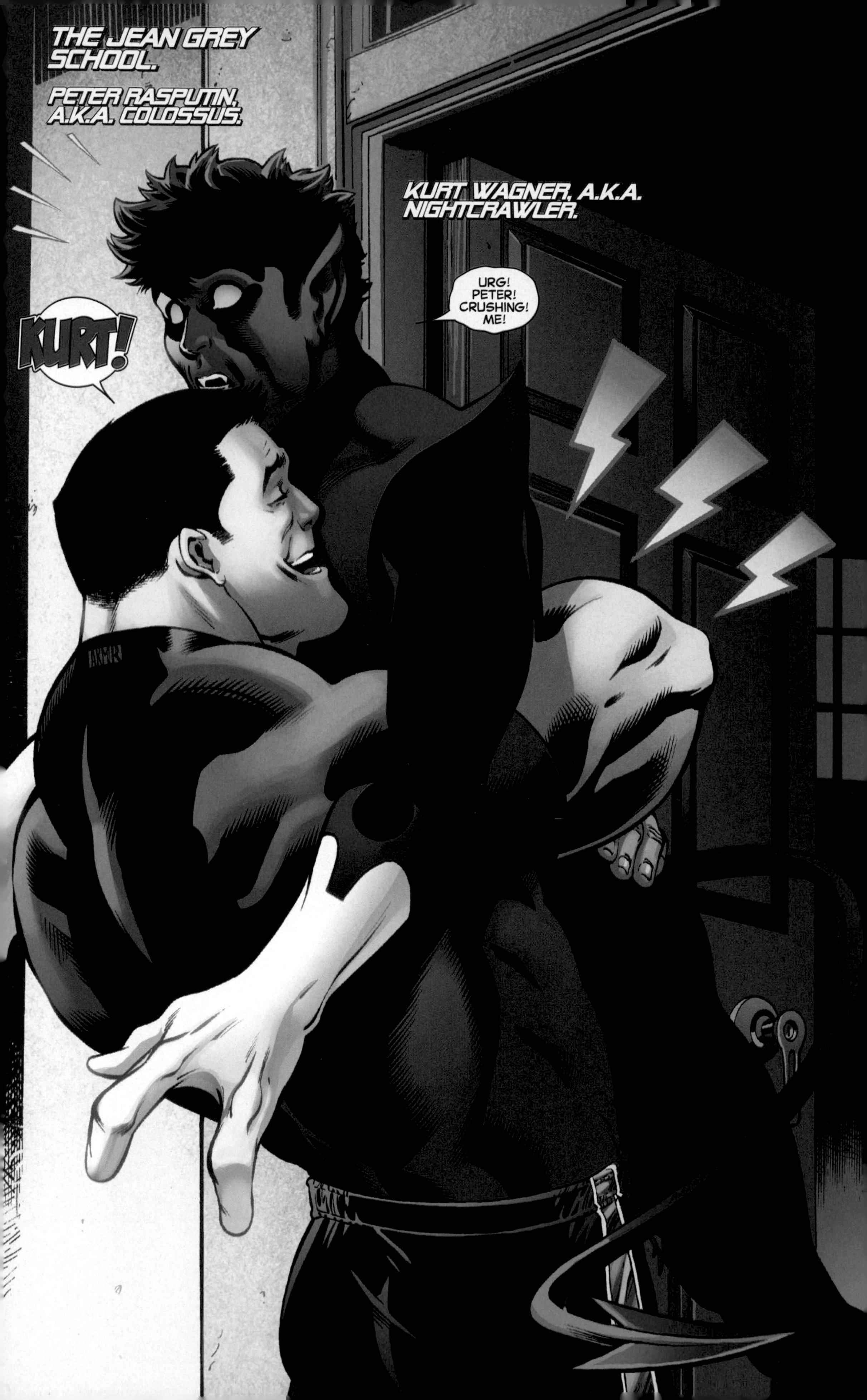
THE JEAN GREY SCHOOL.
PETER RASPUTIN, A.K.A. COLOSSUS.
KURT WAGNER, A.K.A. NIGHTCRAWLER.
KURT!
URG! PETER! CRUSHING! ME!

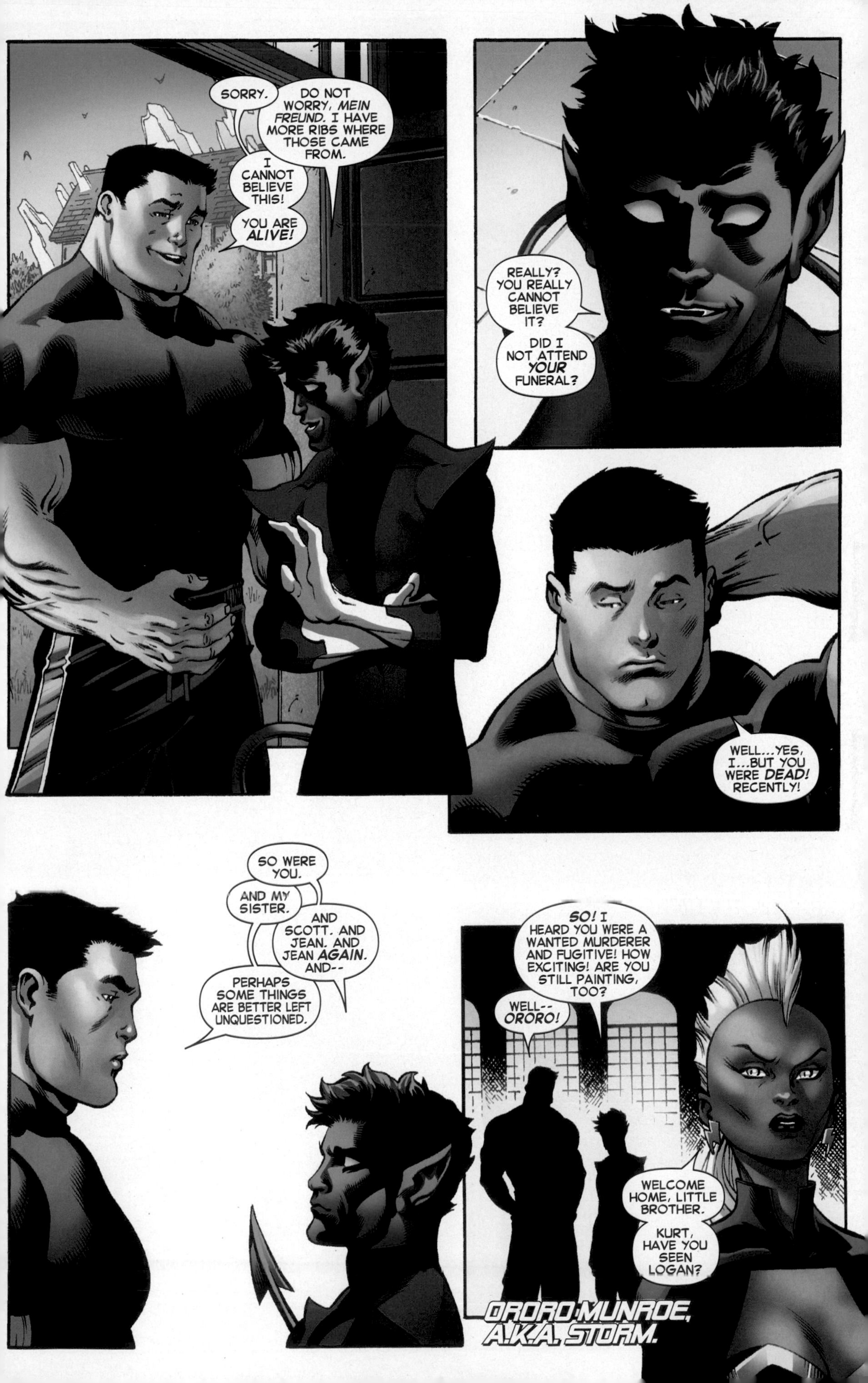
SORRY.
DO NOT WORRY, *MEIN FREUND.* I HAVE MORE RIBS WHERE THOSE CAME FROM.
I CANNOT BELIEVE THIS!
YOU ARE *ALIVE!*
REALLY? YOU REALLY CANNOT BELIEVE IT?
DID I NOT ATTEND *YOUR* FUNERAL?
WELL...YES, I...BUT YOU WERE *DEAD!* RECENTLY!
SO WERE YOU.
AND MY SISTER.
AND SCOTT. AND JEAN. AND JEAN *AGAIN.* AND--
PERHAPS SOME THINGS ARE BETTER LEFT UNQUESTIONED.
SO! I HEARD YOU WERE A WANTED MURDERER AND FUGITIVE! HOW EXCITING! ARE YOU STILL PAINTING, TOO?
WELL-- *ORORO!*
WELCOME HOME, LITTLE BROTHER.
KURT, HAVE YOU SEEN LOGAN?
ORORO MUNROE, A.K.A. STORM.

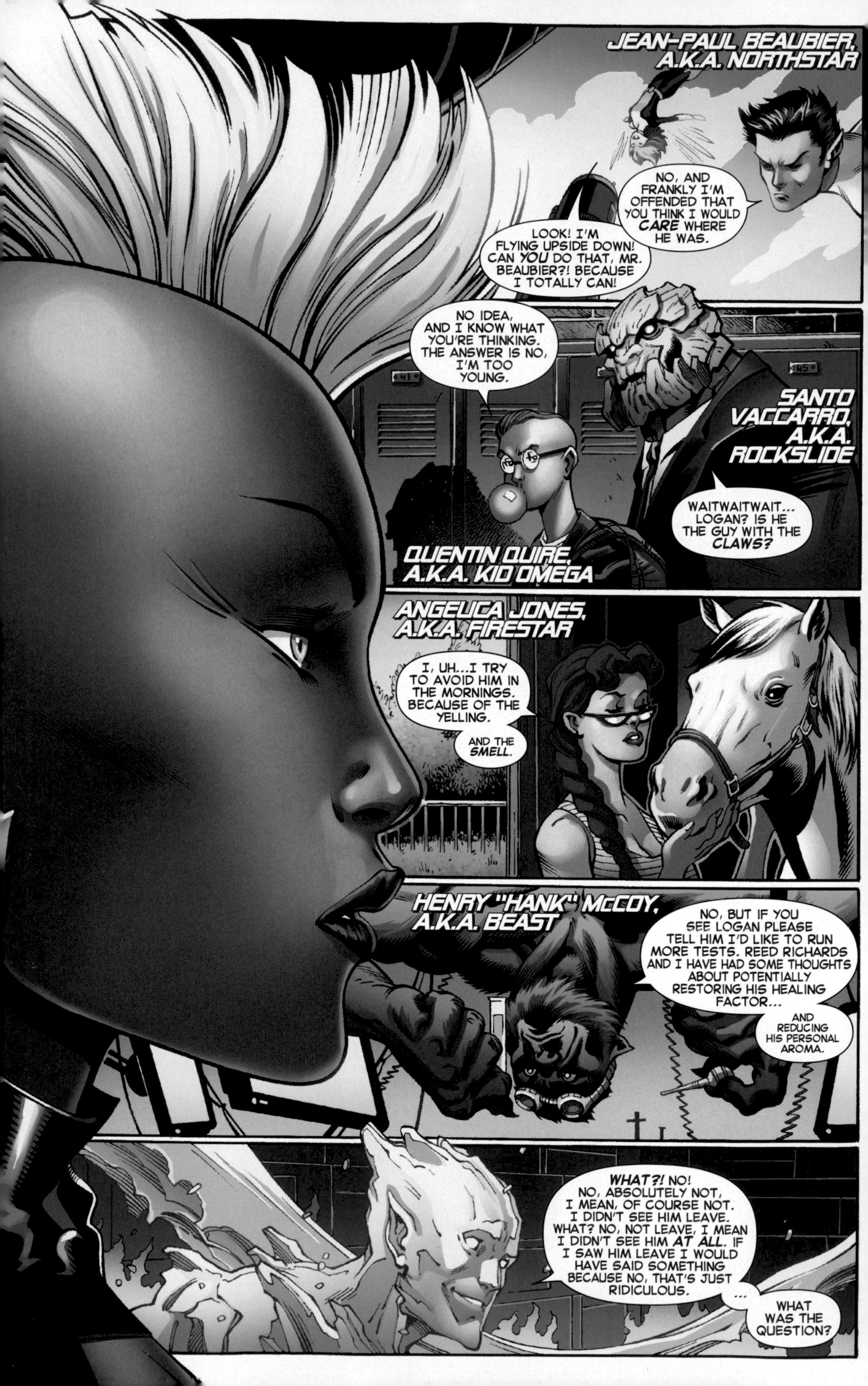

JEAN-PAUL BEAUBIER, A.K.A. NORTHSTAR
LOOK! I'M FLYING UPSIDE DOWN! CAN YOU DO THAT, MR. BEAUBIER?! BECAUSE I TOTALLY CAN!
NO, AND FRANKLY I'M OFFENDED THAT YOU THINK I WOULD CARE WHERE HE WAS.
NO IDEA, AND I KNOW WHAT YOU'RE THINKING. THE ANSWER IS NO, I'M TOO YOUNG.
SANTO VACCARRO, A.K.A. ROCKSLIDE
WAITWAITWAIT... LOGAN? IS HE THE GUY WITH THE CLAWS?
QUENTIN QUIRE, A.K.A. KID OMEGA
ANGELICA JONES, A.K.A. FIRESTAR
I, UH...I TRY TO AVOID HIM IN THE MORNINGS. BECAUSE OF THE YELLING.
AND THE SMELL.
HENRY "HANK" McCOY, A.K.A. BEAST
NO, BUT IF YOU SEE LOGAN PLEASE TELL HIM I'D LIKE TO RUN MORE TESTS. REED RICHARDS AND I HAVE HAD SOME THOUGHTS ABOUT POTENTIALLY RESTORING HIS HEALING FACTOR...
AND REDUCING HIS PERSONAL AROMA.
WHAT?! NO! NO, ABSOLUTELY NOT, I MEAN, OF COURSE NOT. I DIDN'T SEE HIM LEAVE. WHAT? NO, NOT LEAVE, I MEAN I DIDN'T SEE HIM AT ALL. IF I SAW HIM LEAVE I WOULD HAVE SAID SOMETHING BECAUSE NO, THAT'S JUST RIDICULOUS.
...
WHAT WAS THE QUESTION?

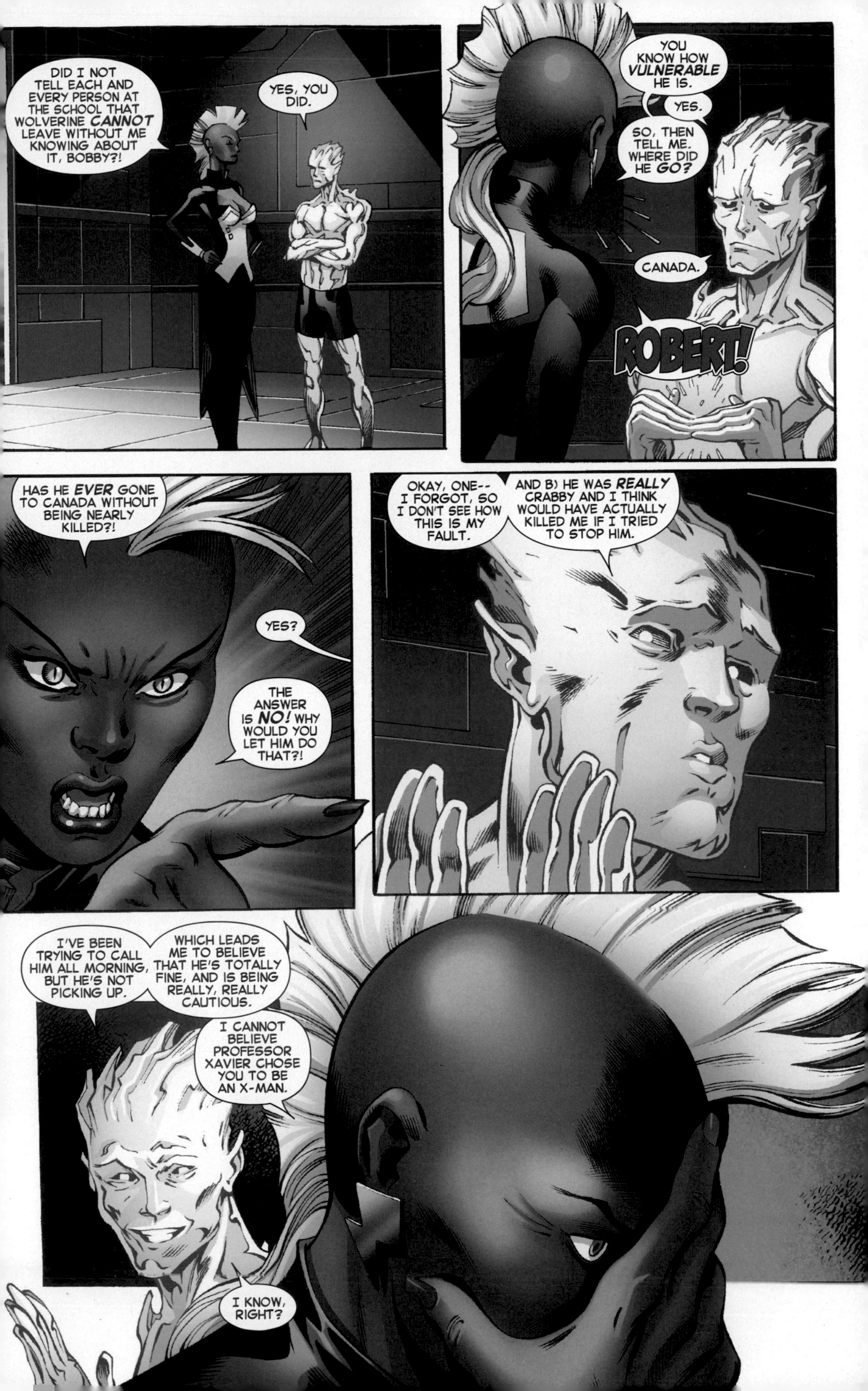
DID I NOT TELL EACH AND EVERY PERSON AT THE SCHOOL THAT WOLVERINE CANNOT LEAVE WITHOUT ME KNOWING ABOUT IT, BOBBY?!
YES, YOU DID.
YOU KNOW HOW VULNERABLE HE IS.
YES.
SO, THEN TELL ME. WHERE DID HE GO?
CANADA.
ROBERT!
HAS HE EVER GONE TO CANADA WITHOUT BEING NEARLY KILLED?!
YES?
THE ANSWER IS NO! WHY WOULD YOU LET HIM DO THAT?!
OKAY, ONE-- I FORGOT, SO I DON'T SEE HOW THIS IS MY FAULT.
AND B) HE WAS REALLY CRABBY AND I THINK WOULD HAVE ACTUALLY KILLED ME IF I TRIED TO STOP HIM.
I'VE BEEN TRYING TO CALL HIM ALL MORNING, BUT HE'S NOT PICKING UP.
WHICH LEADS ME TO BELIEVE THAT HE'S TOTALLY FINE, AND IS BEING REALLY, REALLY CAUTIOUS.
I CANNOT BELIEVE PROFESSOR XAVIER CHOSE YOU TO BE AN X-MAN.
I KNOW, RIGHT?

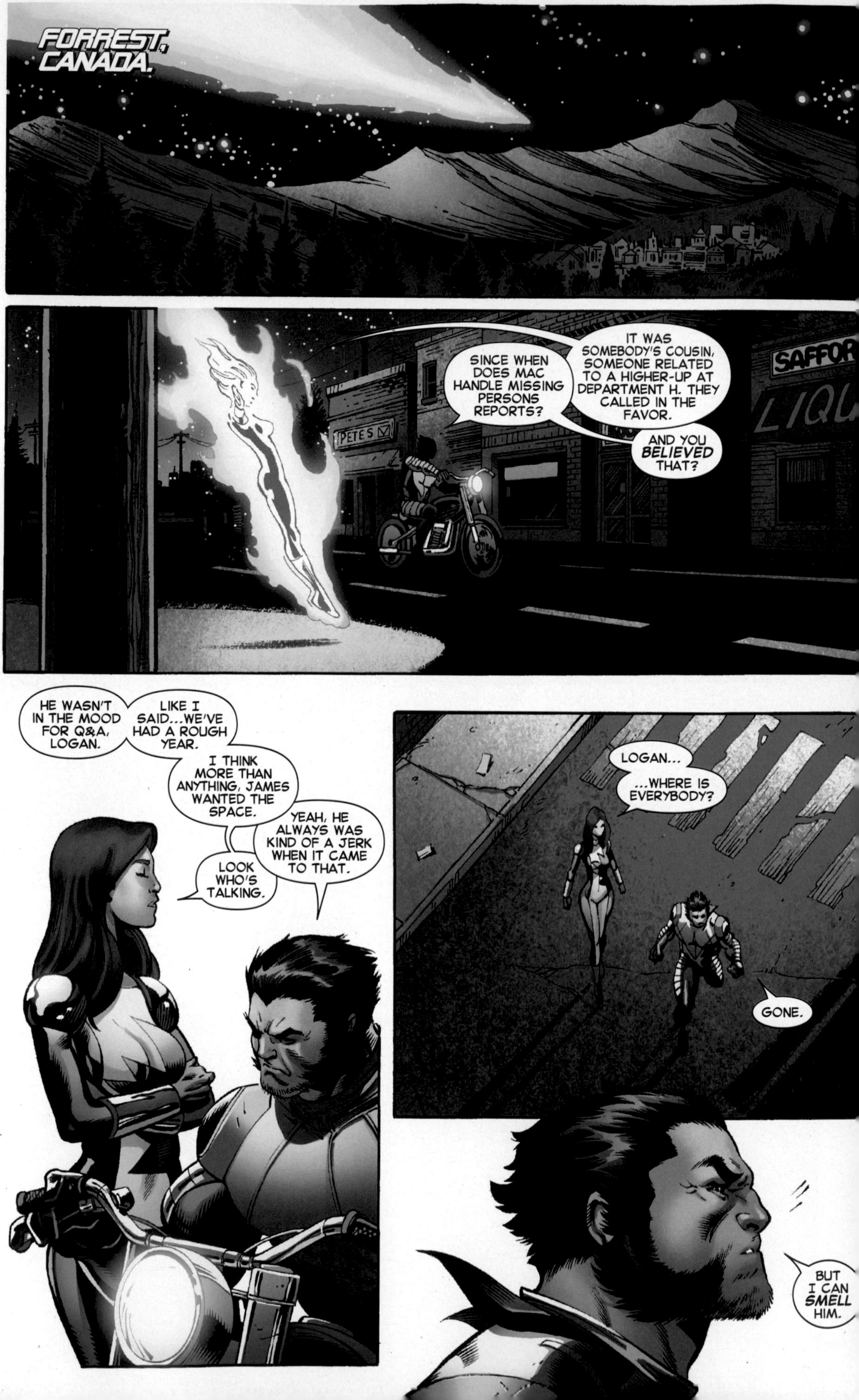
FORREST, CANADA.
SINCE WHEN DOES MAC HANDLE MISSING PERSONS REPORTS?
IT WAS SOMEBODY'S COUSIN, SOMEONE RELATED TO A HIGHER-UP AT DEPARTMENT H. THEY CALLED IN THE FAVOR.
AND YOU BELIEVED THAT?
PETE S
SAFFOR
LIQU
HE WASN'T IN THE MOOD FOR Q&A, LOGAN.
LIKE I SAID...WE'VE HAD A ROUGH YEAR.
I THINK MORE THAN ANYTHING, JAMES WANTED THE SPACE.
YEAH, HE ALWAYS WAS KIND OF A JERK WHEN IT CAME TO THAT.
LOOK WHO'S TALKING.
LOGAN...
...WHERE IS EVERYBODY?
GONE.
BUT I CAN SMELL HIM.

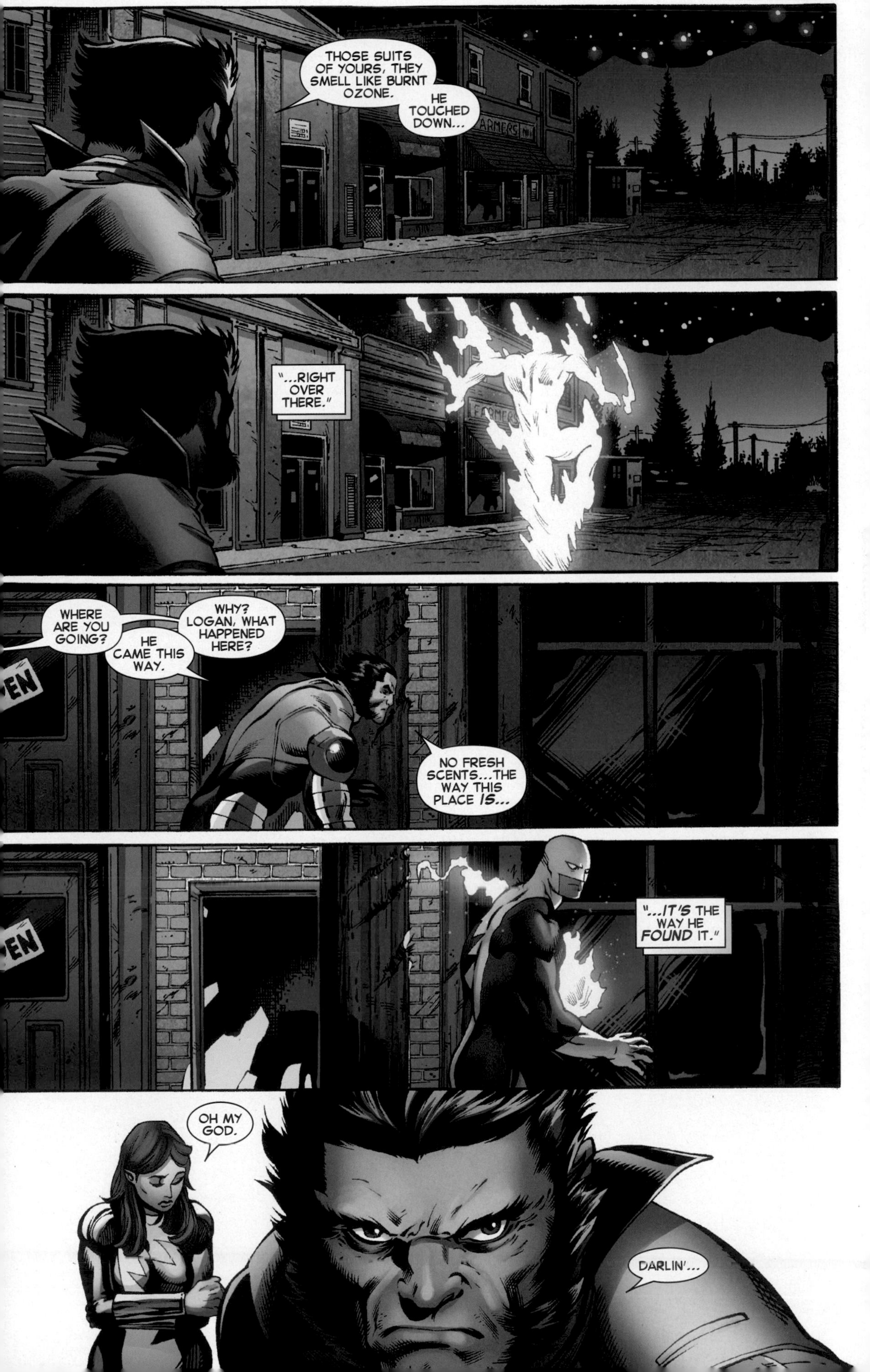
THOSE SUITS OF YOURS, THEY SMELL LIKE BURNT OZONE.
HE TOUCHED DOWN...
FARMERS
"...RIGHT OVER THERE."
WHERE ARE YOU GOING?
HE CAME THIS WAY.
WHY? LOGAN, WHAT HAPPENED HERE?
NO FRESH SCENTS...THE WAY THIS PLACE *IS*...
"...*IT'S* THE WAY HE *FOUND* IT."
OH MY GOD.
DARLIN'...

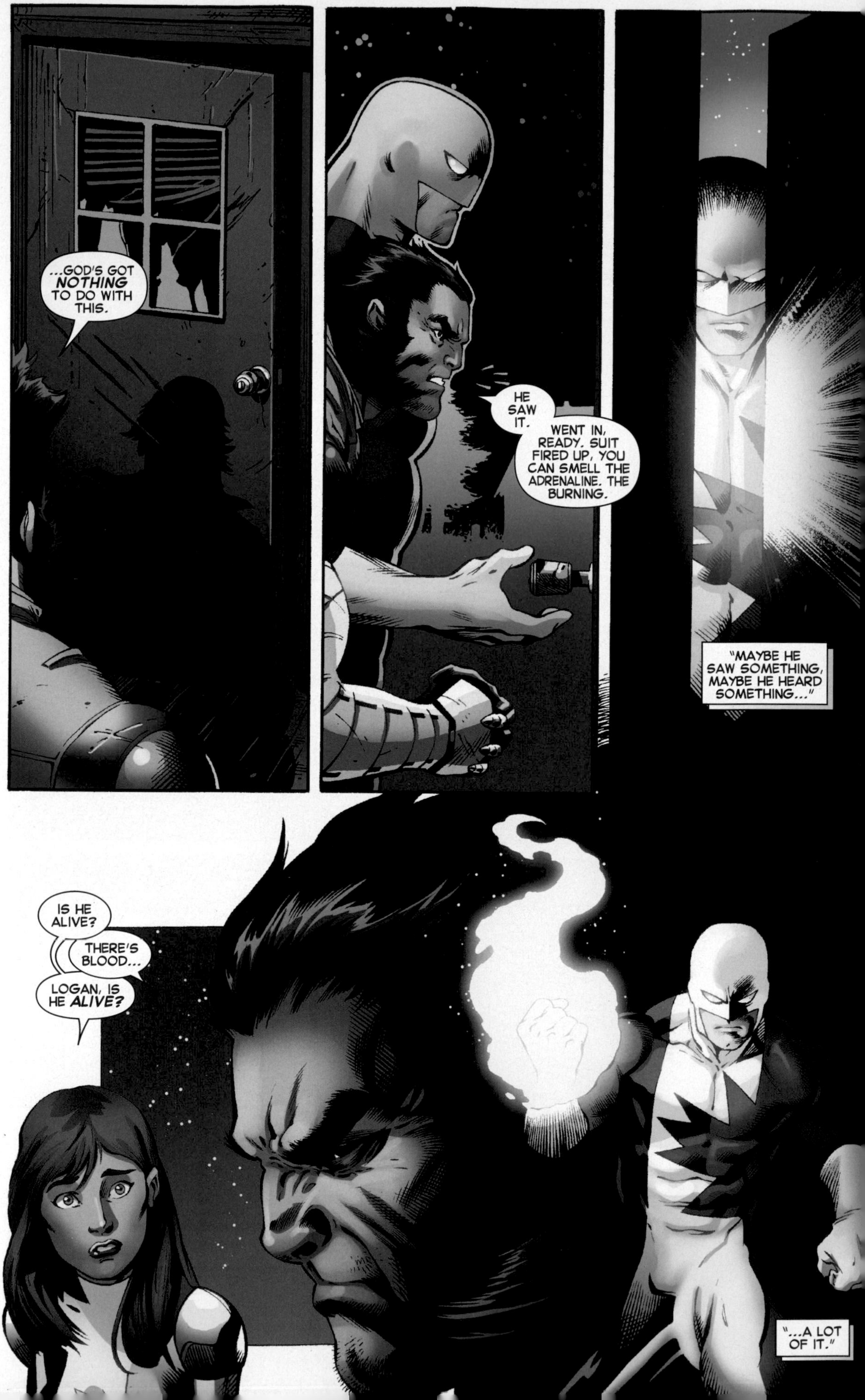
...GOD'S GOT NOTHING TO DO WITH THIS.
HE SAW IT.
WENT IN, READY. SUIT FIRED UP, YOU CAN SMELL THE ADRENALINE. THE BURNING.
"MAYBE HE SAW SOMETHING, MAYBE HE HEARD SOMETHING..."
IS HE ALIVE?
THERE'S BLOOD...
LOGAN, IS HE ALIVE?
"...A LOT OF IT."

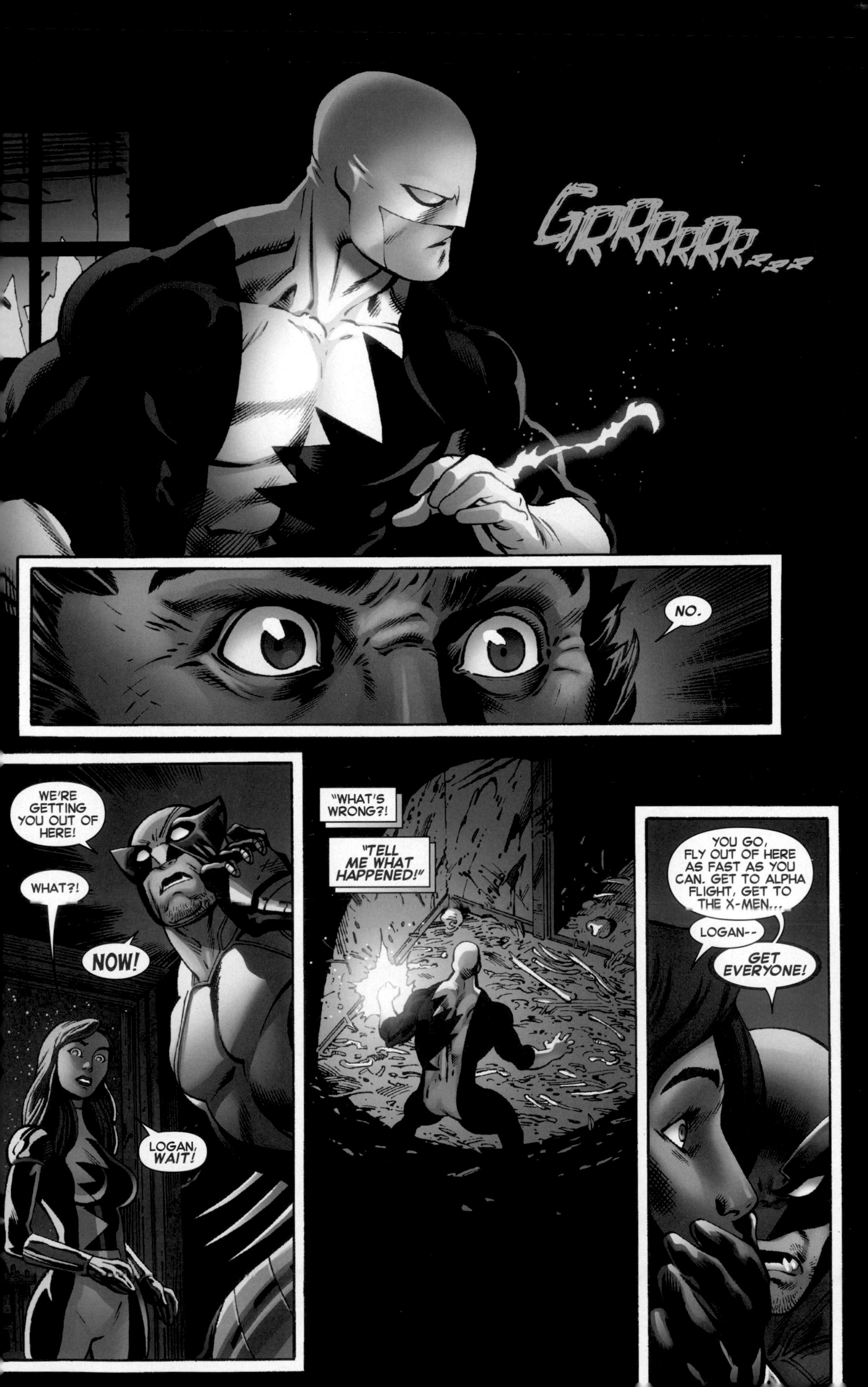
GRRRRRRzzz
NO.
WE'RE GETTING YOU OUT OF HERE!
WHAT?!
NOW!
LOGAN, WAIT!
"WHAT'S WRONG?!
"TELL ME WHAT HAPPENED!"
YOU GO, FLY OUT OF HERE AS FAST AS YOU CAN. GET TO ALPHA FLIGHT, GET TO THE X-MEN...
LOGAN--
GET EVERYONE!

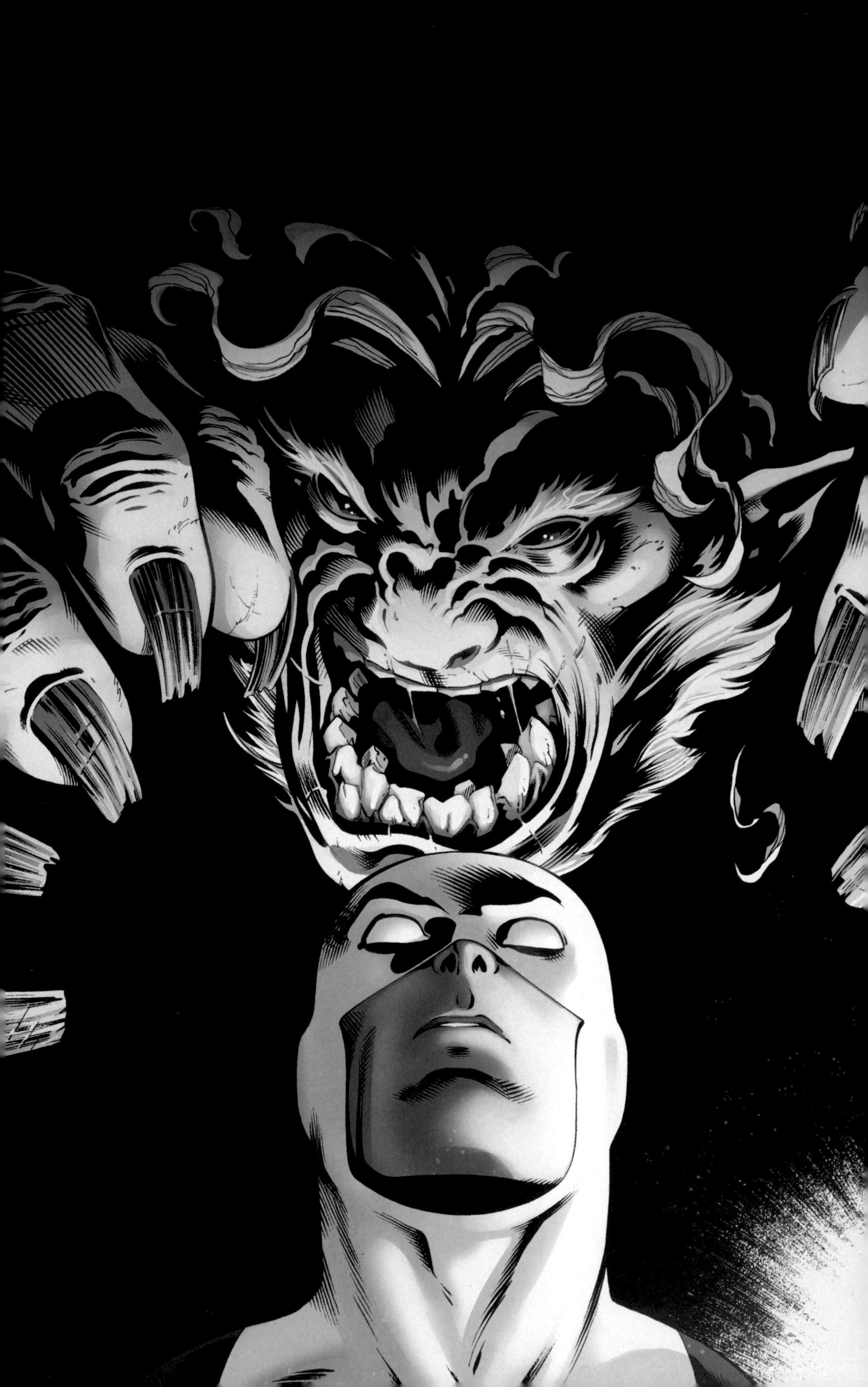

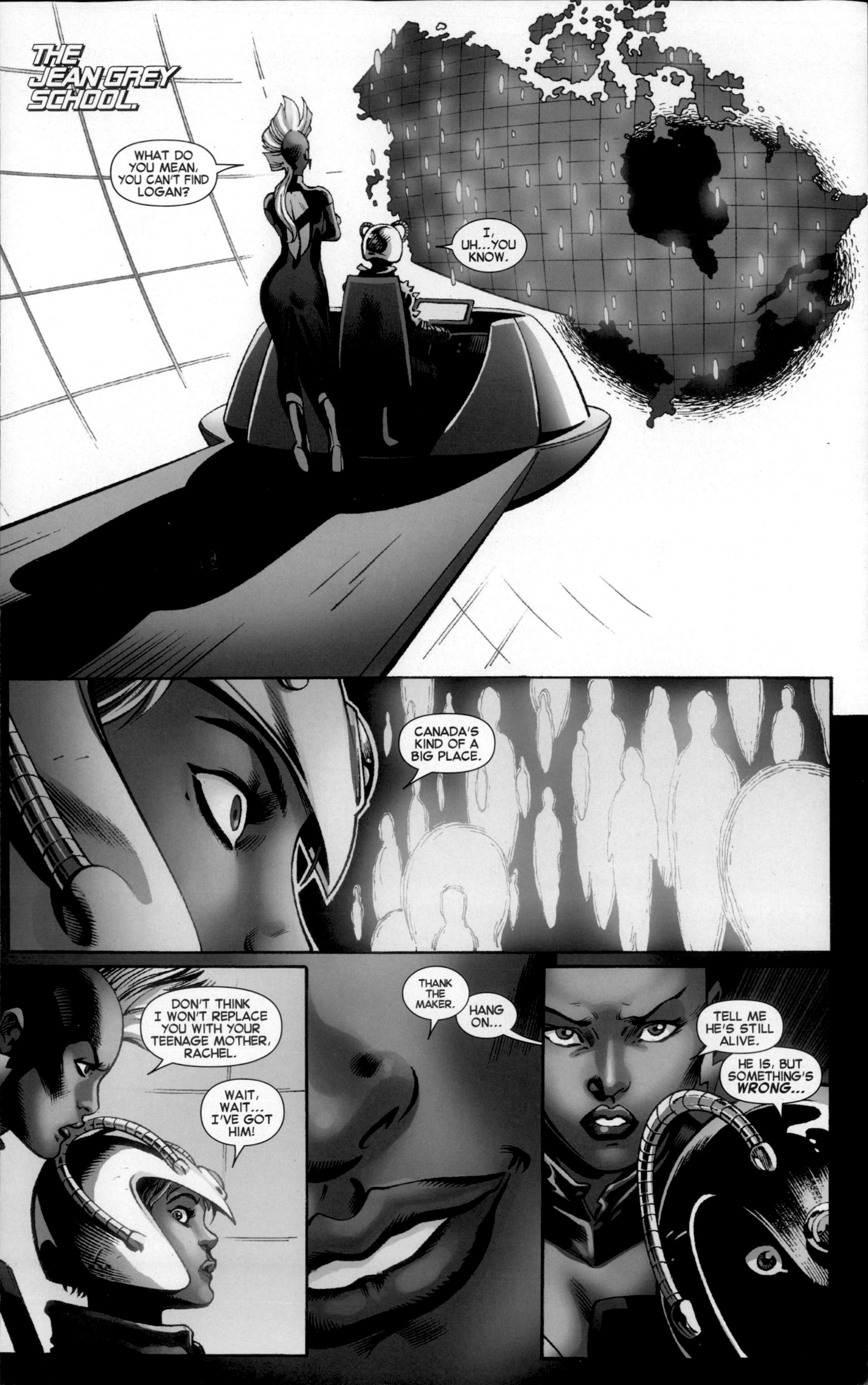
THE JEAN GREY SCHOOL.
WHAT DO YOU MEAN, YOU CAN'T FIND LOGAN?
I, UH...YOU KNOW.
CANADA'S KIND OF A BIG PLACE.
DON'T THINK I WON'T REPLACE YOU WITH YOUR TEENAGE MOTHER, RACHEL.
WAIT, WAIT... I'VE GOT HIM!
THANK THE MAKER.
HANG ON...
TELL ME HE'S STILL ALIVE.
HE IS, BUT SOMETHING'S WRONG...

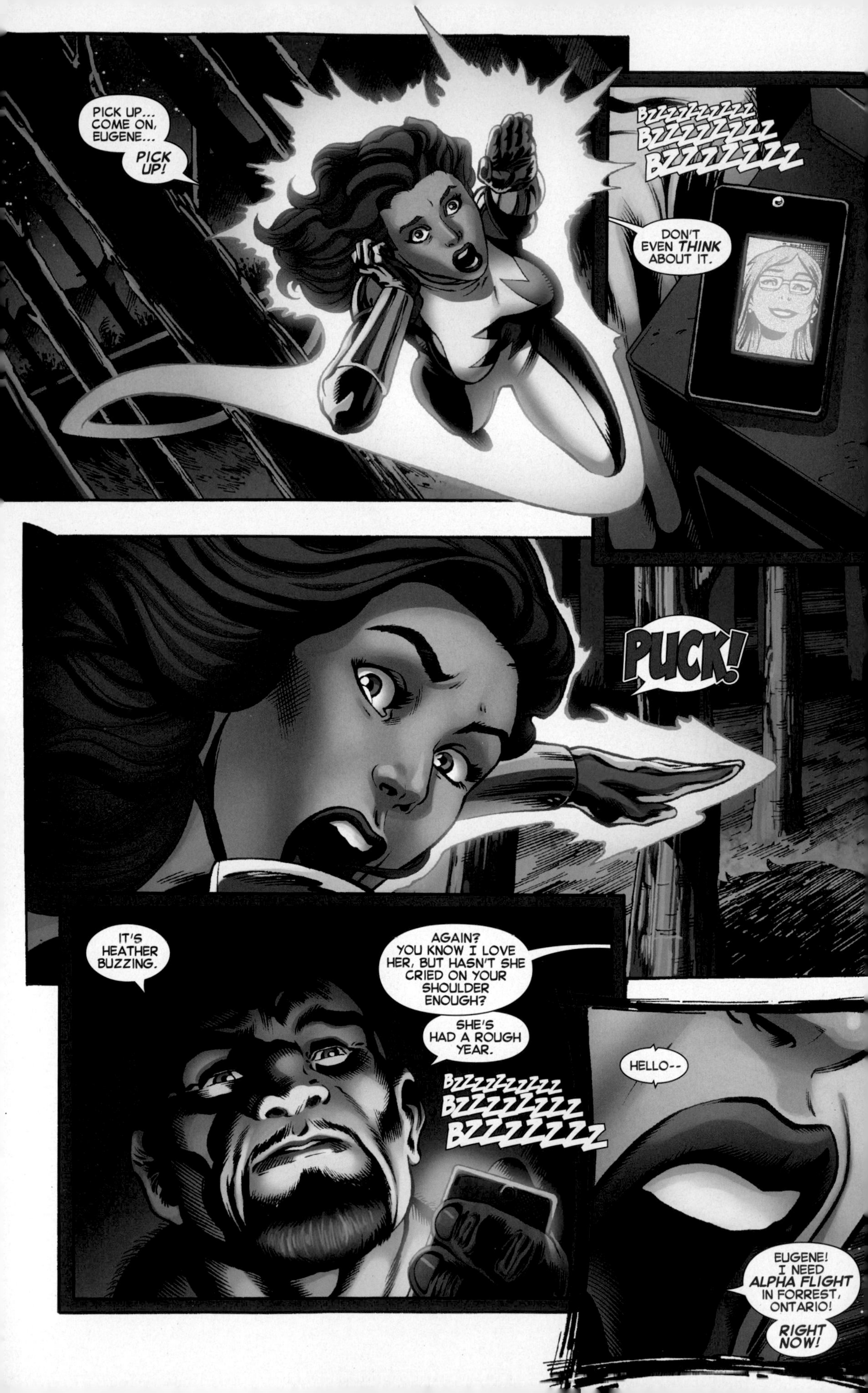
PICK UP... COME ON, EUGENE...
PICK UP!
BZZZZZZZZZZ BZZZZZZZZZ BZZZZZZZ
DON'T EVEN THINK ABOUT IT.
PUCK!
IT'S HEATHER BUZZING.
AGAIN? YOU KNOW I LOVE HER, BUT HASN'T SHE CRIED ON YOUR SHOULDER ENOUGH?
SHE'S HAD A ROUGH YEAR.
BZZZZZZZZZZ BZZZZZZZZZ BZZZZZZZ
HELLO--
EUGENE! I NEED ALPHA FLIGHT IN FORREST, ONTARIO!
RIGHT NOW!

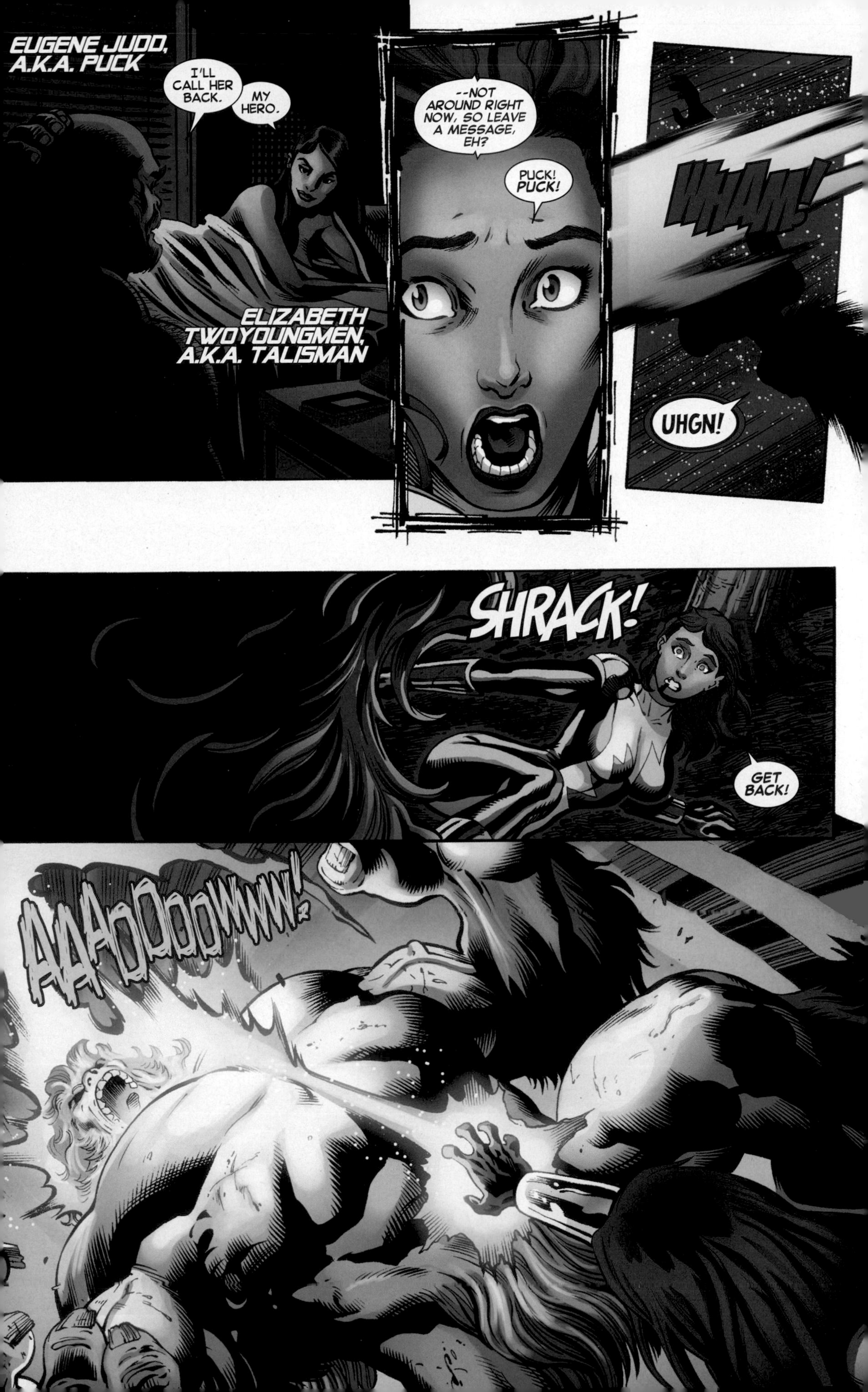
EUGENE JUDD, A.K.A. PUCK
I'LL CALL HER BACK.
MY HERO.
ELIZABETH TWOYOUNGMEN, A.K.A. TALISMAN
--NOT AROUND RIGHT NOW, SO LEAVE A MESSAGE, EH?
PUCK! PUCK!
WHAM!
UHGN!
SHRACK!
GET BACK!
AAAOOOOWWW!

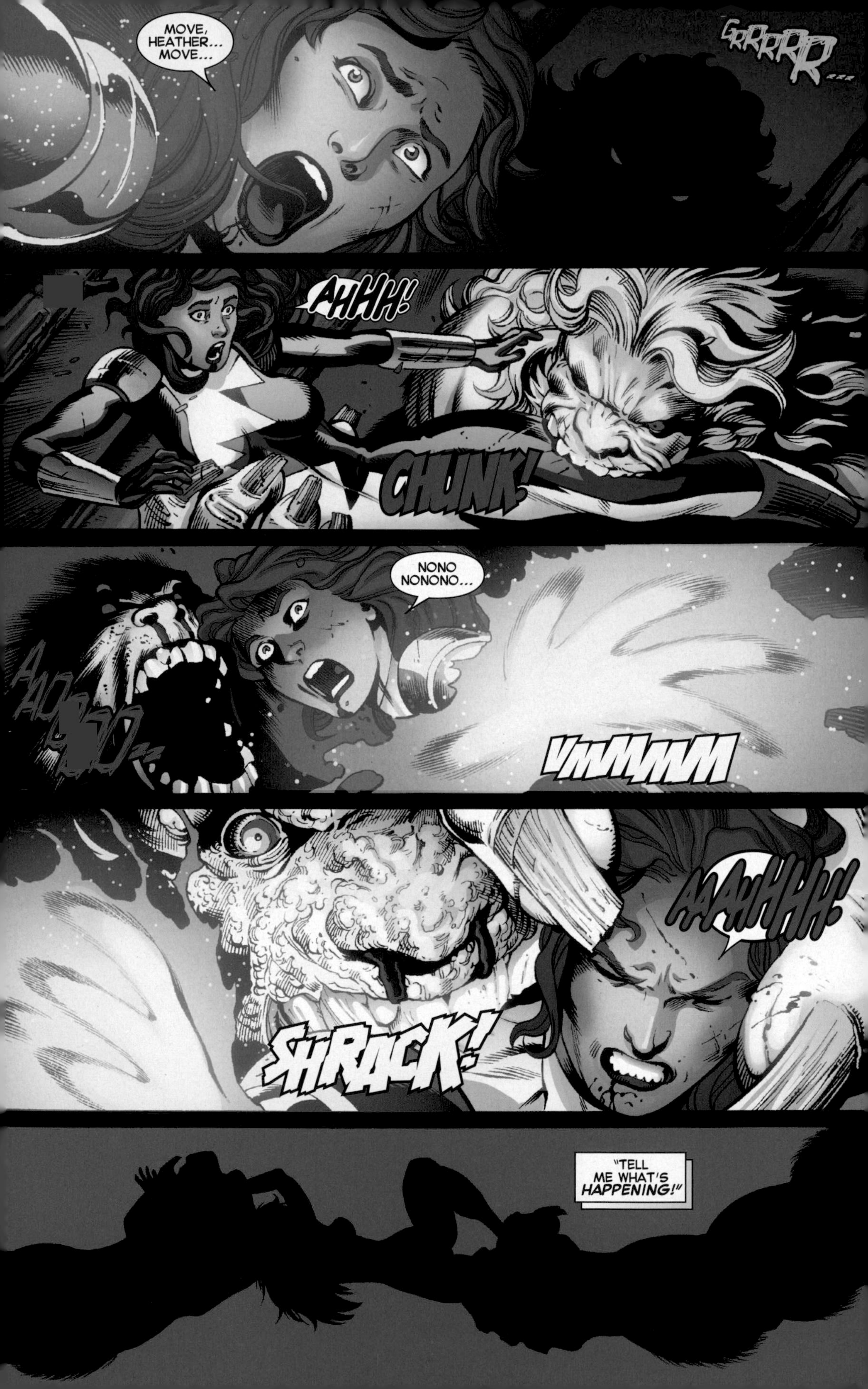
MOVE, HEATHER... MOVE...
GRRRRR...
AHHH!
CHUNK!
NONO NONONO...
VMMMMM
AAAHHHH!
SHRACK!
"TELL ME WHAT'S HAPPENING!"

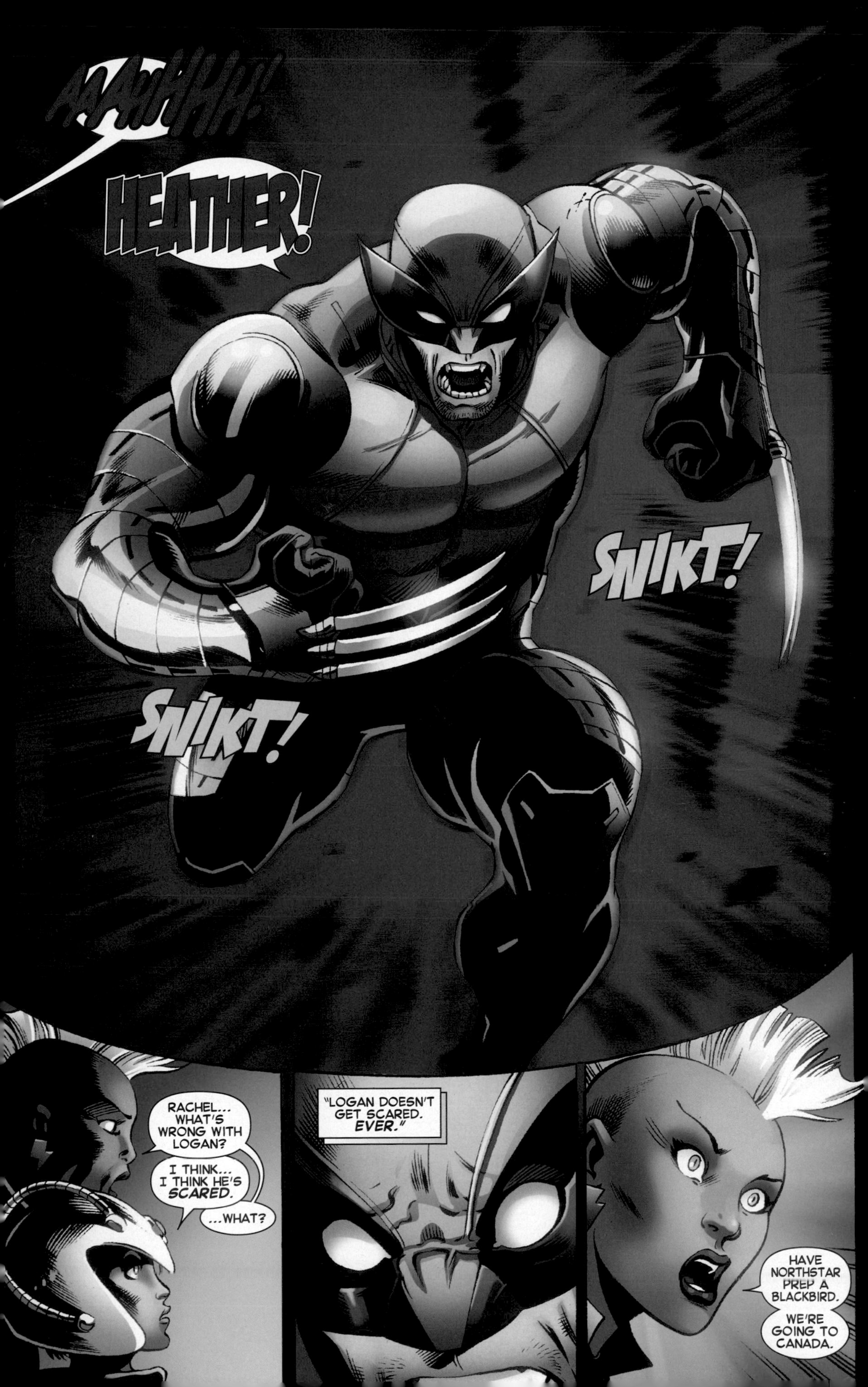
AAAHHHH!
HEATHER!
SNIKT!
SNIKT!
RACHEL... WHAT'S WRONG WITH LOGAN?
I THINK... I THINK HE'S SCARED.
...WHAT?
"LOGAN DOESN'T GET SCARED. EVER."
HAVE NORTHSTAR PREP A BLACKBIRD.
WE'RE GOING TO CANADA.

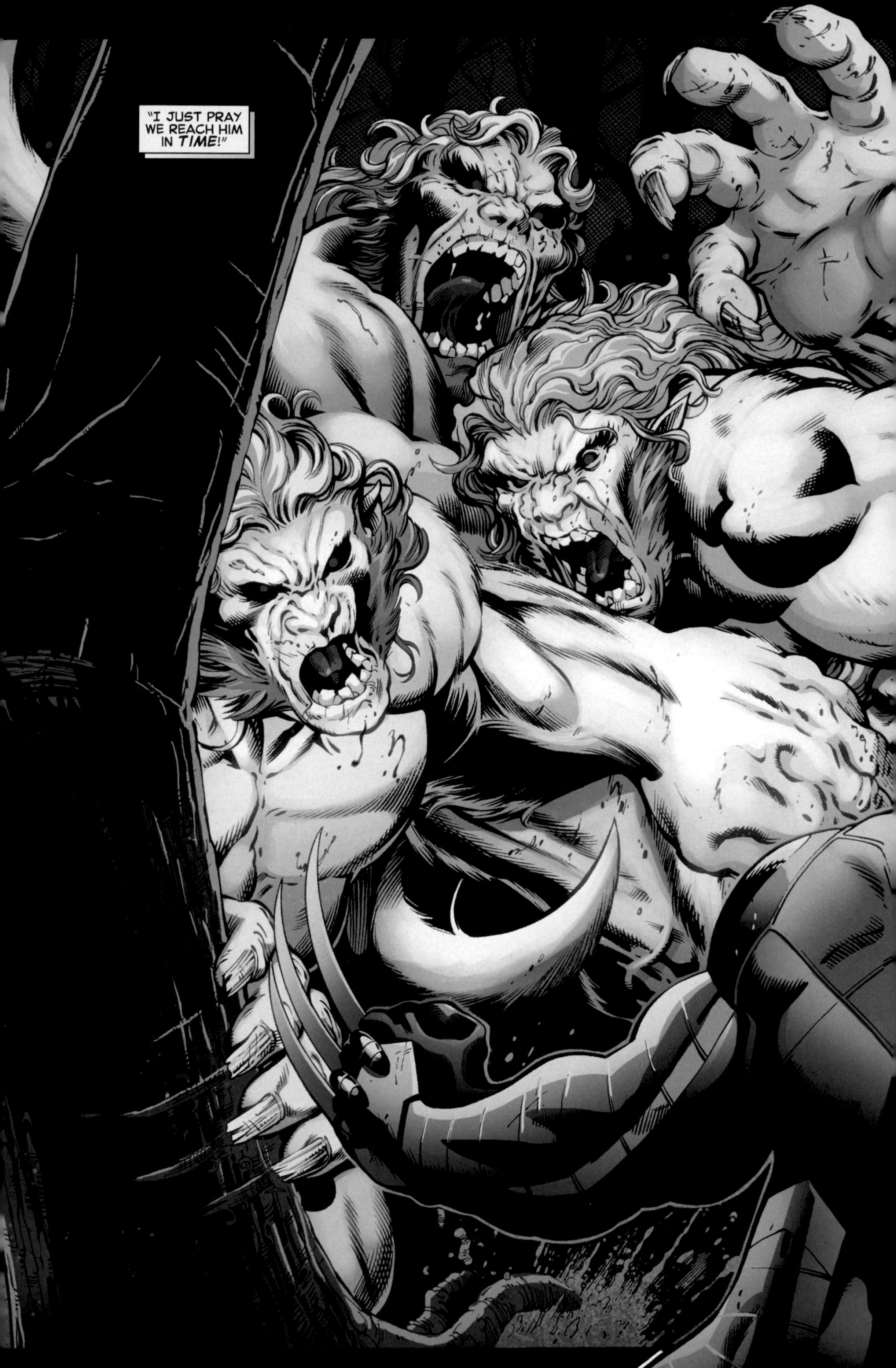
"I JUST PRAY WE REACH HIM IN *TIME*!"

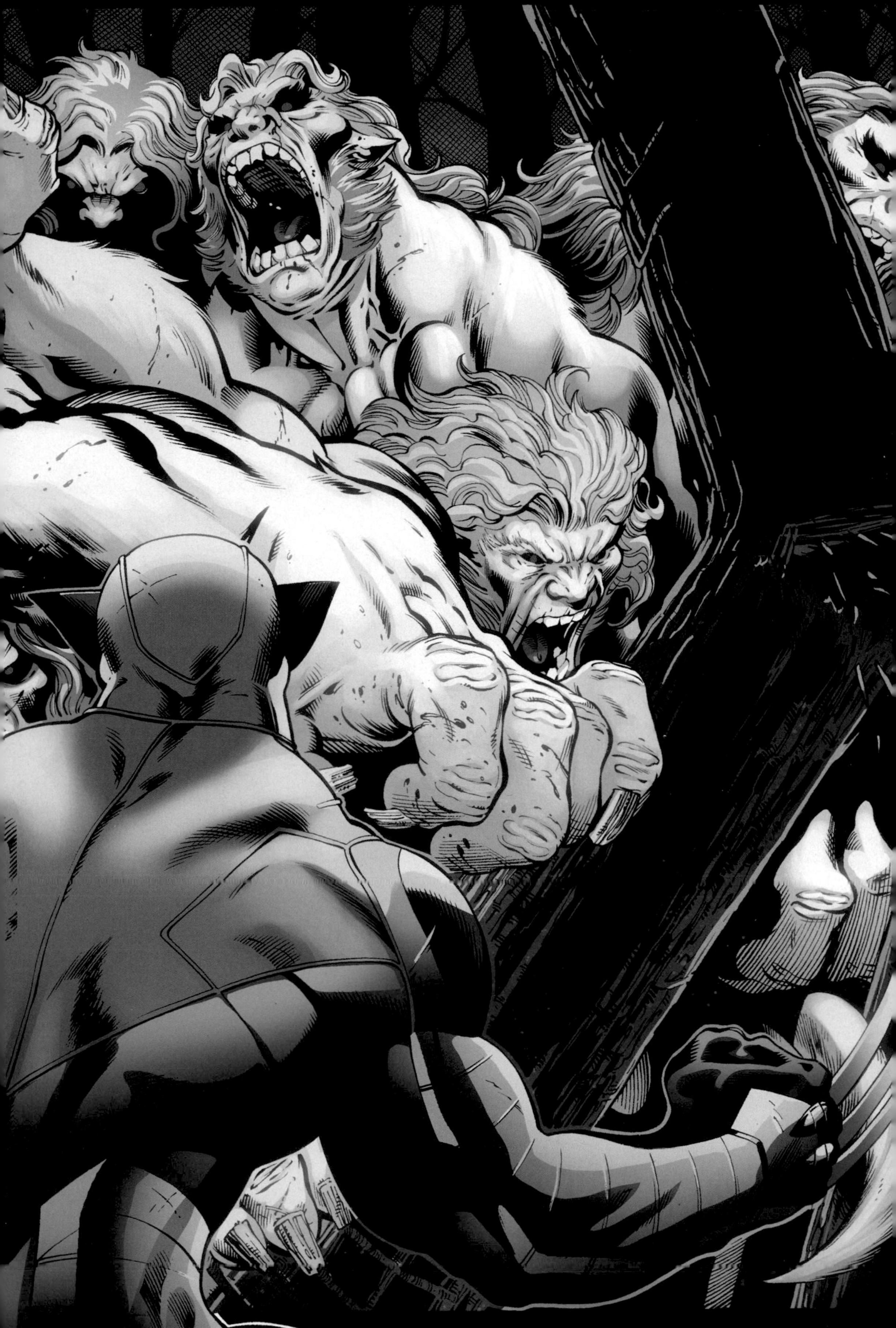

9

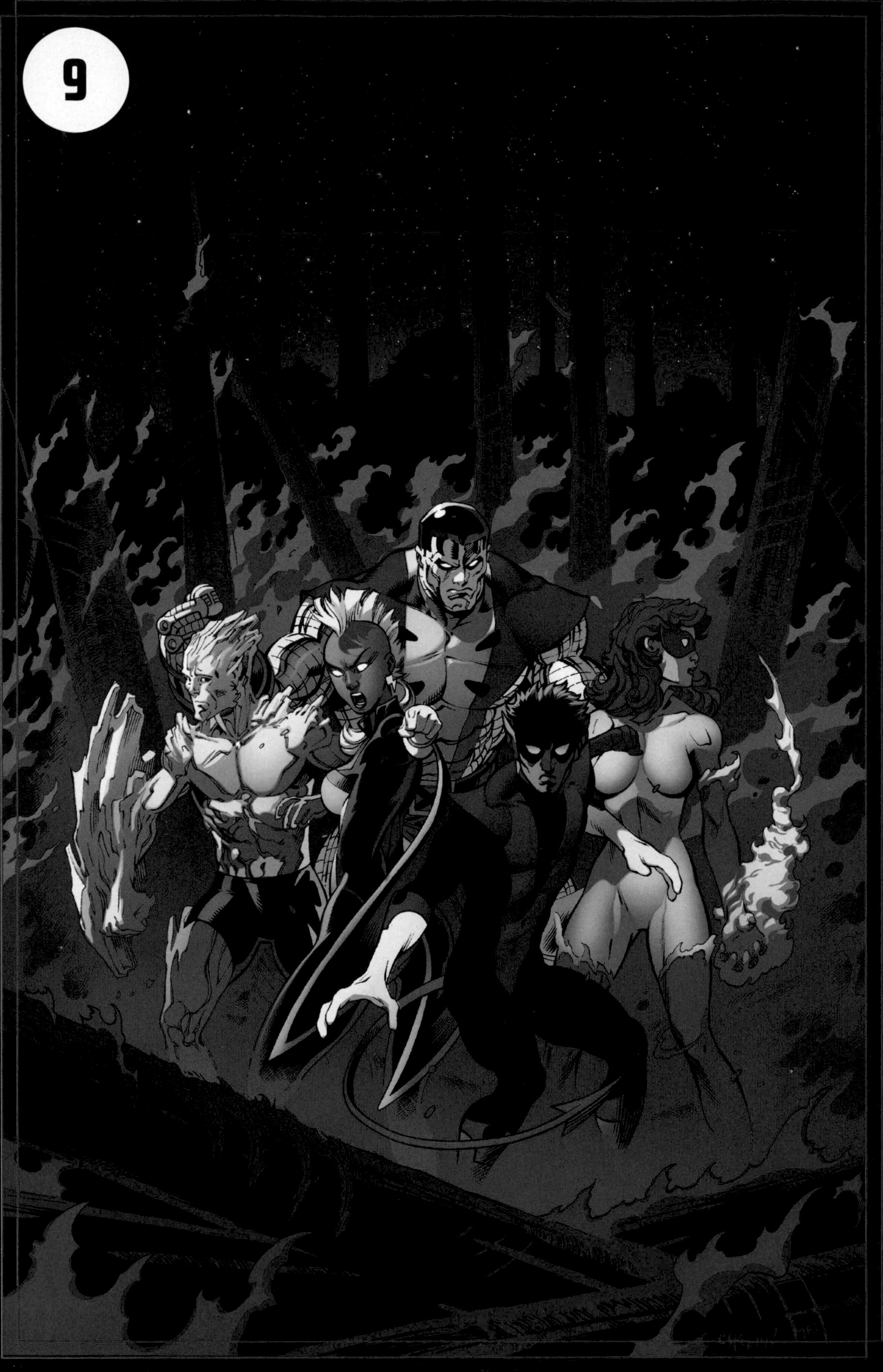

WORLD WAR WENDIGO! PART 2

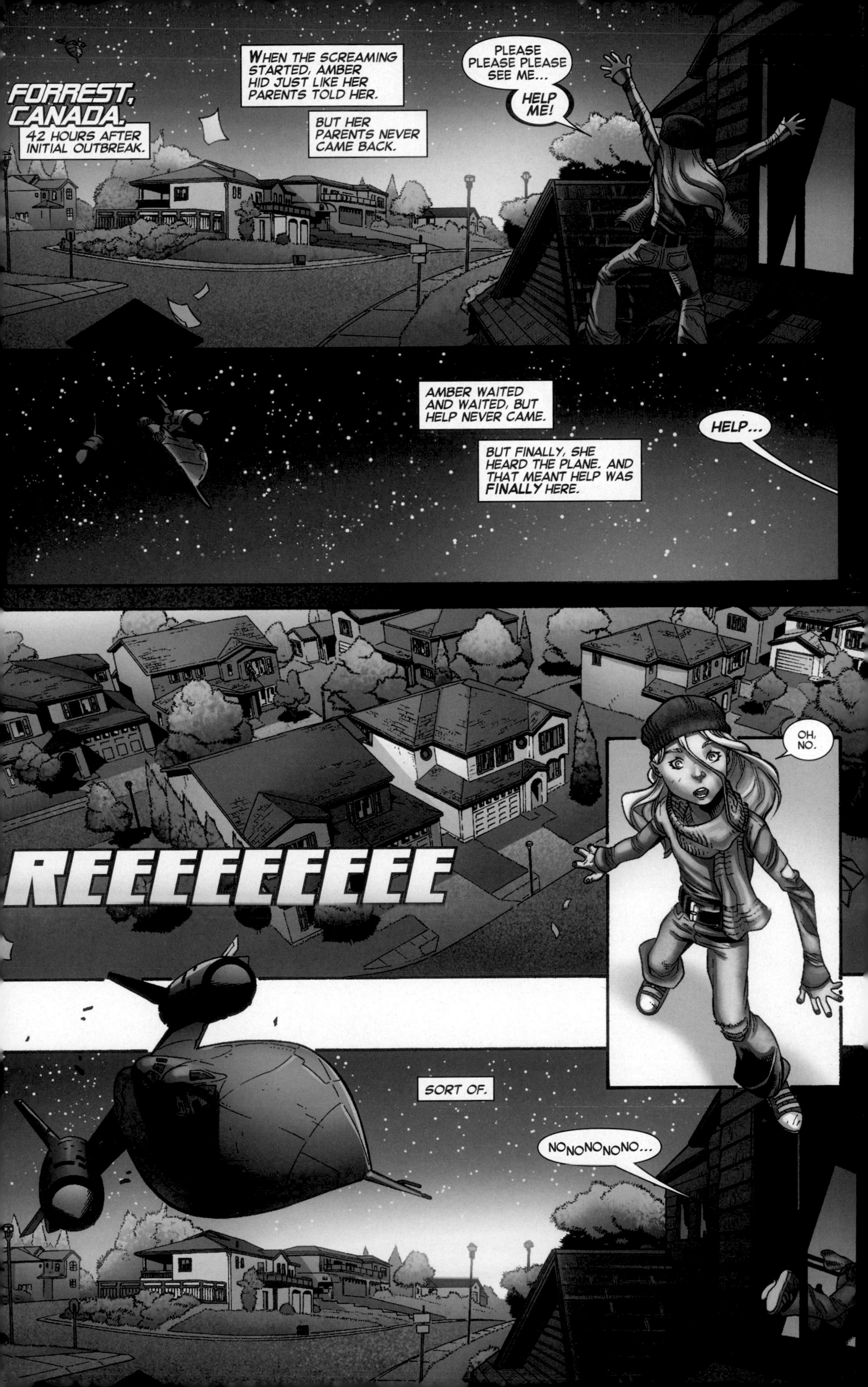
FORREST, CANADA.
42 HOURS AFTER INITIAL OUTBREAK.
WHEN THE SCREAMING STARTED, AMBER HID JUST LIKE HER PARENTS TOLD HER.
BUT HER PARENTS NEVER CAME BACK.
PLEASE PLEASE PLEASE SEE ME...
HELP ME!
AMBER WAITED AND WAITED, BUT HELP NEVER CAME.
BUT FINALLY, SHE HEARD THE PLANE. AND THAT MEANT HELP WAS FINALLY HERE.
HELP...
REEEEEEEEE
OH, NO.
SORT OF.
NONONONONONO...

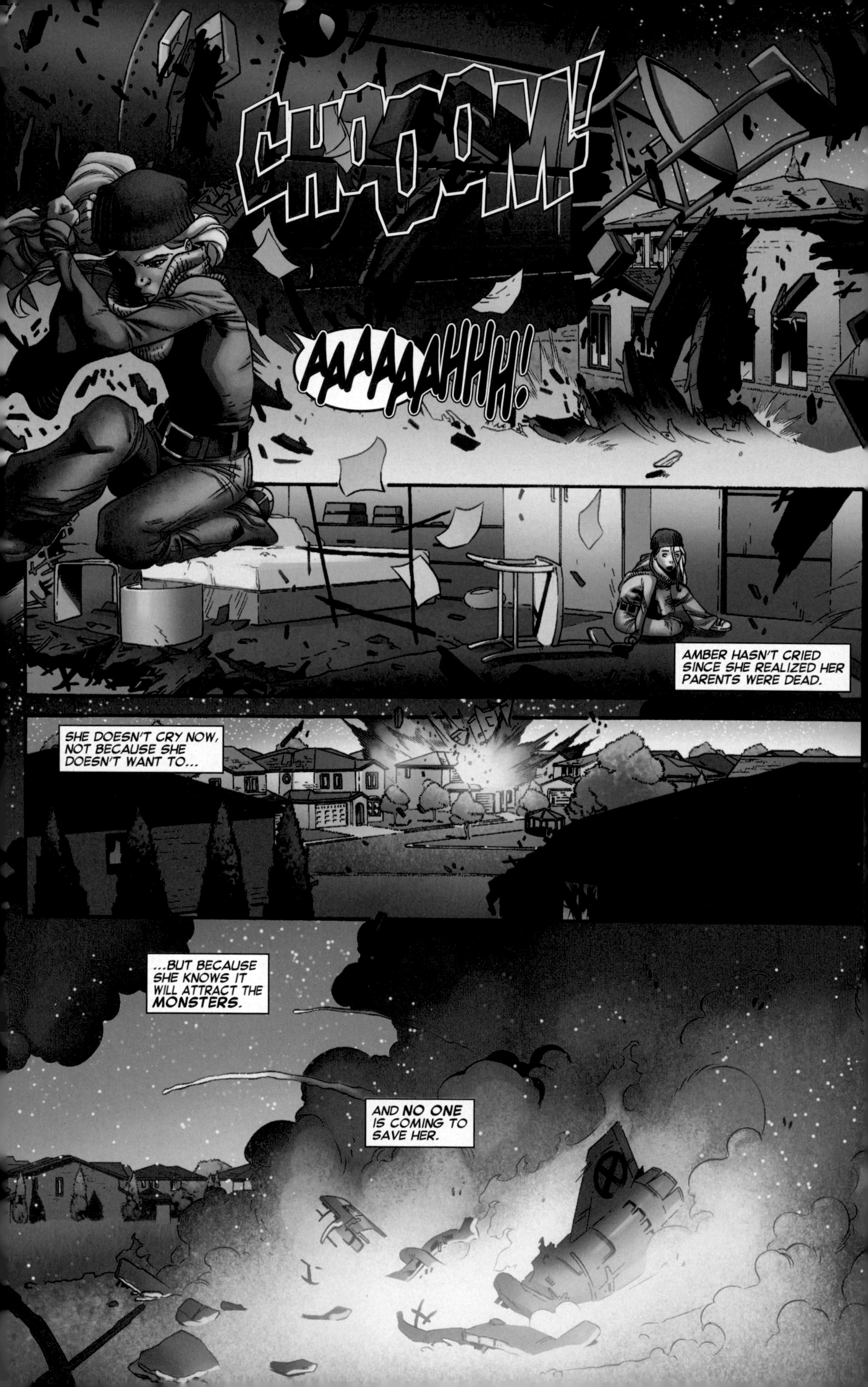
CHOOOM!
AAAAAAHHH!
AMBER HASN'T CRIED SINCE SHE REALIZED HER PARENTS WERE DEAD.
SHE DOESN'T CRY NOW, NOT BECAUSE SHE DOESN'T WANT TO...
...BUT BECAUSE SHE KNOWS IT WILL ATTRACT THE MONSTERS.
AND NO ONE IS COMING TO SAVE HER.

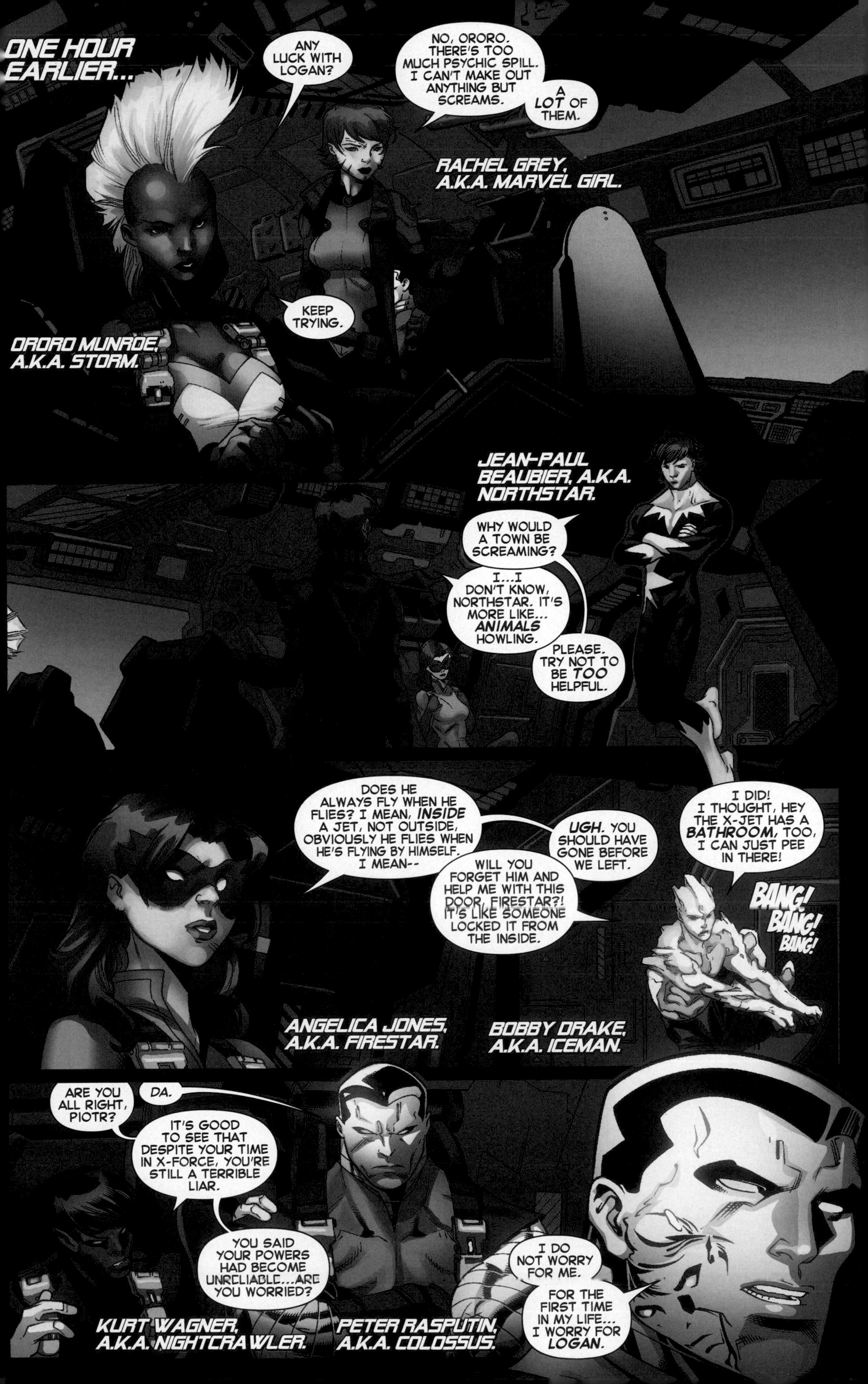
ONE HOUR EARLIER...
ANY LUCK WITH LOGAN?
NO, ORORO. THERE'S TOO MUCH PSYCHIC SPILL. I CAN'T MAKE OUT ANYTHING BUT SCREAMS.
A LOT OF THEM.
RACHEL GREY, A.K.A. MARVEL GIRL.
KEEP TRYING.
ORORO MUNROE, A.K.A. STORM.
JEAN-PAUL BEAUBIER, A.K.A. NORTHSTAR.
WHY WOULD A TOWN BE SCREAMING?
I...I DON'T KNOW, NORTHSTAR. IT'S MORE LIKE... ANIMALS HOWLING.
PLEASE. TRY NOT TO BE TOO HELPFUL.
DOES HE ALWAYS FLY WHEN HE FLIES? I MEAN, INSIDE A JET, NOT OUTSIDE, OBVIOUSLY HE FLIES WHEN HE'S FLYING BY HIMSELF. I MEAN--
UGH. YOU SHOULD HAVE GONE BEFORE WE LEFT.
I DID! I THOUGHT, HEY THE X-JET HAS A BATHROOM, TOO, I CAN JUST PEE IN THERE!
WILL YOU FORGET HIM AND HELP ME WITH THIS DOOR, FIRESTAR?! IT'S LIKE SOMEONE LOCKED IT FROM THE INSIDE.
BANG! BANG! BANG!
ANGELICA JONES, A.K.A. FIRESTAR.
BOBBY DRAKE, A.K.A. ICEMAN.
ARE YOU ALL RIGHT, PIOTR?
DA.
IT'S GOOD TO SEE THAT DESPITE YOUR TIME IN X-FORCE, YOU'RE STILL A TERRIBLE LIAR.
YOU SAID YOUR POWERS HAD BECOME UNRELIABLE...ARE YOU WORRIED?
I DO NOT WORRY FOR ME.
FOR THE FIRST TIME IN MY LIFE... I WORRY FOR LOGAN.
KURT WAGNER, A.K.A. NIGHTCRAWLER.
PETER RASPUTIN, A.K.A. COLOSSUS.

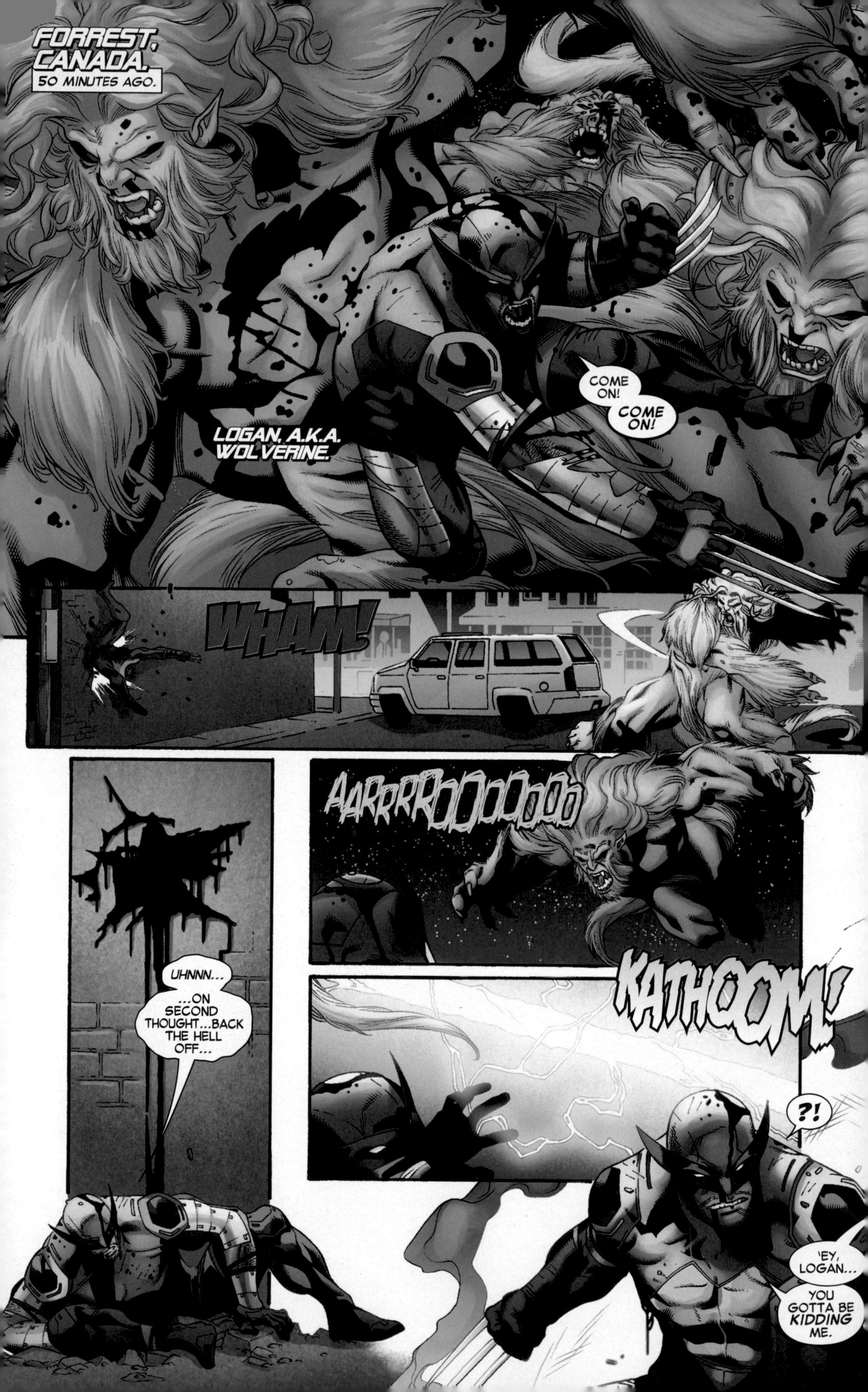
FORREST, CANADA.
50 MINUTES AGO.
LOGAN, A.K.A. WOLVERINE.
COME ON!
COME ON!
WHAM!
AARRRROOOOOOO
UHNNN...
...ON SECOND THOUGHT...BACK THE HELL OFF...
KATHOOM!
?!
'EY, LOGAN...
YOU GOTTA BE KIDDING ME.

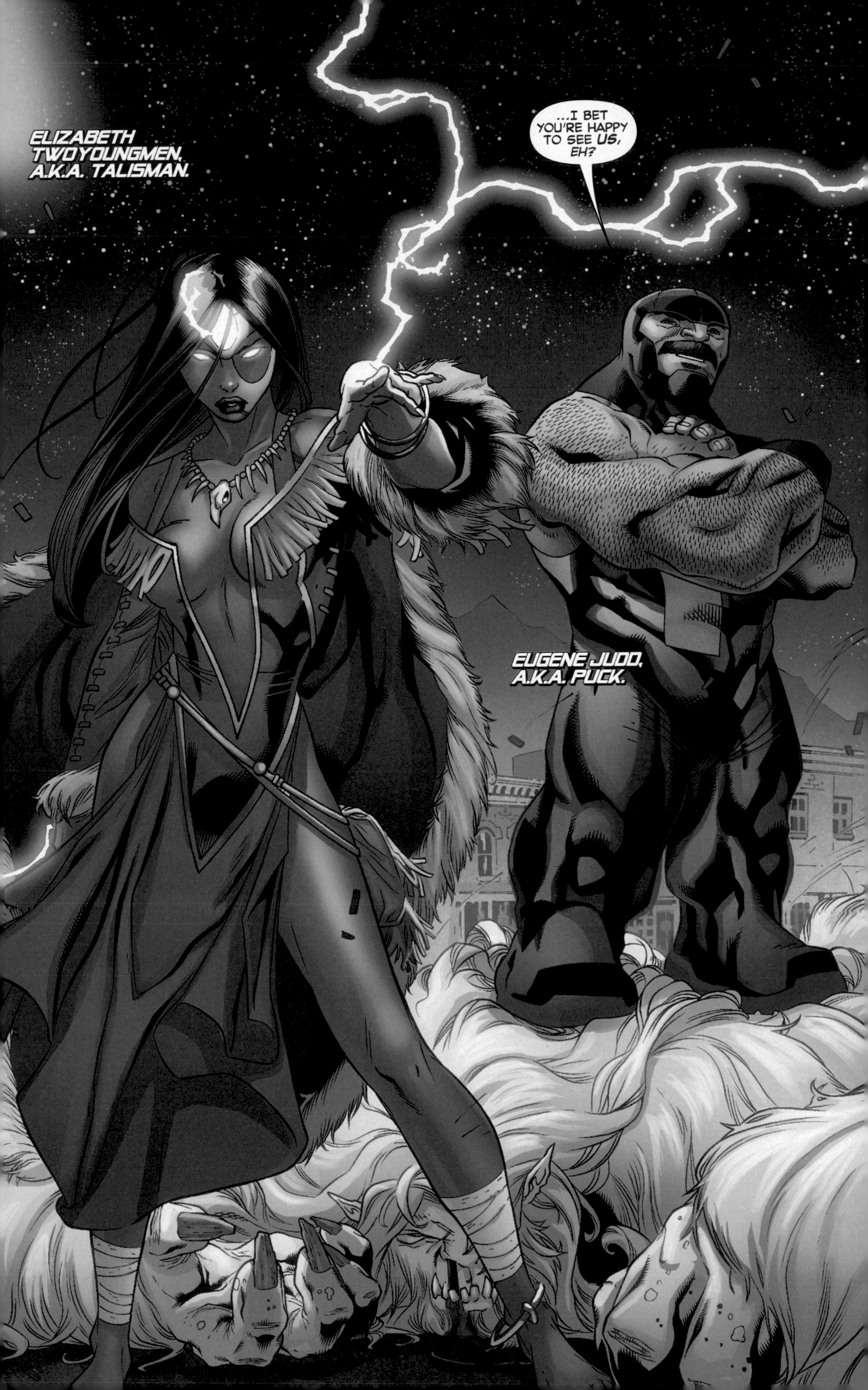
ELIZABETH TWOYOUNGMEN, A.K.A. TALISMAN.
...I BET YOU'RE HAPPY TO SEE US, EH?
EUGENE JUDD, A.K.A. PUCK.

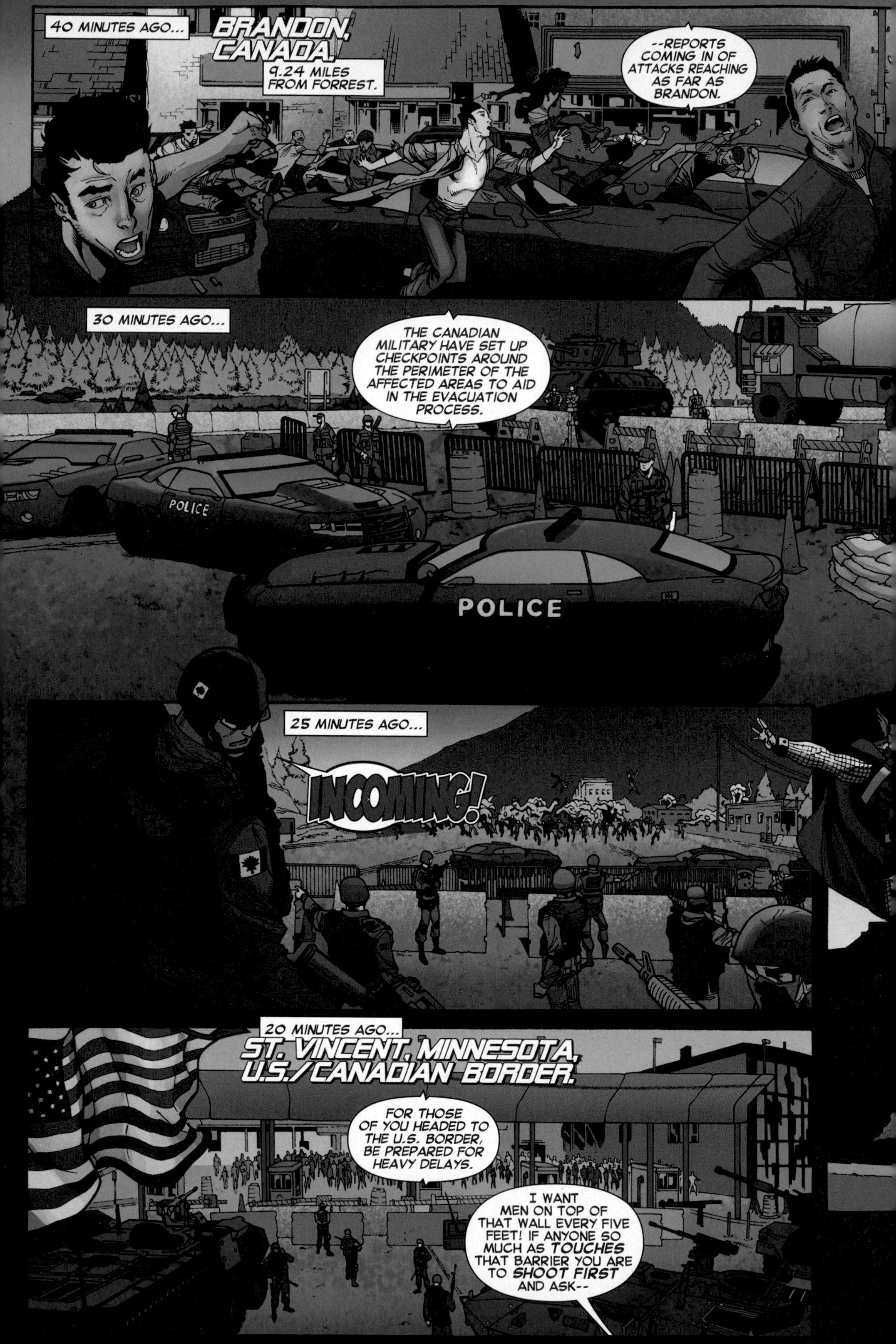
40 MINUTES AGO...
BRANDON, CANADA.
9.24 MILES FROM FORREST.
--REPORTS COMING IN OF ATTACKS REACHING AS FAR AS BRANDON.
30 MINUTES AGO...
THE CANADIAN MILITARY HAVE SET UP CHECKPOINTS AROUND THE PERIMETER OF THE AFFECTED AREAS TO AID IN THE EVACUATION PROCESS.
POLICE
POLICE
25 MINUTES AGO...
INCOMING!
20 MINUTES AGO...
ST. VINCENT, MINNESOTA, U.S./CANADIAN BORDER.
FOR THOSE OF YOU HEADED TO THE U.S. BORDER, BE PREPARED FOR HEAVY DELAYS.
I WANT MEN ON TOP OF THAT WALL EVERY FIVE FEET! IF ANYONE SO MUCH AS TOUCHES THAT BARRIER YOU ARE TO SHOOT FIRST AND ASK--

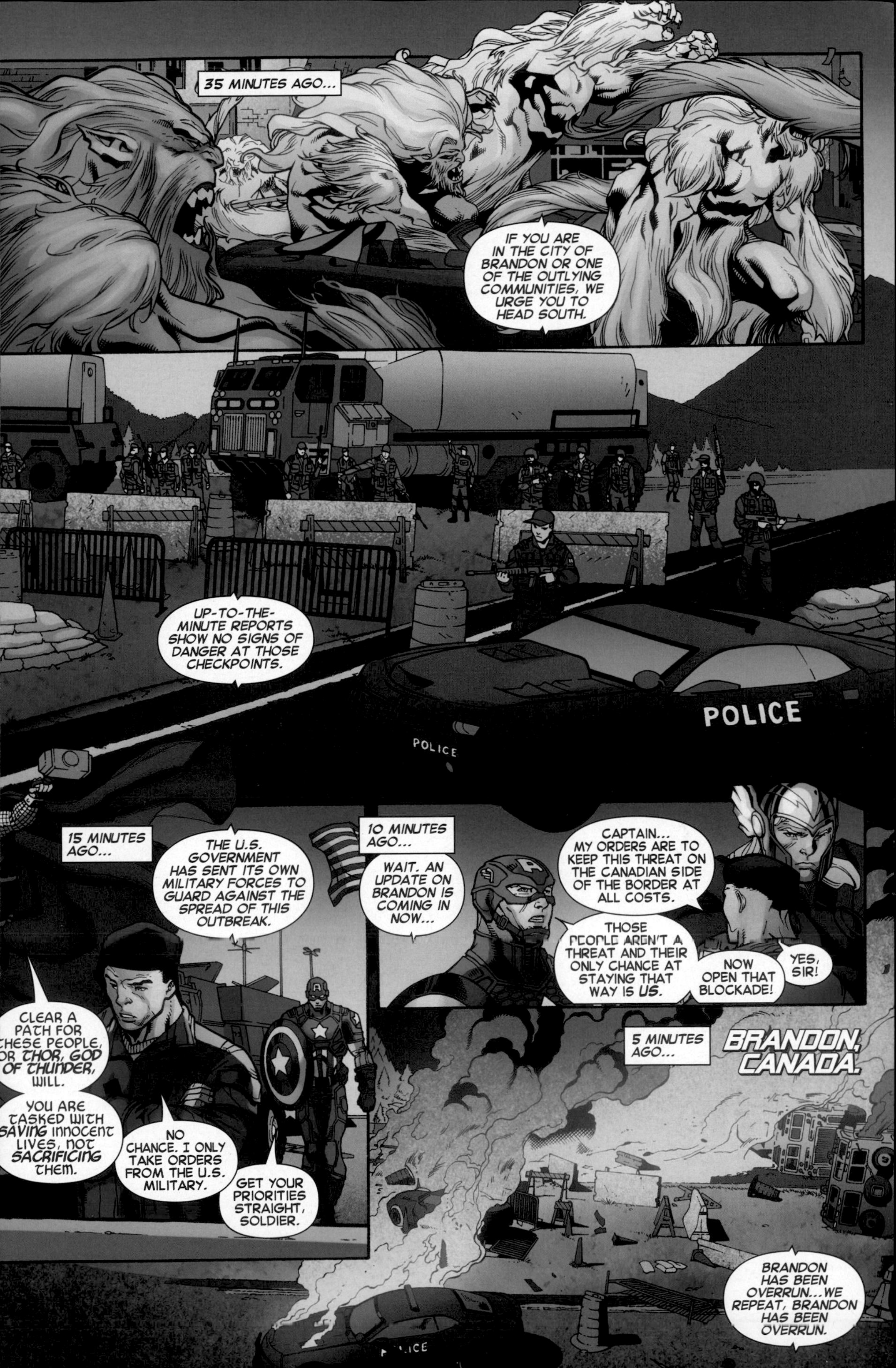
35 MINUTES AGO...
IF YOU ARE IN THE CITY OF BRANDON OR ONE OF THE OUTLYING COMMUNITIES, WE URGE YOU TO HEAD SOUTH.
UP-TO-THE-MINUTE REPORTS SHOW NO SIGNS OF DANGER AT THOSE CHECKPOINTS.
POLICE
POLICE
15 MINUTES AGO...
THE U.S. GOVERNMENT HAS SENT ITS OWN MILITARY FORCES TO GUARD AGAINST THE SPREAD OF THIS OUTBREAK.
CLEAR A PATH FOR THESE PEOPLE, OR THOR, GOD OF THUNDER, WILL.
YOU ARE TASKED WITH SAVING INNOCENT LIVES, NOT SACRIFICING THEM.
NO CHANCE. I ONLY TAKE ORDERS FROM THE U.S. MILITARY.
GET YOUR PRIORITIES STRAIGHT, SOLDIER.
10 MINUTES AGO...
WAIT. AN UPDATE ON BRANDON IS COMING IN NOW...
CAPTAIN... MY ORDERS ARE TO KEEP THIS THREAT ON THE CANADIAN SIDE OF THE BORDER AT ALL COSTS.
THOSE PEOPLE AREN'T A THREAT AND THEIR ONLY CHANCE AT STAYING THAT WAY IS US.
NOW OPEN THAT BLOCKADE!
YES, SIR!
5 MINUTES AGO...
BRANDON, CANADA.
BRANDON HAS BEEN OVERRUN...WE REPEAT, BRANDON HAS BEEN OVERRUN.

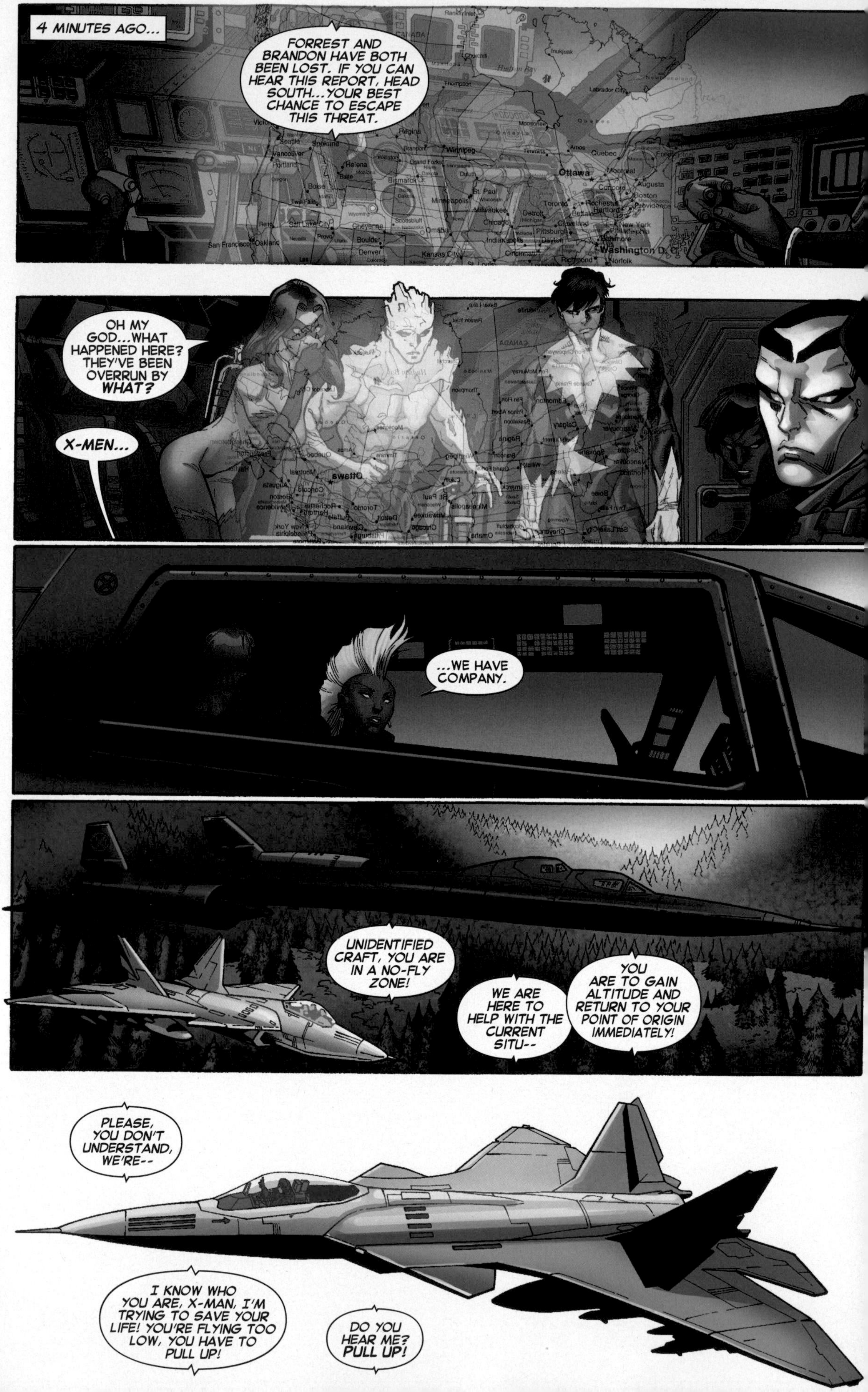
4 MINUTES AGO...
FORREST AND BRANDON HAVE BOTH BEEN LOST. IF YOU CAN HEAR THIS REPORT, HEAD SOUTH...YOUR BEST CHANCE TO ESCAPE THIS THREAT.
OH MY GOD...WHAT HAPPENED HERE? THEY'VE BEEN OVERRUN BY WHAT?
X-MEN...
...WE HAVE COMPANY.
UNIDENTIFIED CRAFT, YOU ARE IN A NO-FLY ZONE!
WE ARE HERE TO HELP WITH THE CURRENT SITU--
YOU ARE TO GAIN ALTITUDE AND RETURN TO YOUR POINT OF ORIGIN IMMEDIATELY!
PLEASE, YOU DON'T UNDERSTAND, WE'RE--
I KNOW WHO YOU ARE, X-MAN, I'M TRYING TO SAVE YOUR LIFE! YOU'RE FLYING TOO LOW, YOU HAVE TO PULL UP!
DO YOU HEAR ME? PULL UP!

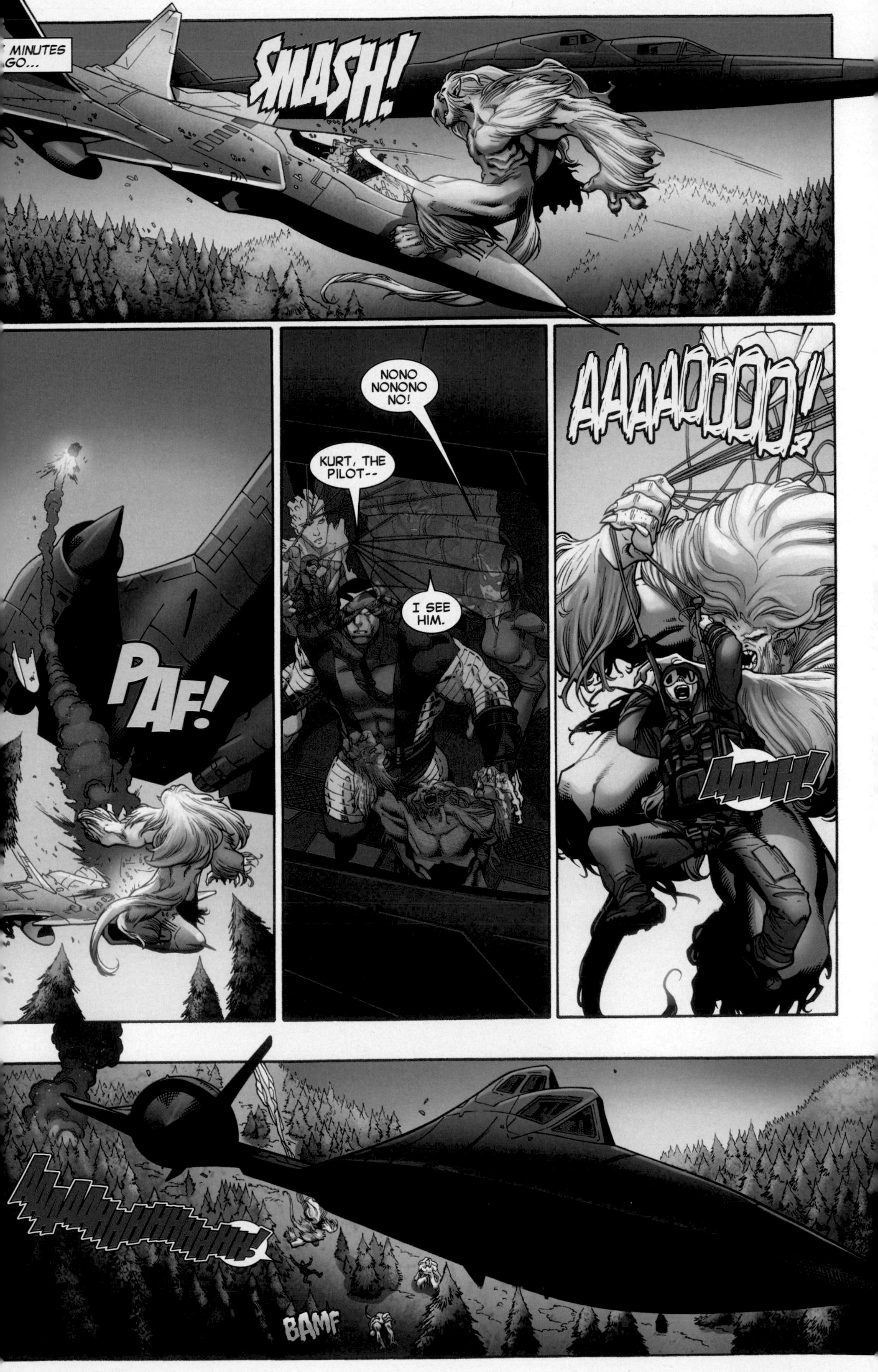
MINUTES
GO...
SMASH!
PAF!
NONO NONONO NO!
KURT, THE PILOT--
I SEE HIM.
AAAAOOOO!
AAHH!
BAMF

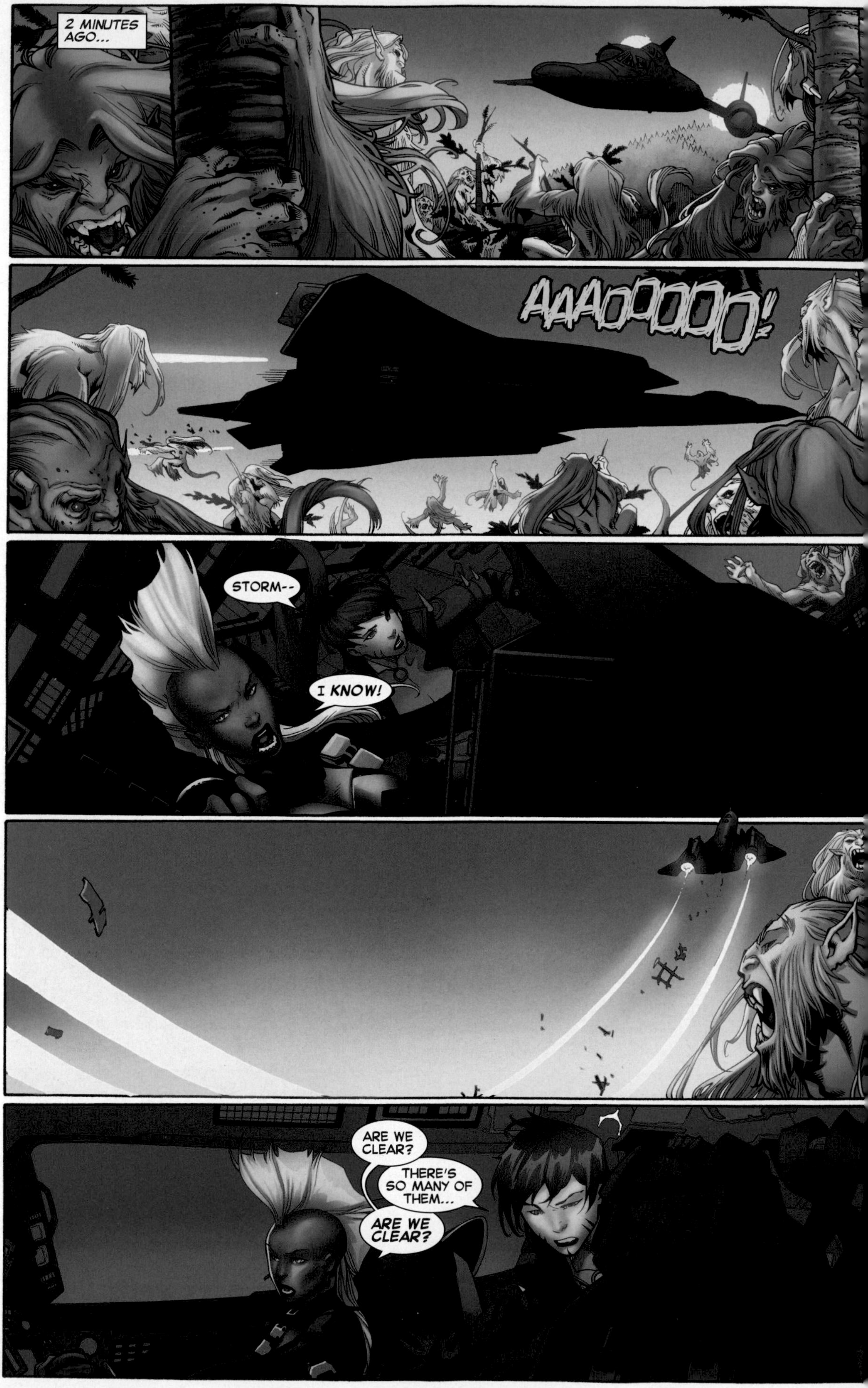
2 MINUTES AGO...
AAAOOOOOO!
STORM--
I KNOW!
ARE WE CLEAR?
THERE'S SO MANY OF THEM...
ARE WE CLEAR?

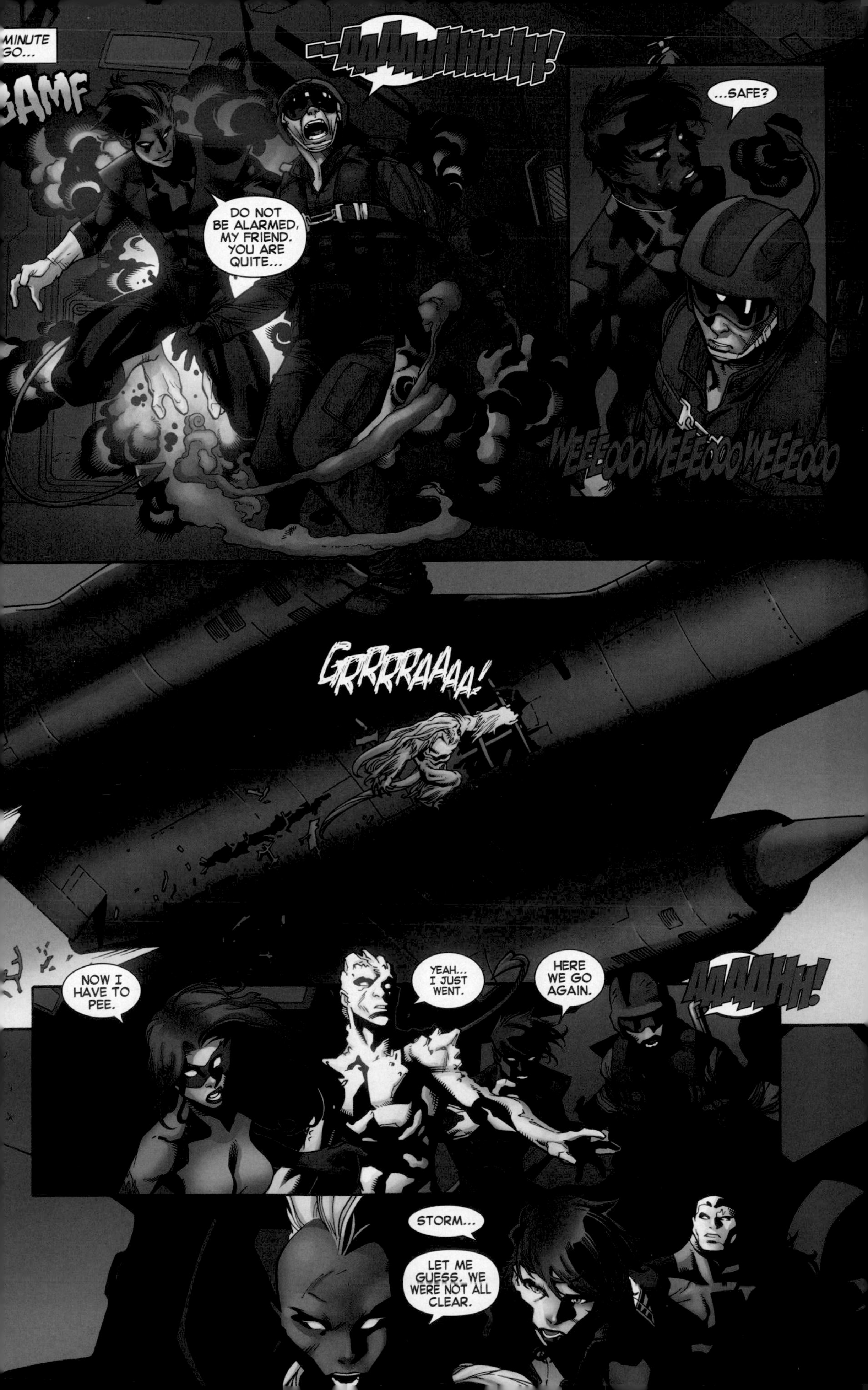
MINUTE
GO...
BAMF
--AAAAHHHHHH!
DO NOT BE ALARMED, MY FRIEND. YOU ARE QUITE...
...SAFE?
WEEEOOO WEEEOOO WEEEOOO
GRRRRAAAA!
NOW I HAVE TO PEE.
YEAH... I JUST WENT.
HERE WE GO AGAIN.
AAAAHH!
STORM...
LET ME GUESS. WE WERE NOT ALL CLEAR.

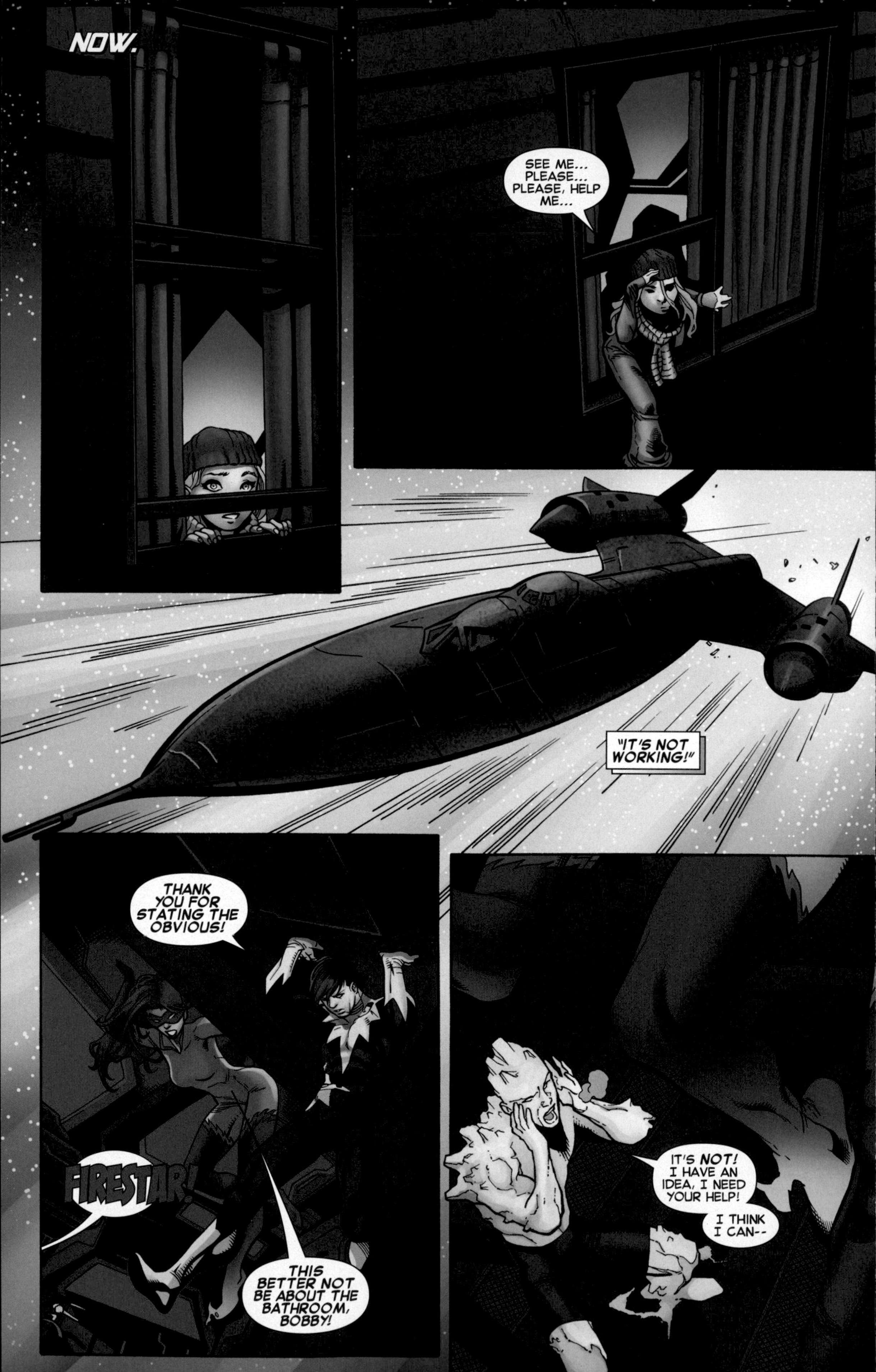
NOW.
SEE ME... PLEASE... PLEASE, HELP ME...
"IT'S NOT WORKING!"
THANK YOU FOR STATING THE OBVIOUS!
FIRESTAR!
THIS BETTER NOT BE ABOUT THE BATHROOM, BOBBY!
IT'S NOT! I HAVE AN IDEA, I NEED YOUR HELP!
I THINK I CAN--

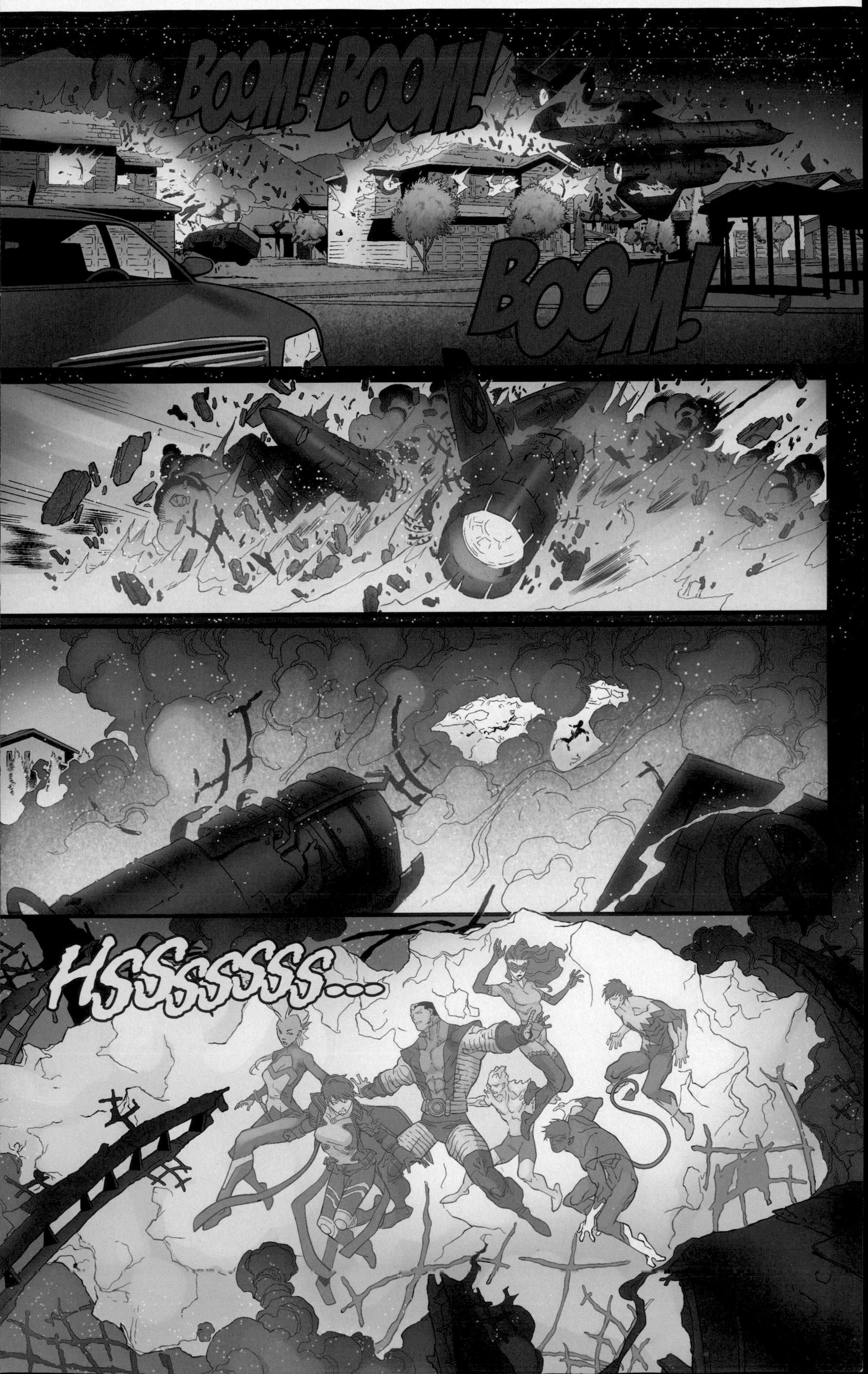
BOOM! BOOM!
BOOM!
HSSSSSSS...

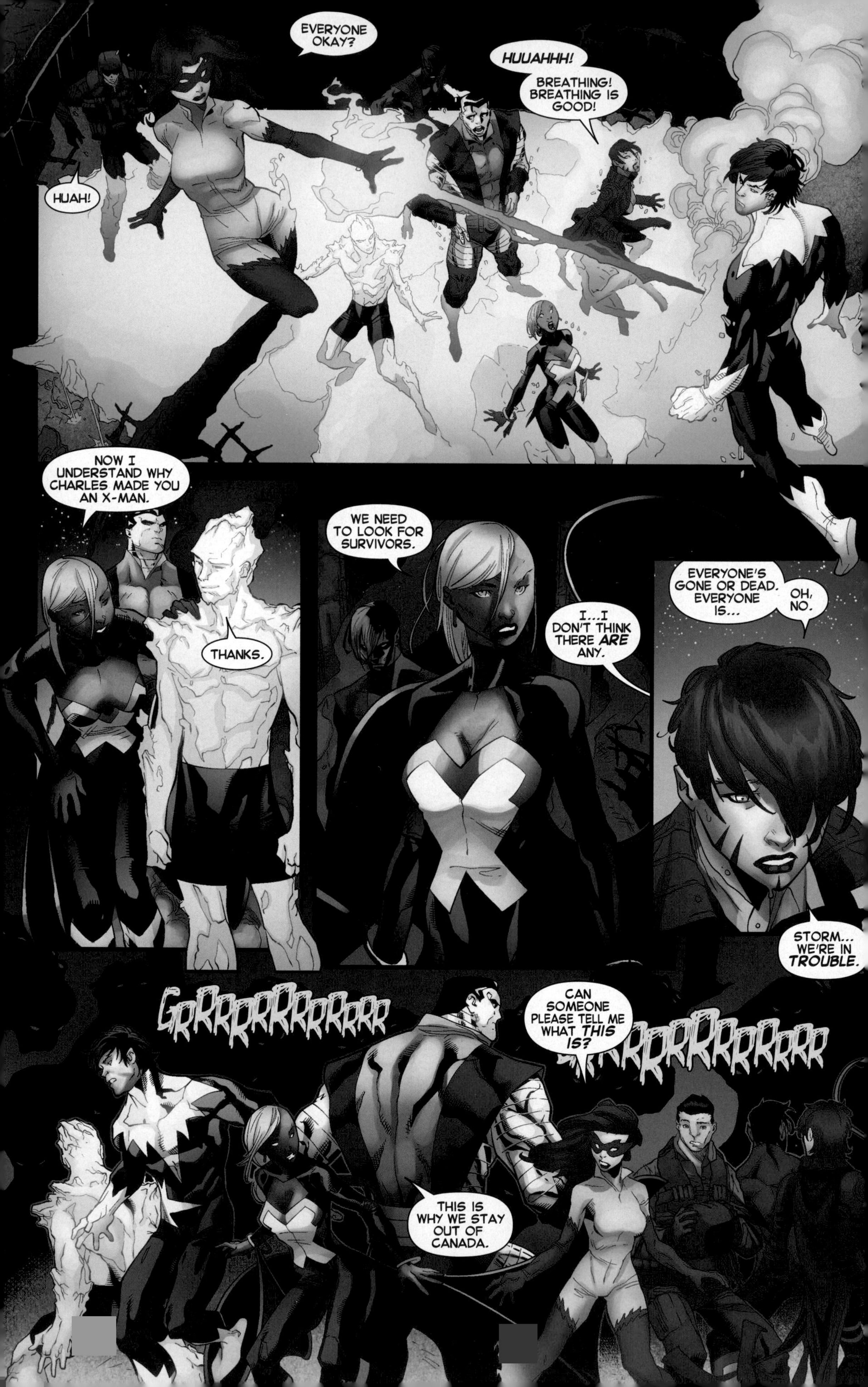
EVERYONE OKAY?
HUUAHHH!
BREATHING! BREATHING IS GOOD!
HUAH!
NOW I UNDERSTAND WHY CHARLES MADE YOU AN X-MAN.
THANKS.
WE NEED TO LOOK FOR SURVIVORS.
I...I DON'T THINK THERE ARE ANY.
EVERYONE'S GONE OR DEAD. EVERYONE IS...
OH, NO.
STORM... WE'RE IN TROUBLE.
GRRRRRRRRRRRR
CAN SOMEONE PLEASE TELL ME WHAT THIS IS?
RRRRRRRRRRRR
THIS IS WHY WE STAY OUT OF CANADA.

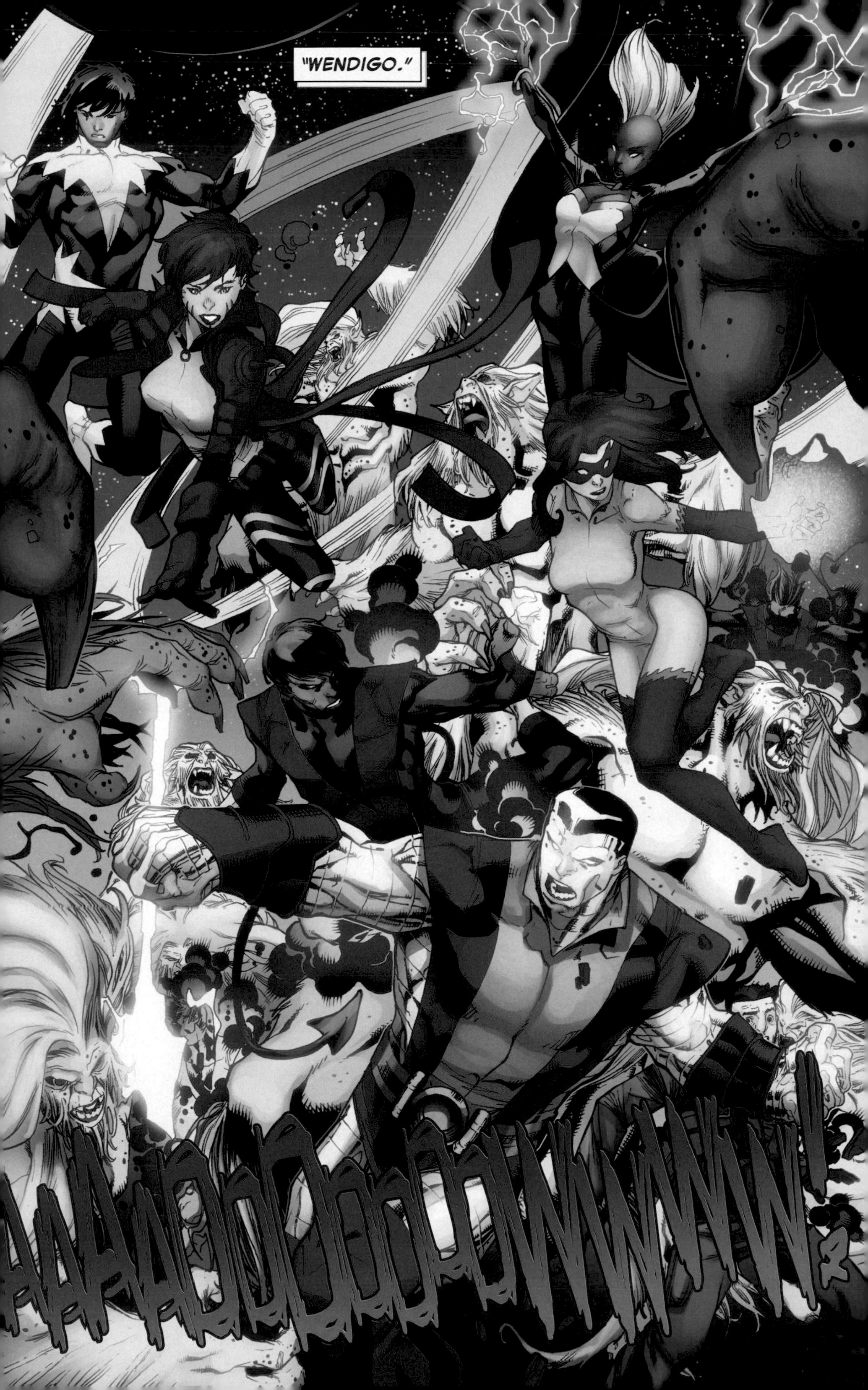
"WENDIGO."
AAAAOOOOOOOWWWWWWW!

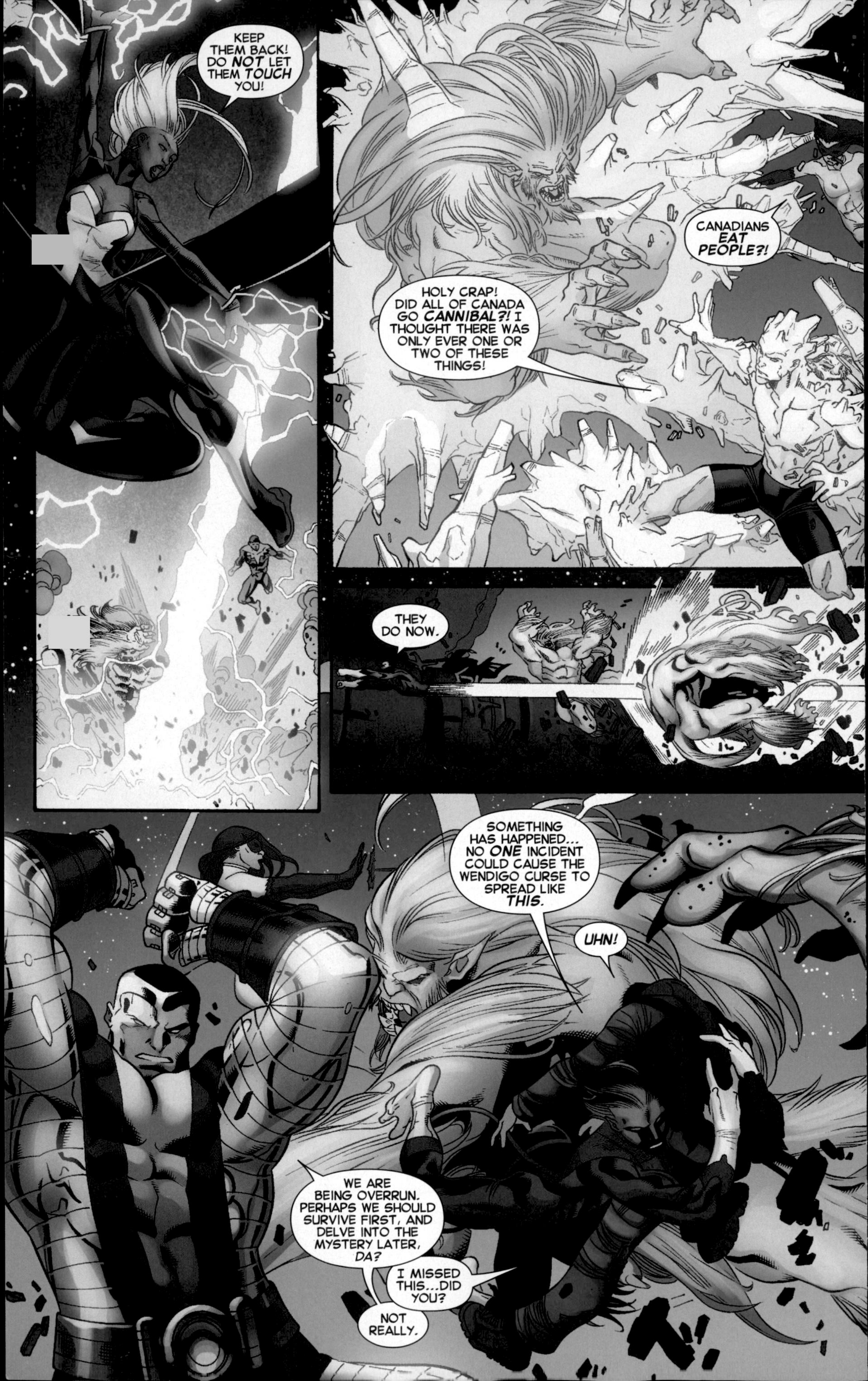
KEEP THEM BACK! DO NOT LET THEM TOUCH YOU!
HOLY CRAP! DID ALL OF CANADA GO CANNIBAL?! I THOUGHT THERE WAS ONLY EVER ONE OR TWO OF THESE THINGS!
CANADIANS EAT PEOPLE?!
THEY DO NOW.
SOMETHING HAS HAPPENED... NO ONE INCIDENT COULD CAUSE THE WENDIGO CURSE TO SPREAD LIKE THIS.
UHN!
WE ARE BEING OVERRUN. PERHAPS WE SHOULD SURVIVE FIRST, AND DELVE INTO THE MYSTERY LATER, DA?
I MISSED THIS...DID YOU?
NOT REALLY.

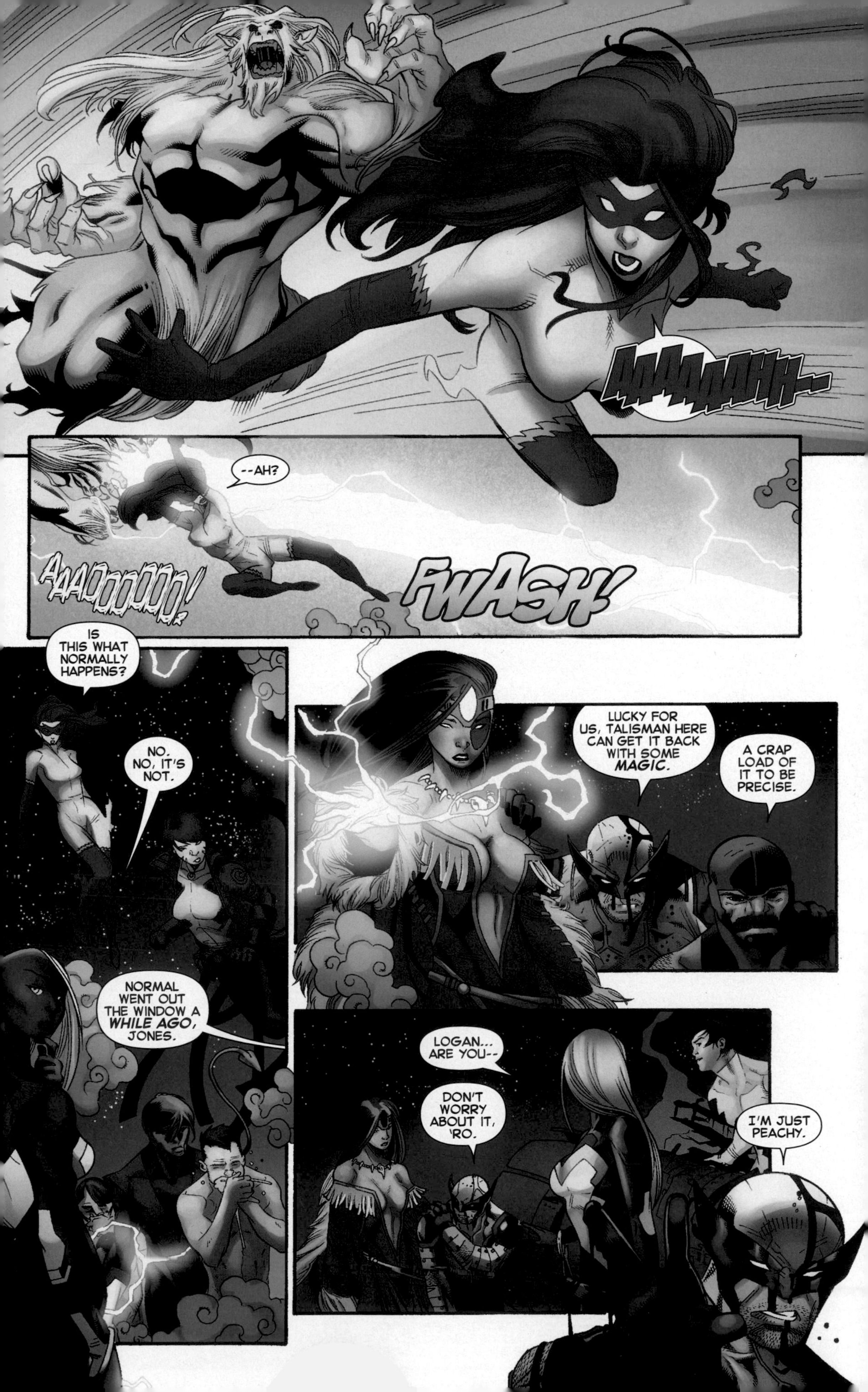
AAAAAAAHH--
--AH?
AAAOOOOOOO!
FWASH!
IS THIS WHAT NORMALLY HAPPENS?
NO. NO, IT'S NOT.
LUCKY FOR US, TALISMAN HERE CAN GET IT BACK WITH SOME MAGIC.
A CRAP LOAD OF IT TO BE PRECISE.
NORMAL WENT OUT THE WINDOW A WHILE AGO, JONES.
LOGAN... ARE YOU--
DON'T WORRY ABOUT IT, 'RO.
I'M JUST PEACHY.

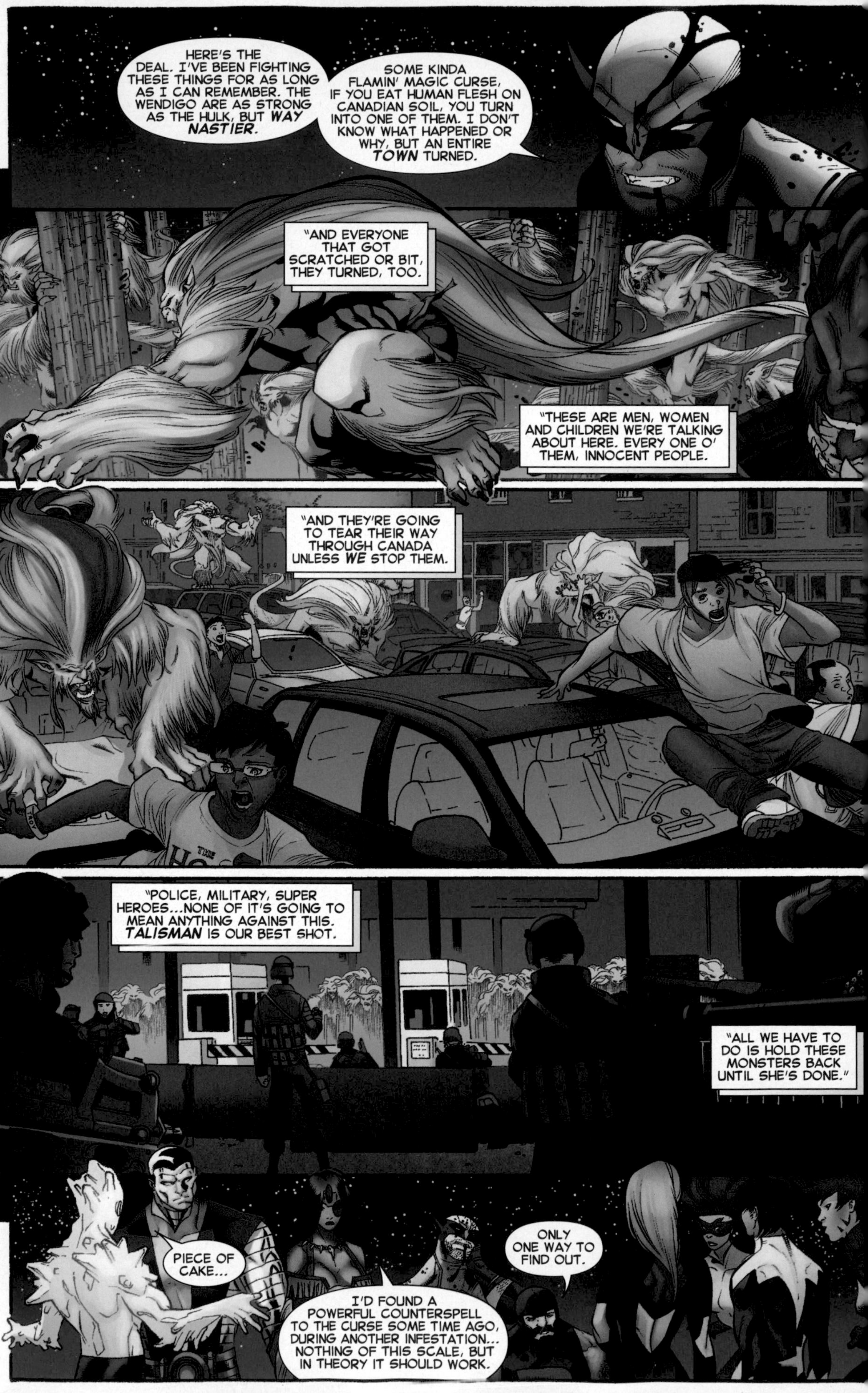
HERE'S THE DEAL. I'VE BEEN FIGHTING THESE THINGS FOR AS LONG AS I CAN REMEMBER. THE WENDIGO ARE AS STRONG AS THE HULK, BUT WAY NASTIER.
SOME KINDA FLAMIN' MAGIC CURSE, IF YOU EAT HUMAN FLESH ON CANADIAN SOIL, YOU TURN INTO ONE OF THEM. I DON'T KNOW WHAT HAPPENED OR WHY, BUT AN ENTIRE TOWN TURNED.
"AND EVERYONE THAT GOT SCRATCHED OR BIT, THEY TURNED, TOO.
"THESE ARE MEN, WOMEN AND CHILDREN WE'RE TALKING ABOUT HERE. EVERY ONE O' THEM, INNOCENT PEOPLE.
"AND THEY'RE GOING TO TEAR THEIR WAY THROUGH CANADA UNLESS WE STOP THEM.
"POLICE, MILITARY, SUPER HEROES...NONE OF IT'S GOING TO MEAN ANYTHING AGAINST THIS. TALISMAN IS OUR BEST SHOT.
"ALL WE HAVE TO DO IS HOLD THESE MONSTERS BACK UNTIL SHE'S DONE."
PIECE OF CAKE...
I'D FOUND A POWERFUL COUNTERSPELL TO THE CURSE SOME TIME AGO, DURING ANOTHER INFESTATION... NOTHING OF THIS SCALE, BUT IN THEORY IT SHOULD WORK.
ONLY ONE WAY TO FIND OUT.

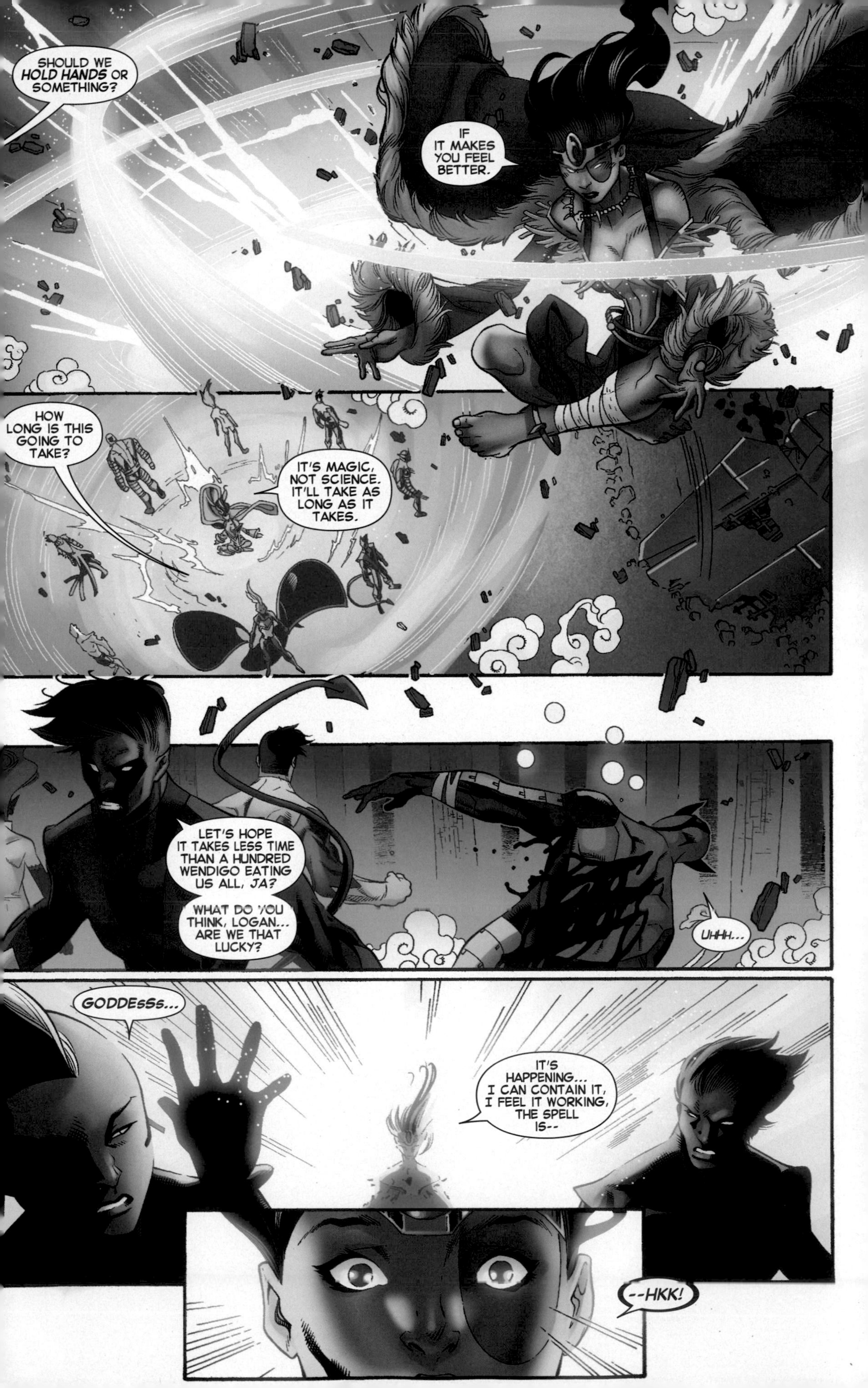
SHOULD WE HOLD HANDS OR SOMETHING?
IF IT MAKES YOU FEEL BETTER.
HOW LONG IS THIS GOING TO TAKE?
IT'S MAGIC, NOT SCIENCE. IT'LL TAKE AS LONG AS IT TAKES.
LET'S HOPE IT TAKES LESS TIME THAN A HUNDRED WENDIGO EATING US ALL, JA?
WHAT DO YOU THINK, LOGAN... ARE WE THAT LUCKY?
UHHH...
GODDESsS...
IT'S HAPPENING... I CAN CONTAIN IT, I FEEL IT WORKING, THE SPELL IS--
--HKK!

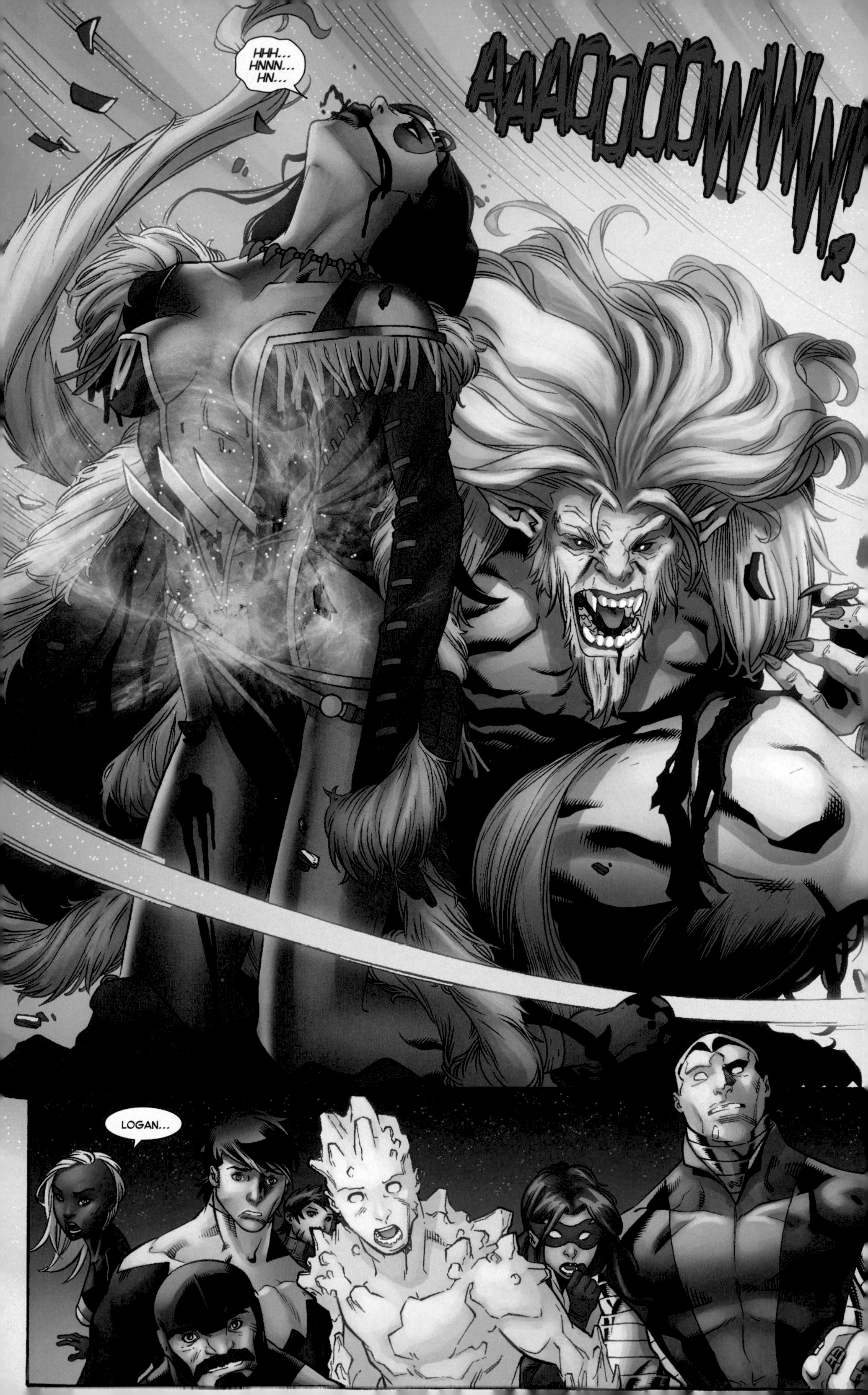
HHH... HNNN... HN...
AAAOOOOWWW!
LOGAN...

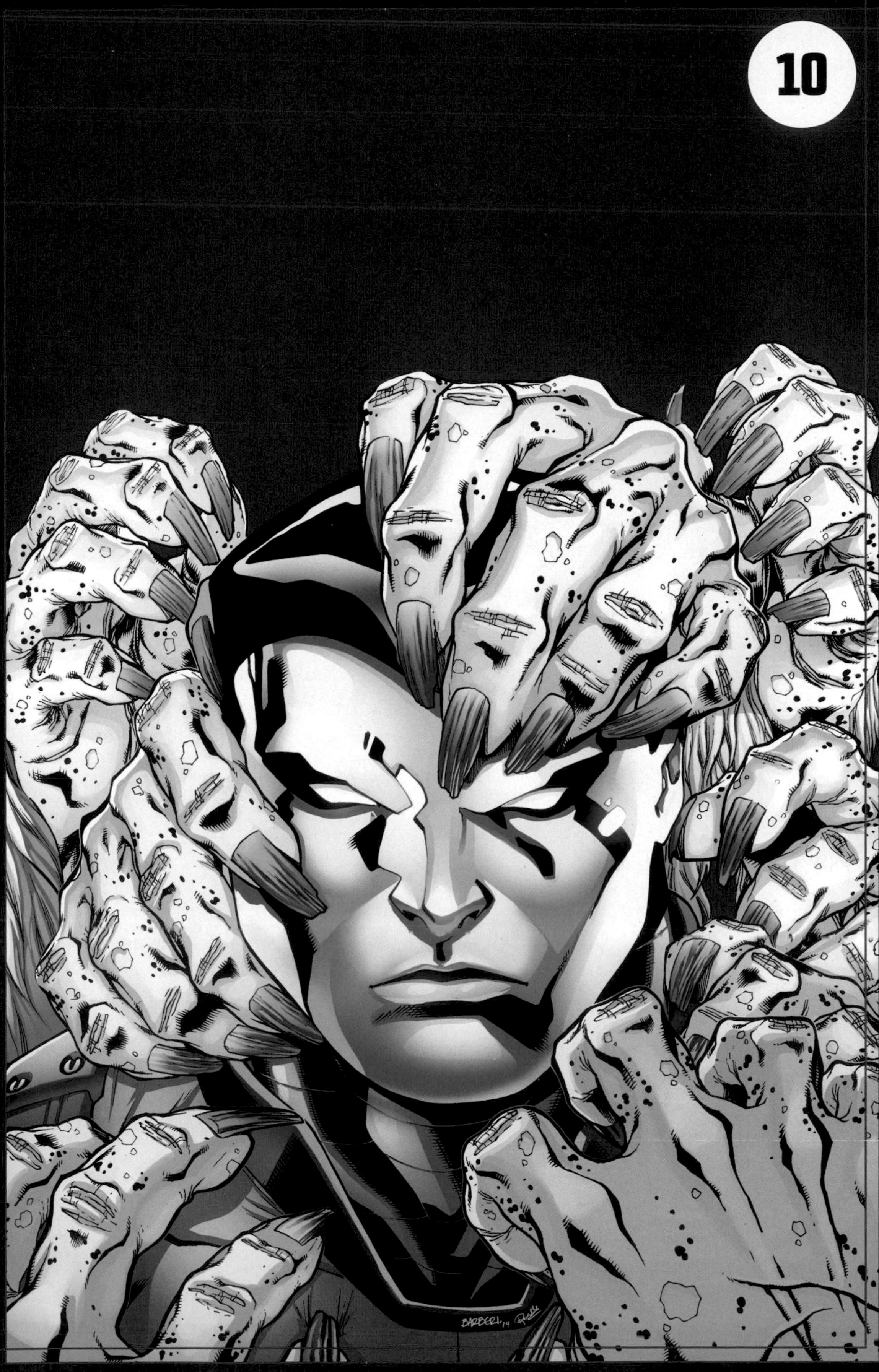
10

WORLD WAR WENDIGO! PART 3

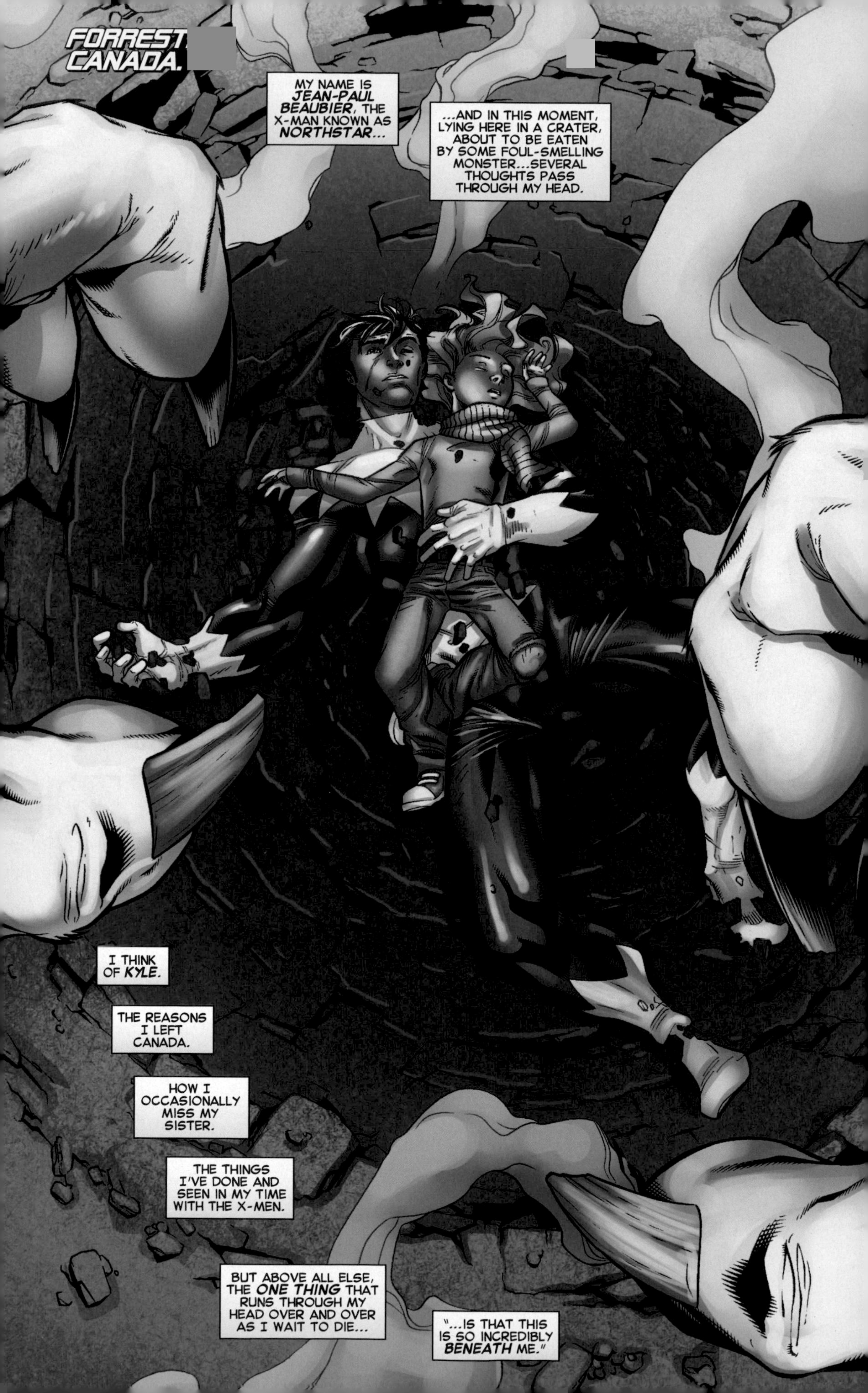
FORREST, CANADA.
MY NAME IS JEAN-PAUL BEAUBIER, THE X-MAN KNOWN AS NORTHSTAR...
...AND IN THIS MOMENT, LYING HERE IN A CRATER, ABOUT TO BE EATEN BY SOME FOUL-SMELLING MONSTER...SEVERAL THOUGHTS PASS THROUGH MY HEAD.
I THINK OF KYLE.
THE REASONS I LEFT CANADA.
HOW I OCCASIONALLY MISS MY SISTER.
THE THINGS I'VE DONE AND SEEN IN MY TIME WITH THE X-MEN.
BUT ABOVE ALL ELSE, THE ONE THING THAT RUNS THROUGH MY HEAD OVER AND OVER AS I WAIT TO DIE...
"...IS THAT THIS IS SO INCREDIBLY BENEATH ME."

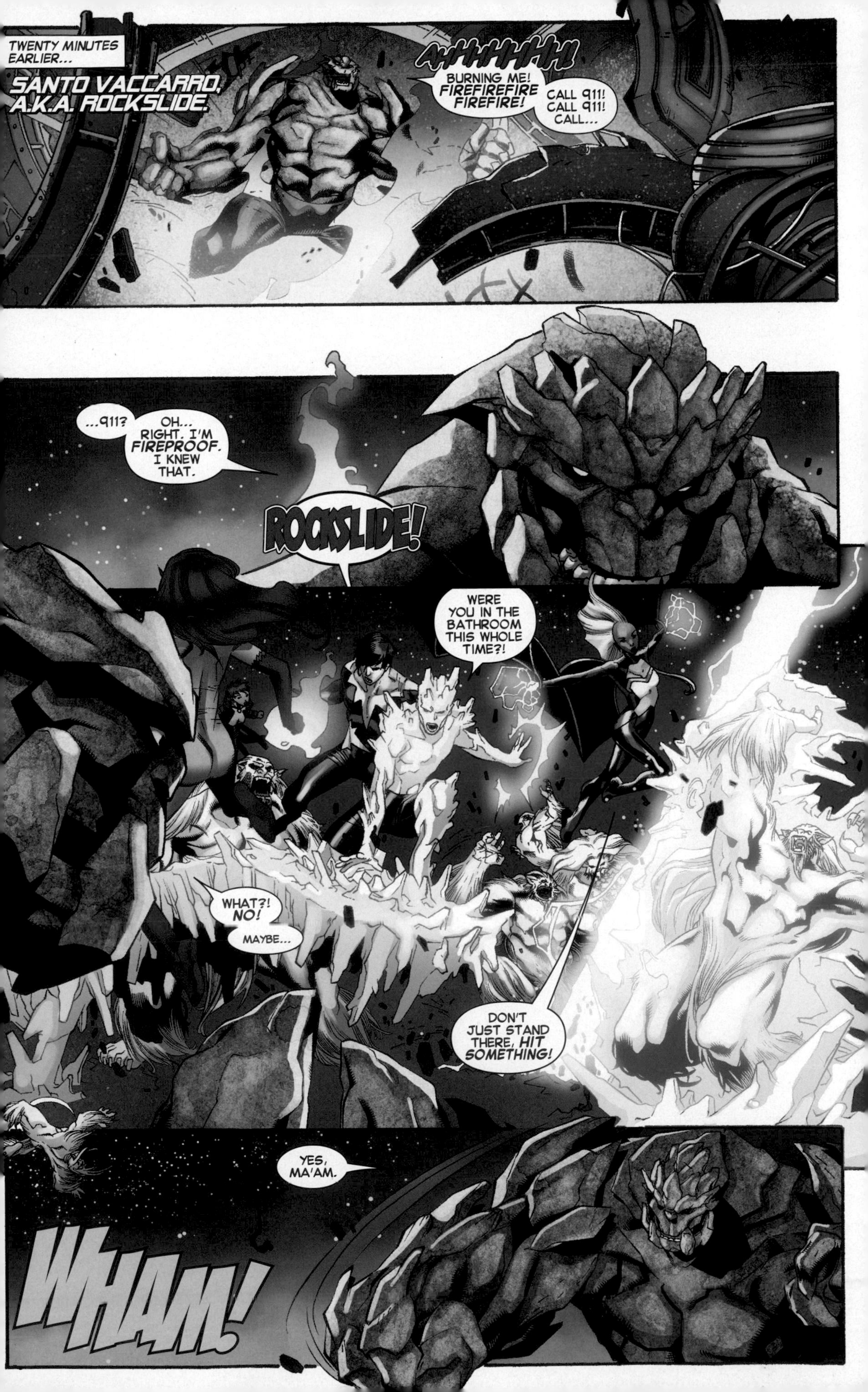
TWENTY MINUTES EARLIER...
SANTO VACCARRO, A.K.A. ROCKSLIDE.
AHHHHHHH!
BURNING ME! FIREFIREFIRE FIREFIRE!
CALL 911! CALL 911! CALL...
...911?
OH... RIGHT. I'M FIREPROOF. I KNEW THAT.
ROCKSLIDE!
WERE YOU IN THE BATHROOM THIS WHOLE TIME?!
WHAT?! NO!
MAYBE...
DON'T JUST STAND THERE, HIT SOMETHING!
YES, MA'AM.
WHAM!

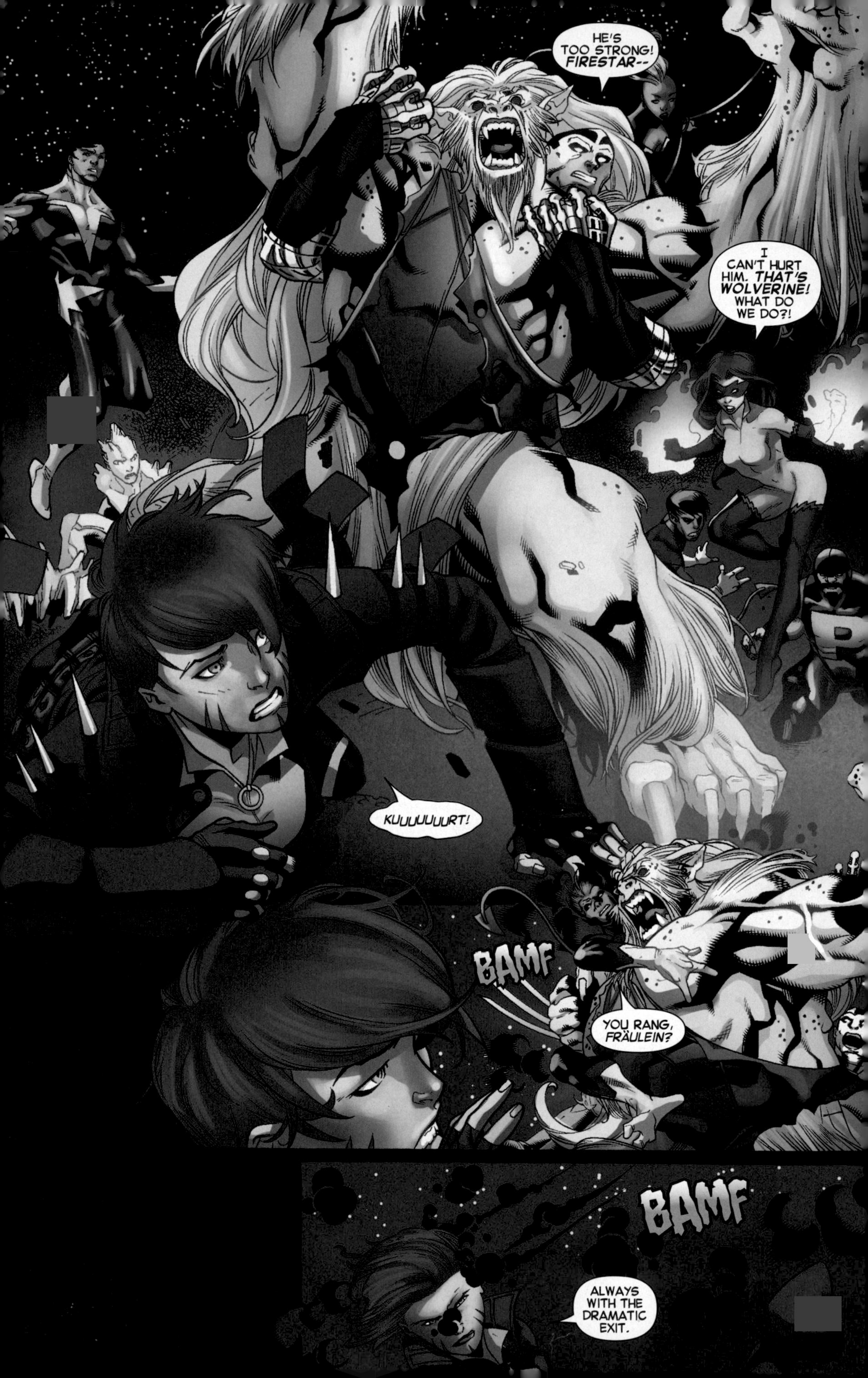
HE'S TOO STRONG! FIRESTAR--
I CAN'T HURT HIM. THAT'S WOLVERINE! WHAT DO WE DO?!
KUUUUUUURT!
BAMF
YOU RANG, FRÄULEIN?
BAMF
ALWAYS WITH THE DRAMATIC EXIT.

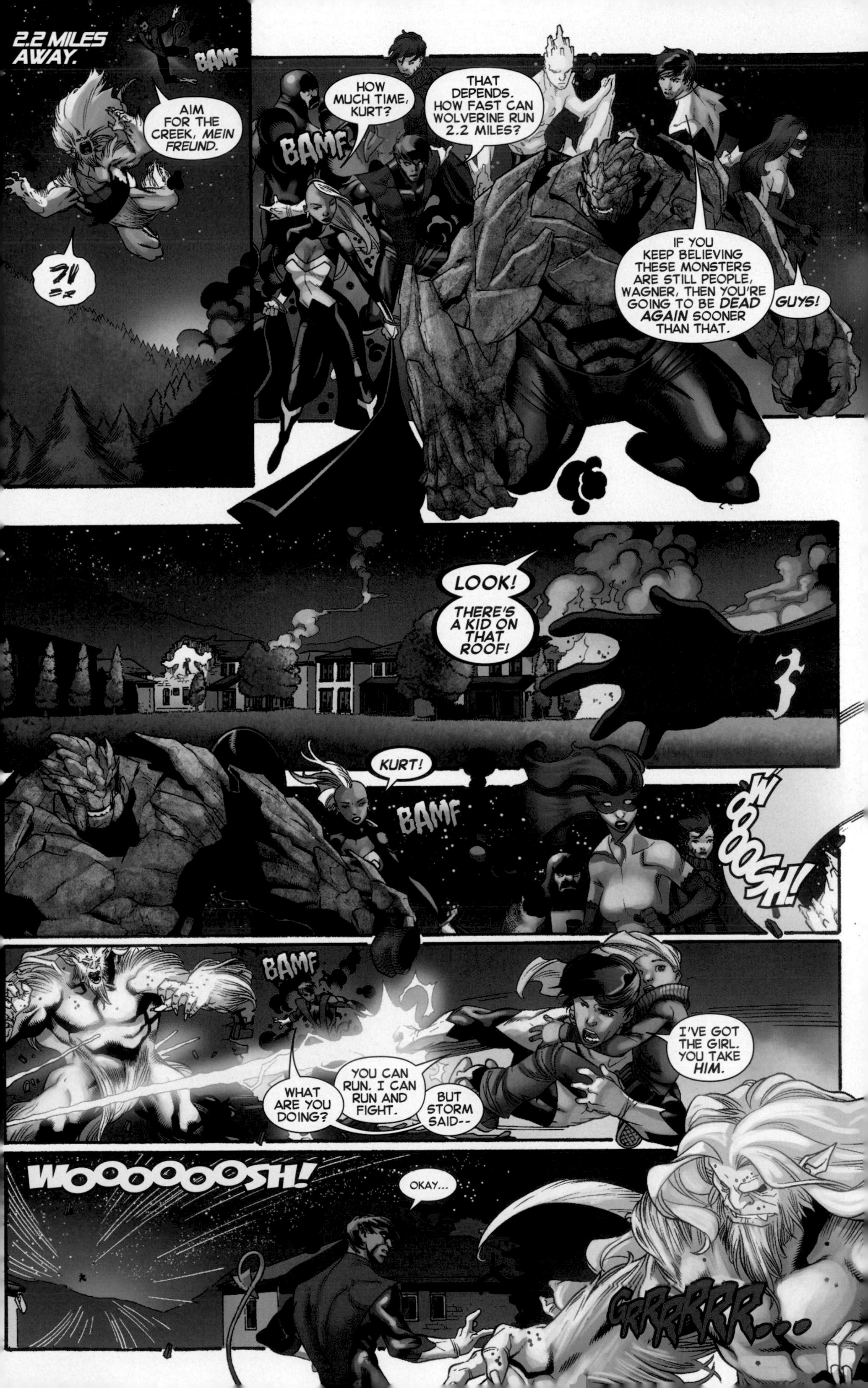
2.2 MILES AWAY.
BAMF
AIM FOR THE CREEK, MEIN FREUND.
HOW MUCH TIME, KURT?
BAMF
THAT DEPENDS. HOW FAST CAN WOLVERINE RUN 2.2 MILES?
IF YOU KEEP BELIEVING THESE MONSTERS ARE STILL PEOPLE, WAGNER, THEN YOU'RE GOING TO BE DEAD AGAIN SOONER THAN THAT.
GUYS!
LOOK!
THERE'S A KID ON THAT ROOF!
KURT!
BAMF
WOOOOSH!
BAMF
I'VE GOT THE GIRL. YOU TAKE HIM.
WHAT ARE YOU DOING?
YOU CAN RUN. I CAN RUN AND FIGHT.
BUT STORM SAID--
WOOOOOOOSH!
OKAY...
GRRRRRR...

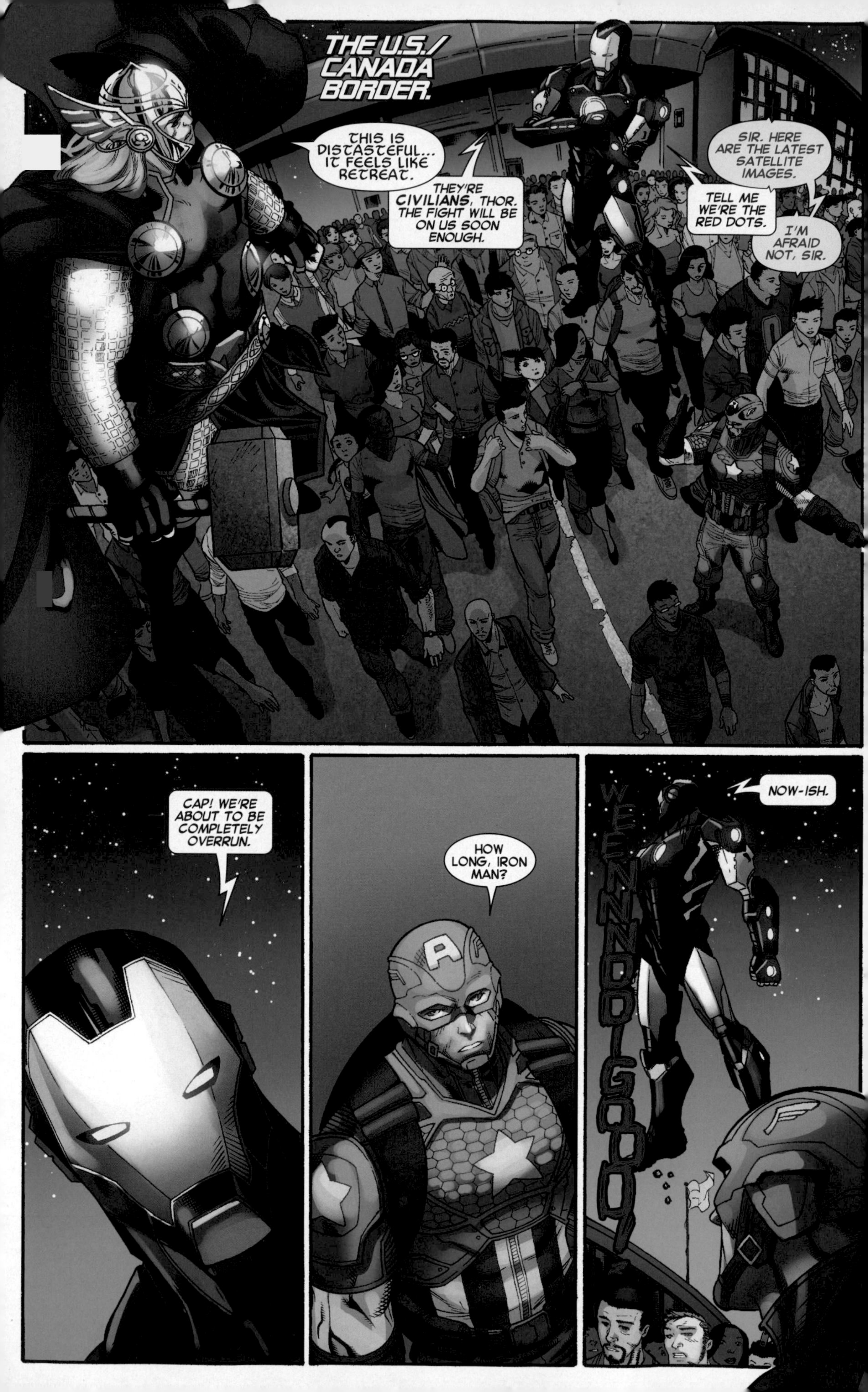
THE U.S./ CANADA BORDER.
THIS IS DISTASTEFUL... IT FEELS LIKE RETREAT.
THEY'RE CIVILIANS, THOR. THE FIGHT WILL BE ON US SOON ENOUGH.
SIR. HERE ARE THE LATEST SATELLITE IMAGES.
TELL ME WE'RE THE RED DOTS.
I'M AFRAID NOT, SIR.
CAP! WE'RE ABOUT TO BE COMPLETELY OVERRUN.
HOW LONG, IRON MAN?
NOW-ISH.

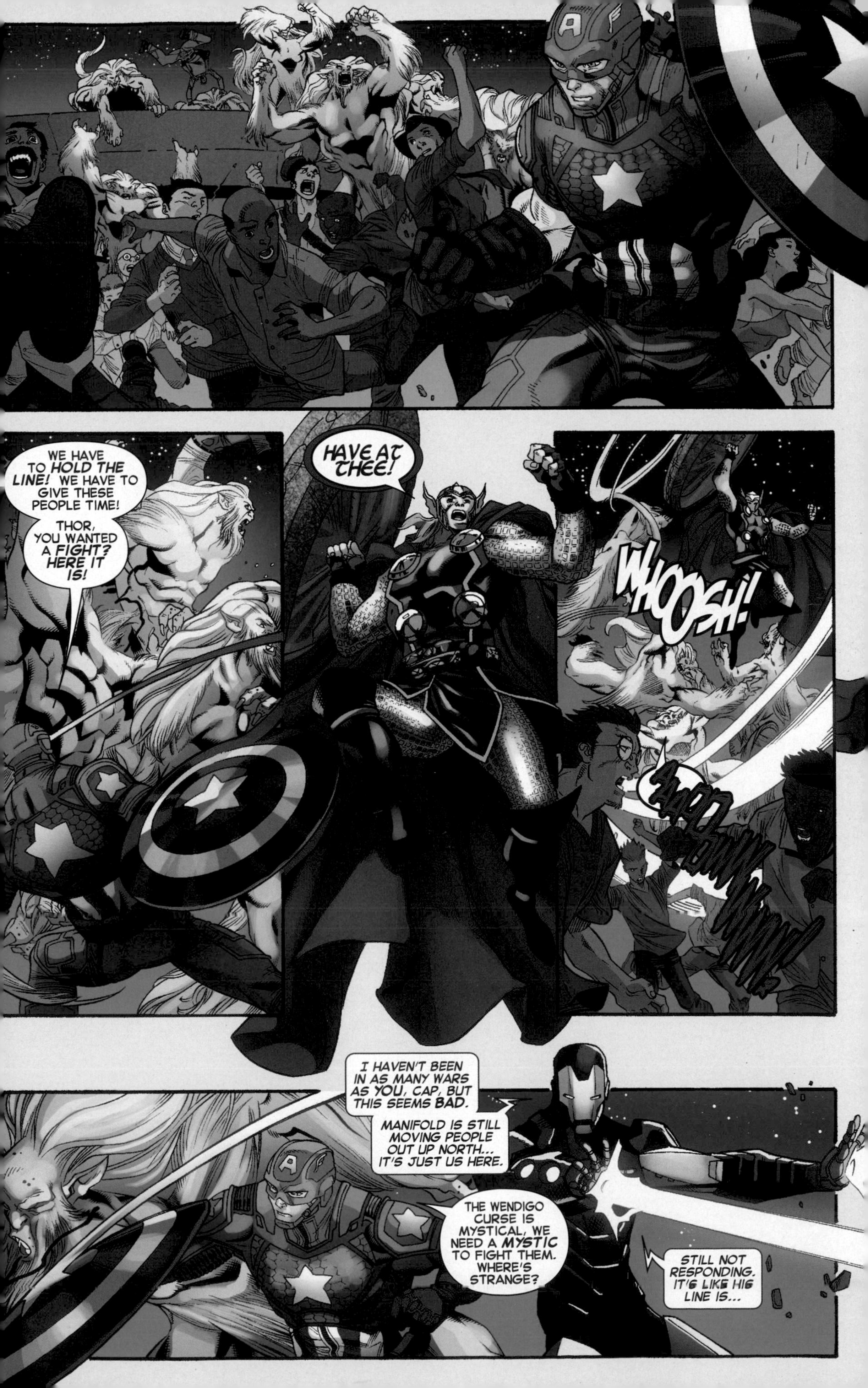
WE HAVE TO HOLD THE LINE! WE HAVE TO GIVE THESE PEOPLE TIME!
THOR, YOU WANTED A FIGHT? HERE IT IS!
HAVE AT THEE!
WHOOSH!
I HAVEN'T BEEN IN AS MANY WARS AS YOU, CAP, BUT THIS SEEMS BAD.
MANIFOLD IS STILL MOVING PEOPLE OUT UP NORTH... IT'S JUST US HERE.
THE WENDIGO CURSE IS MYSTICAL, WE NEED A MYSTIC TO FIGHT THEM. WHERE'S STRANGE?
STILL NOT RESPONDING. IT'S LIKE HIS LINE IS...

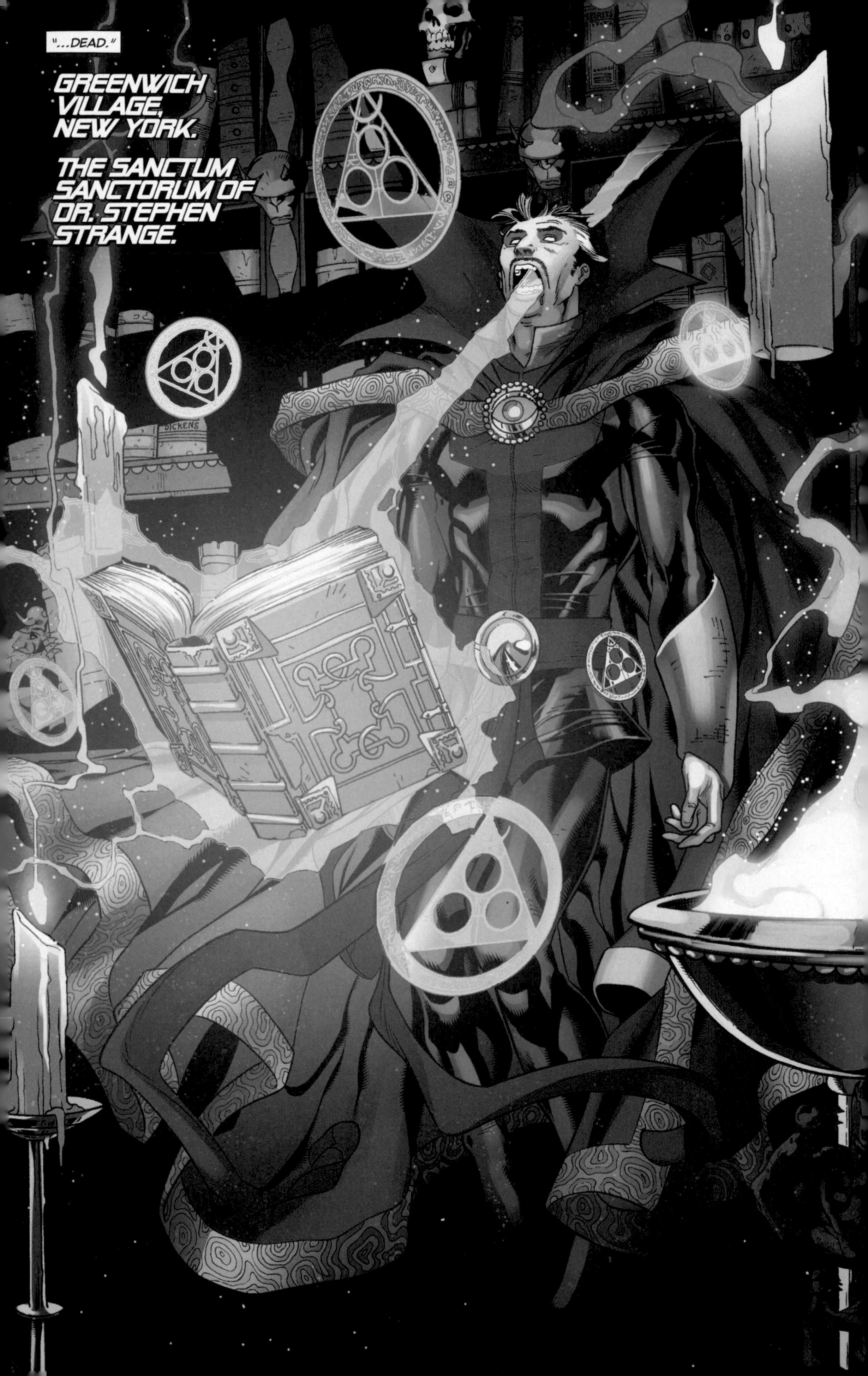
"...DEAD."
GREENWICH VILLAGE, NEW YORK.
THE SANCTUM SANCTORUM OF DR. STEPHEN STRANGE.
DICKENS

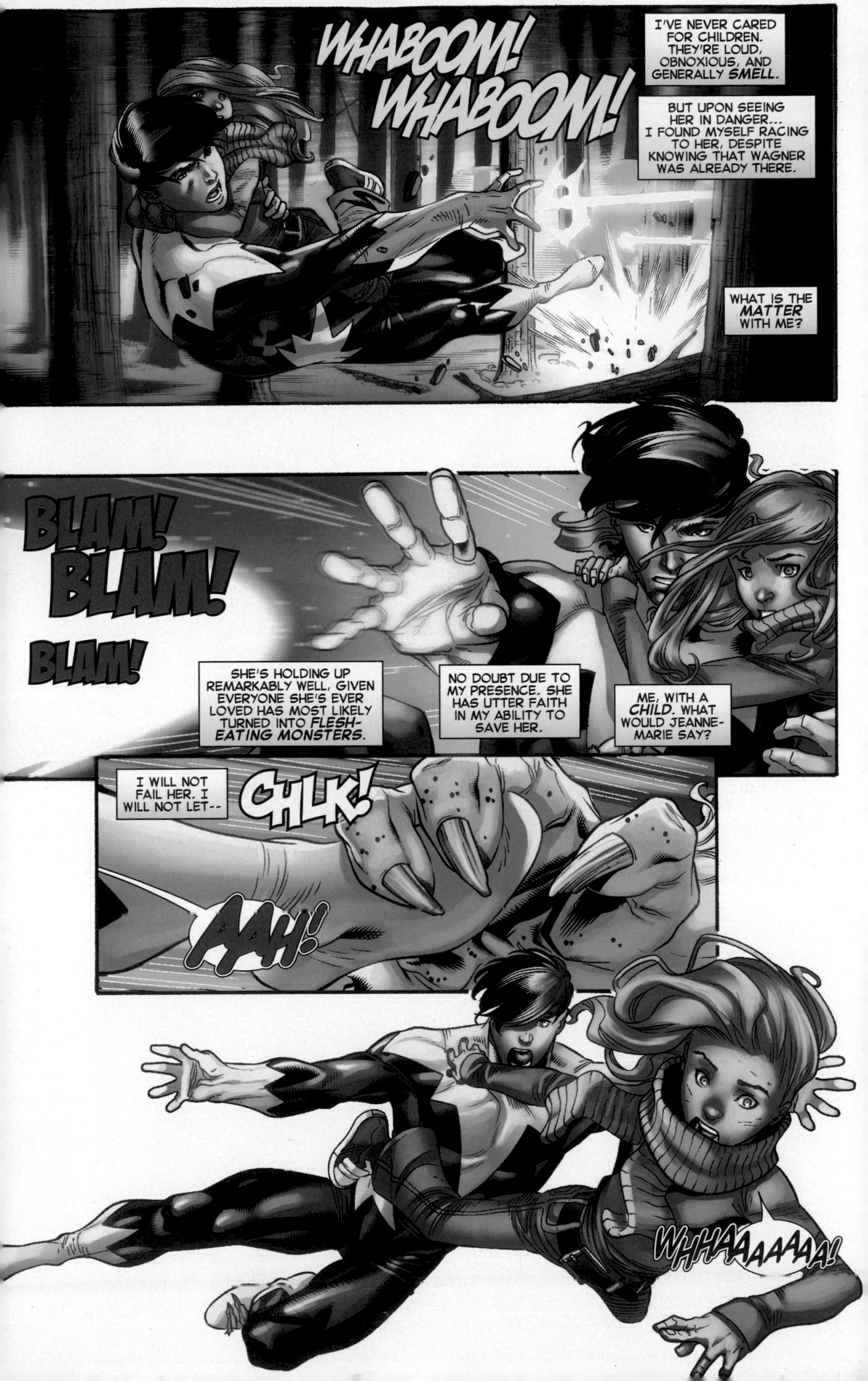
WHABOOM! WHABOOM!
I'VE NEVER CARED FOR CHILDREN. THEY'RE LOUD, OBNOXIOUS, AND GENERALLY SMELL.
BUT UPON SEEING HER IN DANGER... I FOUND MYSELF RACING TO HER, DESPITE KNOWING THAT WAGNER WAS ALREADY THERE.
WHAT IS THE MATTER WITH ME?
BLAM! BLAM!
BLAM!
SHE'S HOLDING UP REMARKABLY WELL, GIVEN EVERYONE SHE'S EVER LOVED HAS MOST LIKELY TURNED INTO FLESH-EATING MONSTERS.
NO DOUBT DUE TO MY PRESENCE. SHE HAS UTTER FAITH IN MY ABILITY TO SAVE HER.
ME, WITH A CHILD. WHAT WOULD JEANNE-MARIE SAY?
I WILL NOT FAIL HER. I WILL NOT LET--
CHLK!
AAH!
WHHAAAAAAA!

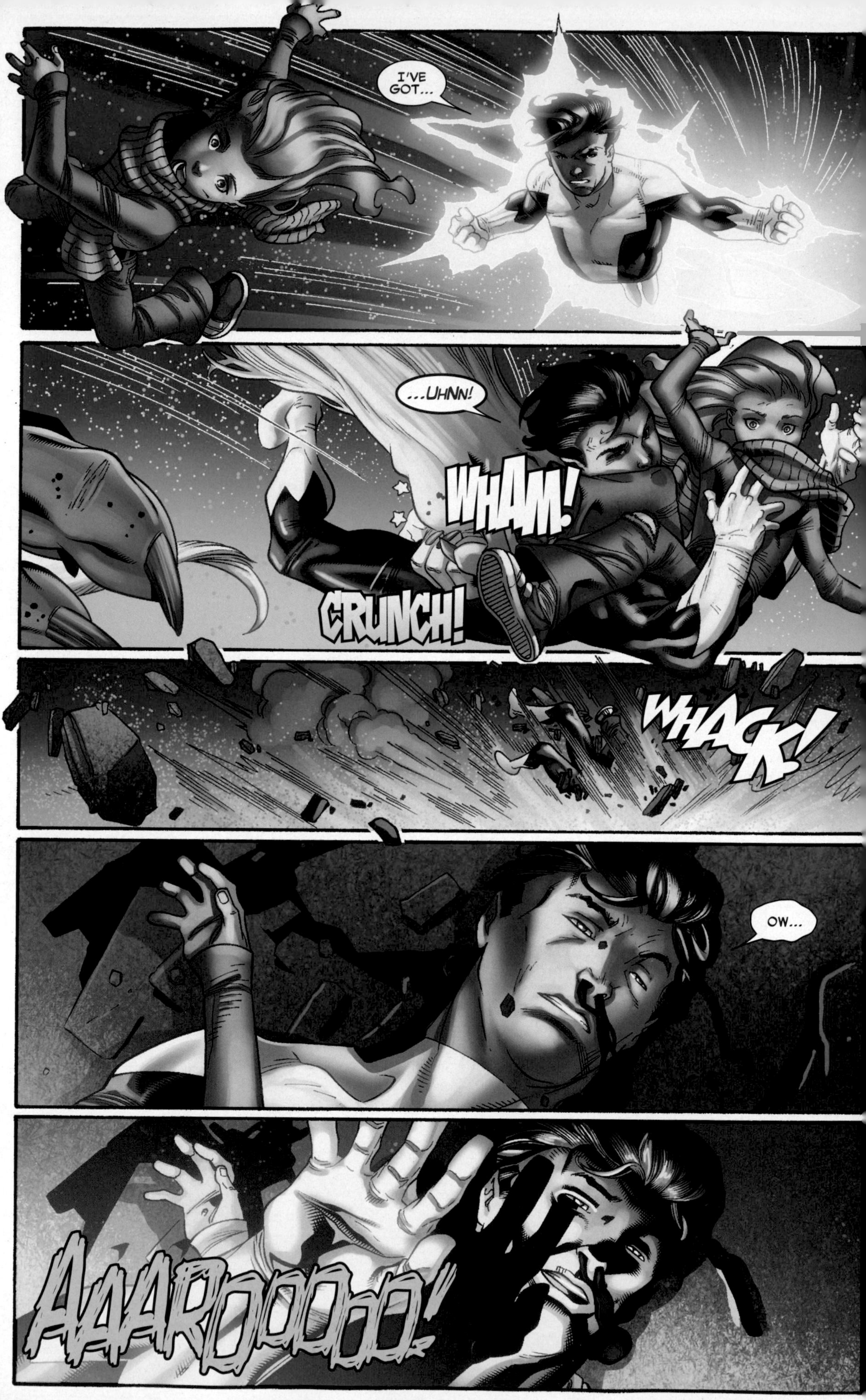
I'VE GOT...
...UHNN!
WHAM!
CRUNCH!
WHACK!
OW...
AAARDOOOOO!

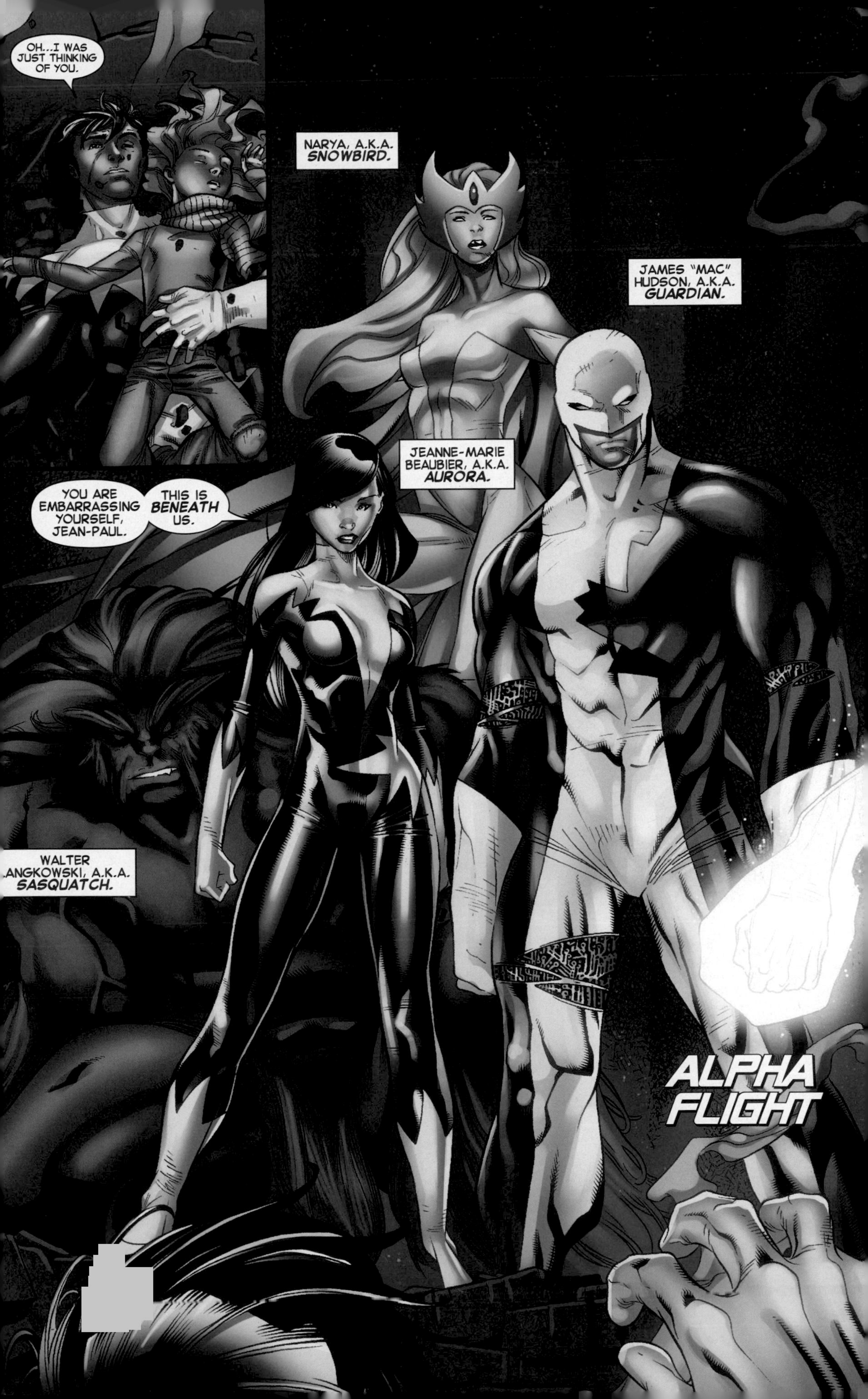
OH...I WAS JUST THINKING OF YOU.
NARYA, A.K.A. SNOWBIRD.
JAMES "MAC" HUDSON, A.K.A. GUARDIAN.
JEANNE-MARIE BEAUBIER, A.K.A. AURORA.
YOU ARE EMBARRASSING YOURSELF, JEAN-PAUL.
THIS IS BENEATH US.
WALTER ANGKOWSKI, A.K.A. SASQUATCH.
ALPHA FLIGHT

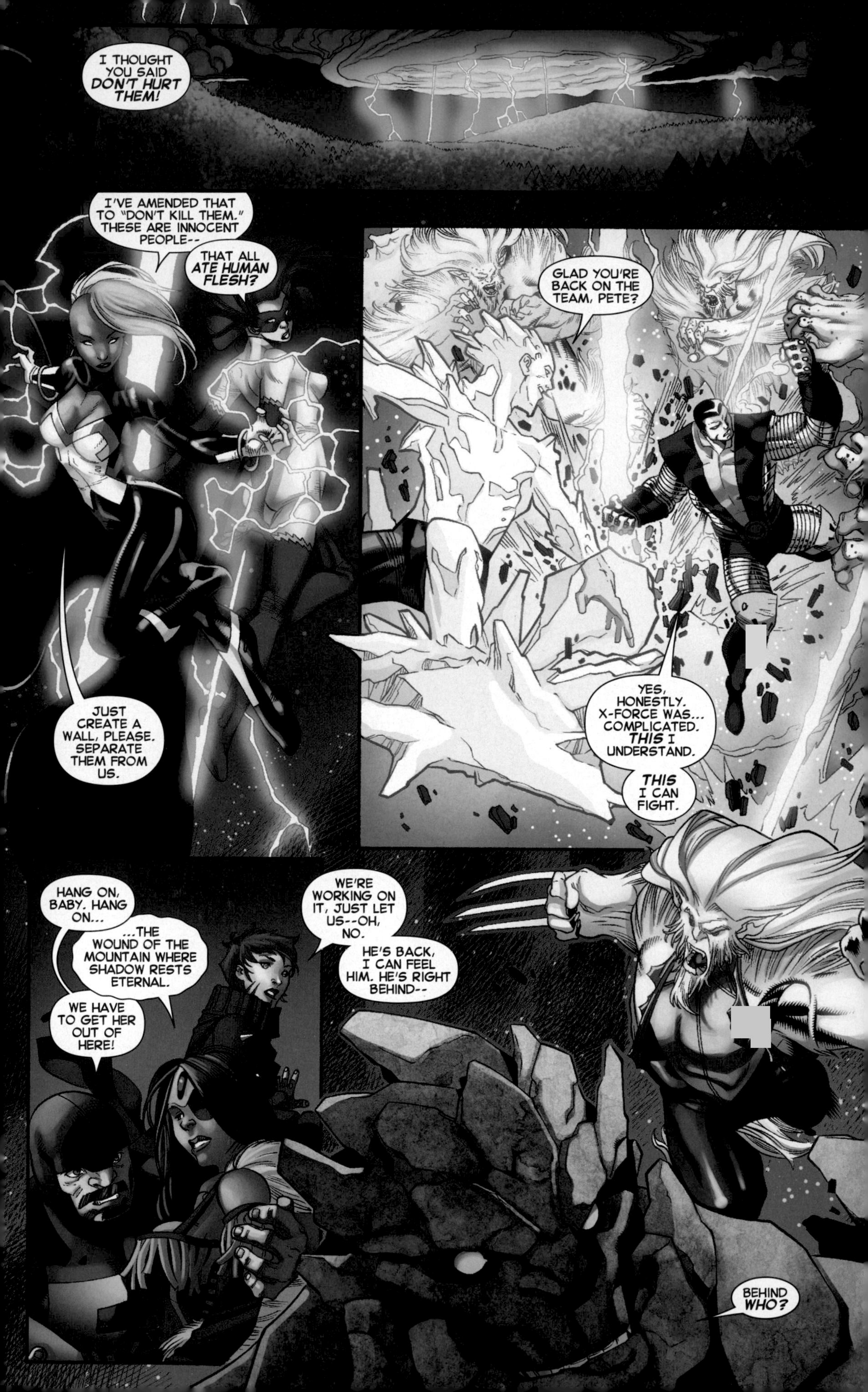

I THOUGHT YOU SAID DON'T HURT THEM!
I'VE AMENDED THAT TO "DON'T KILL THEM." THESE ARE INNOCENT PEOPLE--
THAT ALL ATE HUMAN FLESH?
JUST CREATE A WALL, PLEASE. SEPARATE THEM FROM US.
GLAD YOU'RE BACK ON THE TEAM, PETE?
YES, HONESTLY. X-FORCE WAS... COMPLICATED. THIS I UNDERSTAND.
THIS I CAN FIGHT.
HANG ON, BABY. HANG ON...
...THE WOUND OF THE MOUNTAIN WHERE SHADOW RESTS ETERNAL.
WE HAVE TO GET HER OUT OF HERE!
WE'RE WORKING ON IT, JUST LET US--OH, NO.
HE'S BACK, I CAN FEEL HIM. HE'S RIGHT BEHIND--
BEHIND WHO?

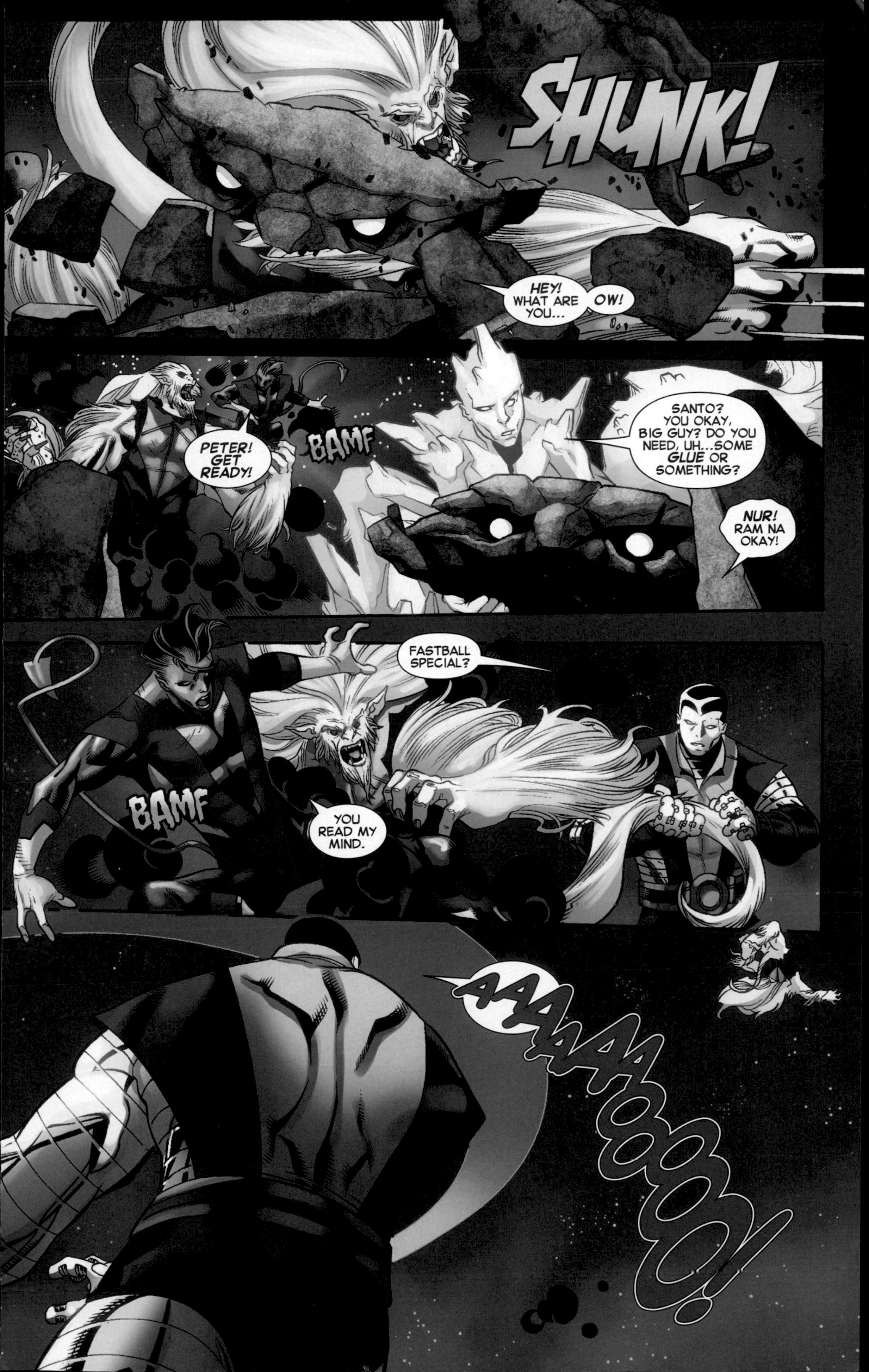
SHUNK!
HEY! WHAT ARE YOU...
OW!
PETER! GET READY!
BAMF
SANTO? YOU OKAY, BIG GUY? DO YOU NEED, UH...SOME GLUE OR SOMETHING?
NUR! RAM NA OKAY!
FASTBALL SPECIAL?
BAMF
YOU READ MY MIND.
AAAAAAOOOOOO!

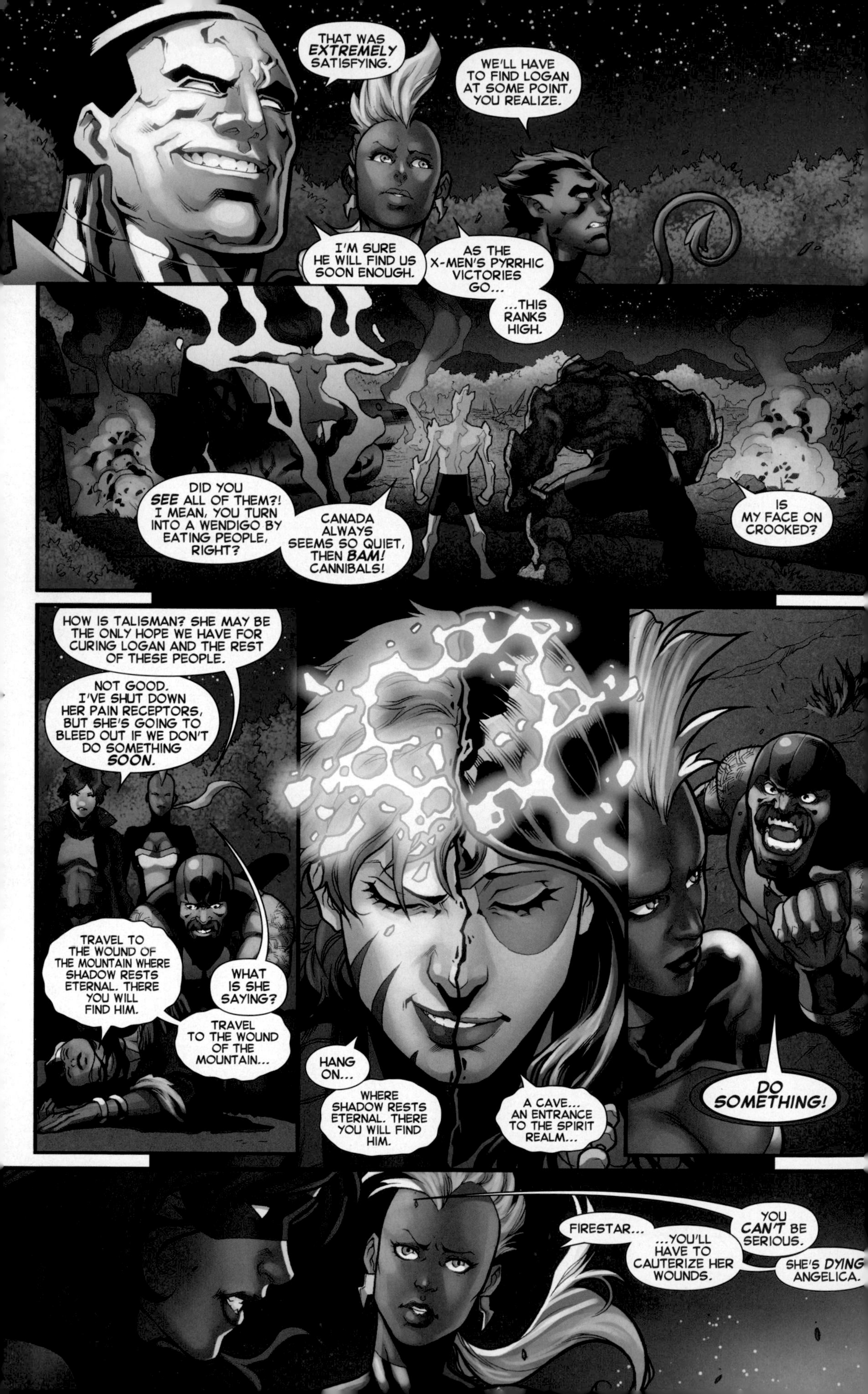
THAT WAS EXTREMELY SATISFYING.
WE'LL HAVE TO FIND LOGAN AT SOME POINT, YOU REALIZE.
I'M SURE HE WILL FIND US SOON ENOUGH.
AS THE X-MEN'S PYRRHIC VICTORIES GO...
...THIS RANKS HIGH.
DID YOU SEE ALL OF THEM?! I MEAN, YOU TURN INTO A WENDIGO BY EATING PEOPLE, RIGHT?
CANADA ALWAYS SEEMS SO QUIET, THEN BAM! CANNIBALS!
IS MY FACE ON CROOKED?
HOW IS TALISMAN? SHE MAY BE THE ONLY HOPE WE HAVE FOR CURING LOGAN AND THE REST OF THESE PEOPLE.
NOT GOOD. I'VE SHUT DOWN HER PAIN RECEPTORS, BUT SHE'S GOING TO BLEED OUT IF WE DON'T DO SOMETHING SOON.
TRAVEL TO THE WOUND OF THE MOUNTAIN WHERE SHADOW RESTS ETERNAL. THERE YOU WILL FIND HIM.
WHAT IS SHE SAYING?
TRAVEL TO THE WOUND OF THE MOUNTAIN...
HANG ON...
WHERE SHADOW RESTS ETERNAL. THERE YOU WILL FIND HIM.
A CAVE... AN ENTRANCE TO THE SPIRIT REALM...
DO SOMETHING!
FIRESTAR...
...YOU'LL HAVE TO CAUTERIZE HER WOUNDS.
YOU CAN'T BE SERIOUS.
SHE'S DYING ANGELICA.

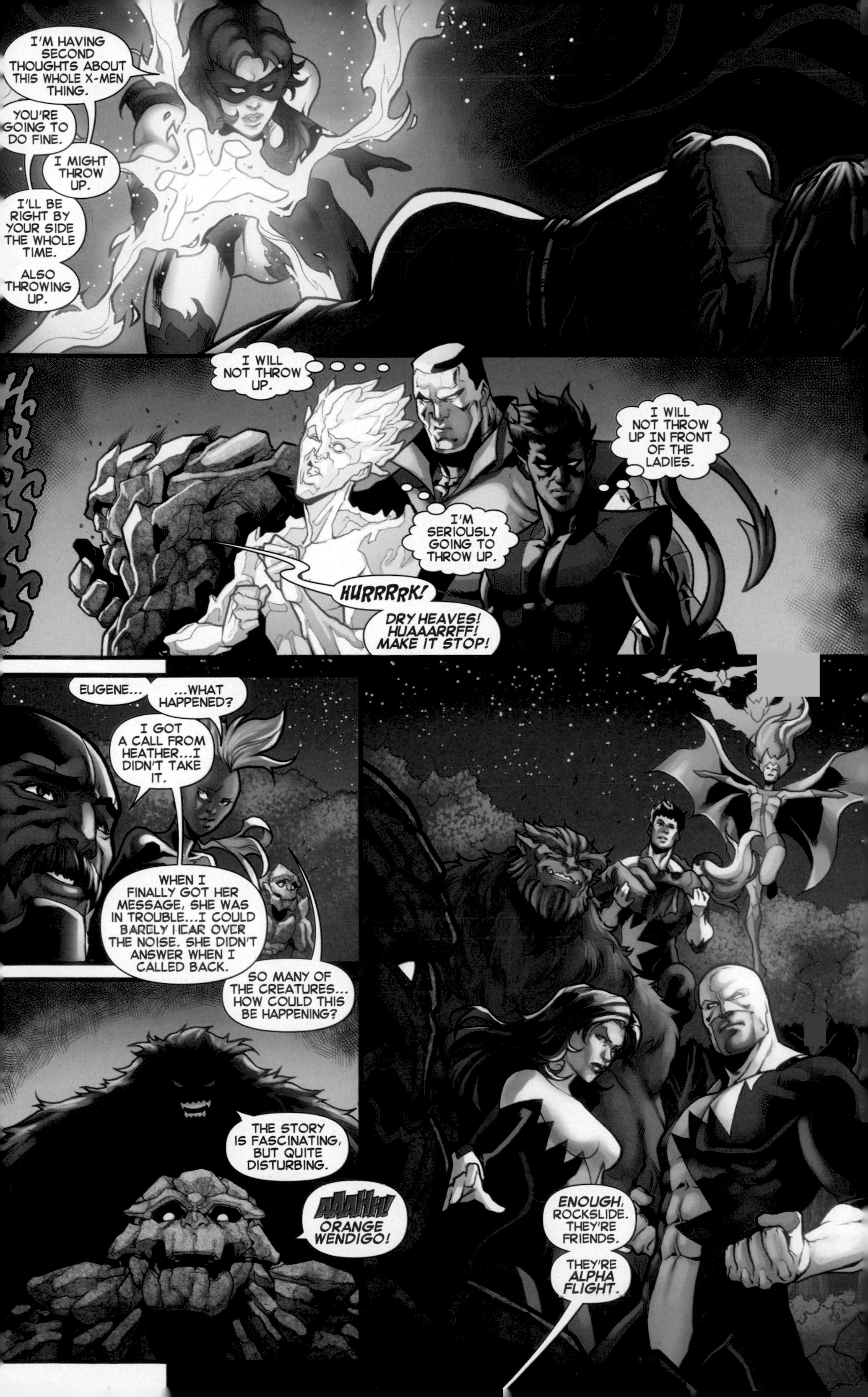
I'M HAVING SECOND THOUGHTS ABOUT THIS WHOLE X-MEN THING.
YOU'RE GOING TO DO FINE.
I MIGHT THROW UP.
I'LL BE RIGHT BY YOUR SIDE THE WHOLE TIME.
ALSO THROWING UP.
I WILL NOT THROW UP.
I WILL NOT THROW UP IN FRONT OF THE LADIES.
I'M SERIOUSLY GOING TO THROW UP.
HURRRRK!
DRY HEAVES! HUAAARRFF! MAKE IT STOP!
EUGENE...
...WHAT HAPPENED?
I GOT A CALL FROM HEATHER...I DIDN'T TAKE IT.
WHEN I FINALLY GOT HER MESSAGE, SHE WAS IN TROUBLE...I COULD BARELY HEAR OVER THE NOISE. SHE DIDN'T ANSWER WHEN I CALLED BACK.
SO MANY OF THE CREATURES... HOW COULD THIS BE HAPPENING?
THE STORY IS FASCINATING, BUT QUITE DISTURBING.
AAAHH! ORANGE WENDIGO!
ENOUGH, ROCKSLIDE. THEY'RE FRIENDS.
THEY'RE ALPHA FLIGHT.

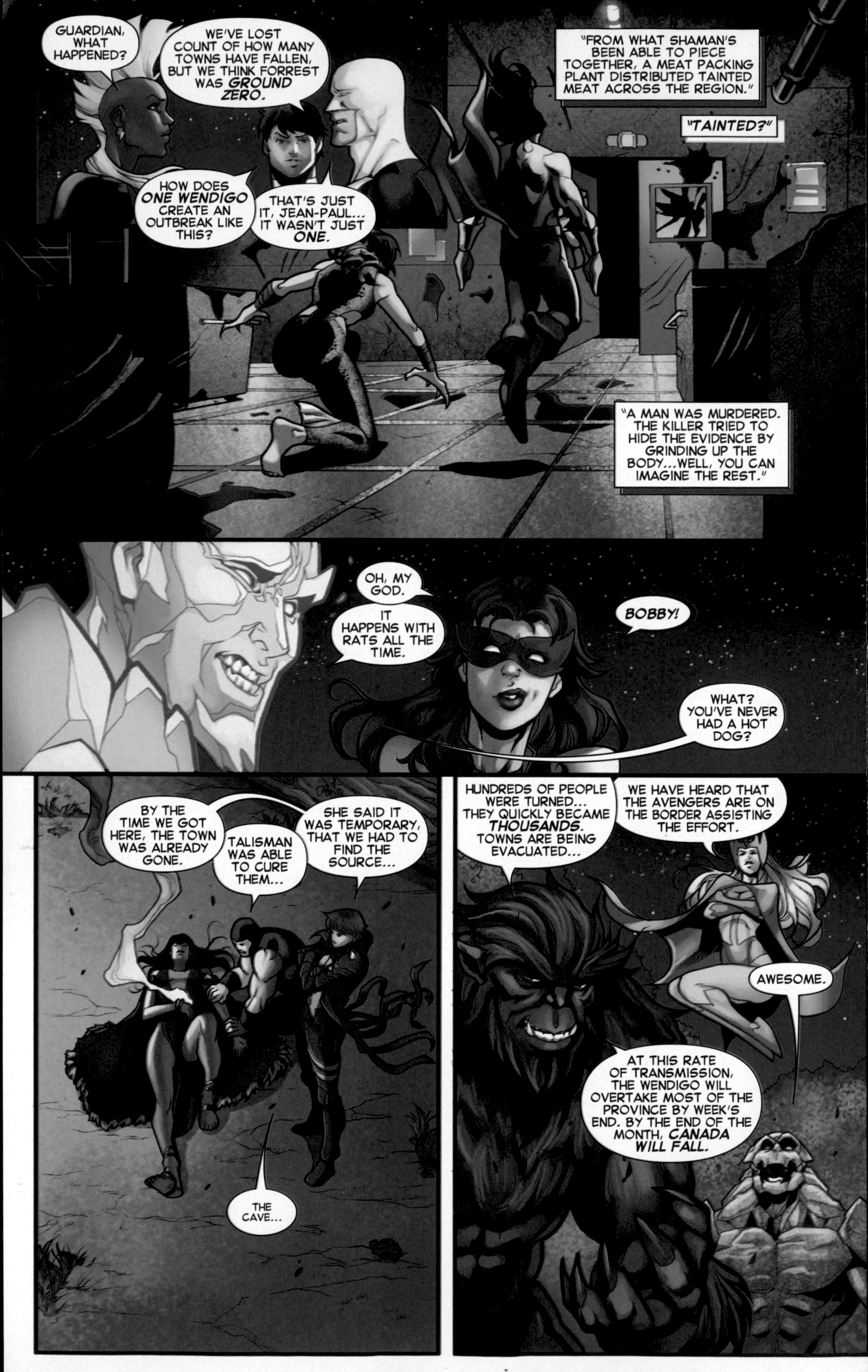

GUARDIAN, WHAT HAPPENED?
WE'VE LOST COUNT OF HOW MANY TOWNS HAVE FALLEN, BUT WE THINK FORREST WAS GROUND ZERO.
HOW DOES ONE WENDIGO CREATE AN OUTBREAK LIKE THIS?
THAT'S JUST IT, JEAN-PAUL... IT WASN'T JUST ONE.
"FROM WHAT SHAMAN'S BEEN ABLE TO PIECE TOGETHER, A MEAT PACKING PLANT DISTRIBUTED TAINTED MEAT ACROSS THE REGION."
"TAINTED?"
"A MAN WAS MURDERED. THE KILLER TRIED TO HIDE THE EVIDENCE BY GRINDING UP THE BODY...WELL, YOU CAN IMAGINE THE REST."
OH, MY GOD.
IT HAPPENS WITH RATS ALL THE TIME.
BOBBY!
WHAT? YOU'VE NEVER HAD A HOT DOG?
BY THE TIME WE GOT HERE, THE TOWN WAS ALREADY GONE.
TALISMAN WAS ABLE TO CURE THEM...
SHE SAID IT WAS TEMPORARY, THAT WE HAD TO FIND THE SOURCE...
THE CAVE...
HUNDREDS OF PEOPLE WERE TURNED... THEY QUICKLY BECAME THOUSANDS. TOWNS ARE BEING EVACUATED...
WE HAVE HEARD THAT THE AVENGERS ARE ON THE BORDER ASSISTING THE EFFORT.
AWESOME.
AT THIS RATE OF TRANSMISSION, THE WENDIGO WILL OVERTAKE MOST OF THE PROVINCE BY WEEK'S END. BY THE END OF THE MONTH, CANADA WILL FALL.

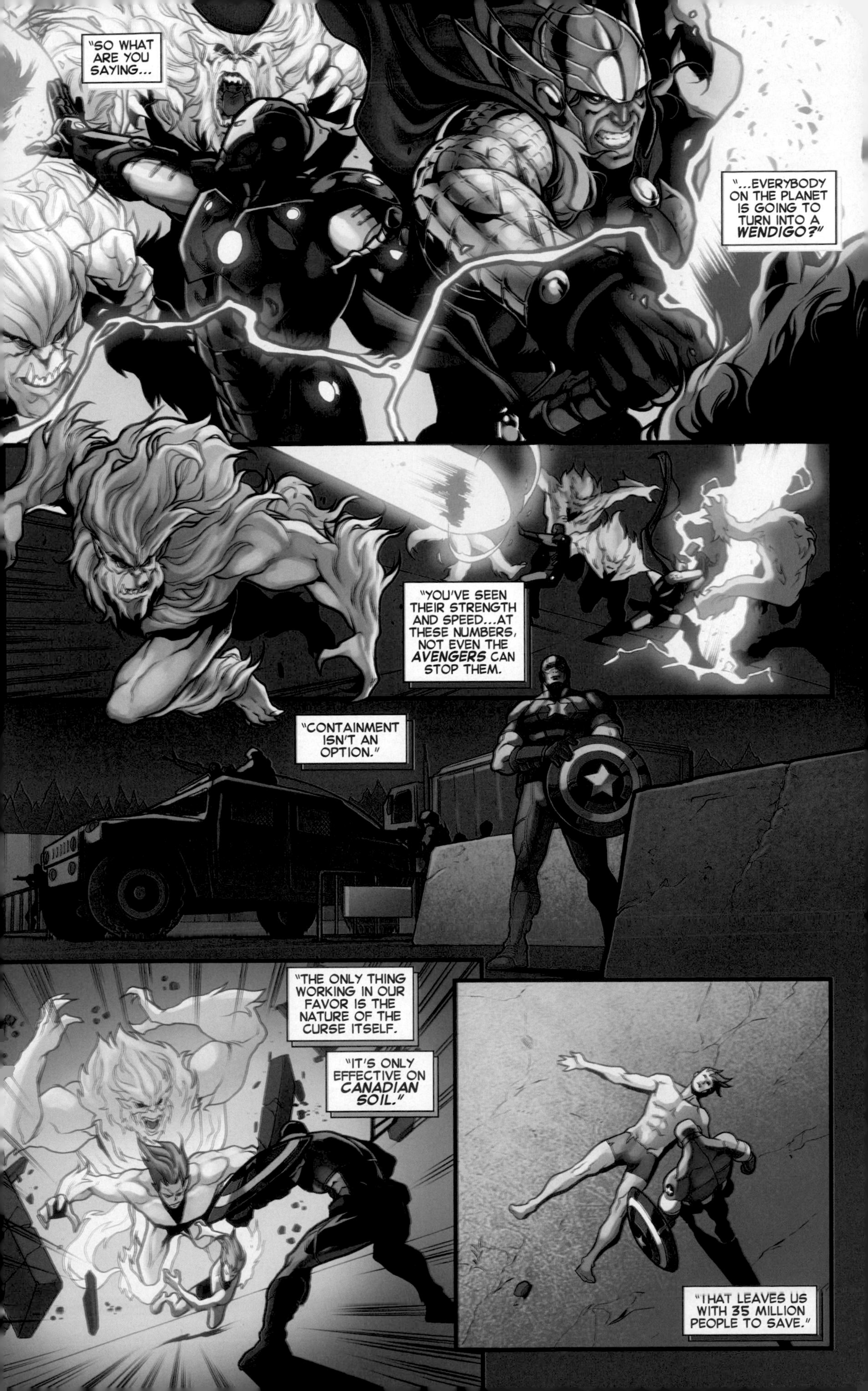
"SO WHAT ARE YOU SAYING...
"...EVERYBODY ON THE PLANET IS GOING TO TURN INTO A *WENDIGO?*"
"YOU'VE SEEN THEIR STRENGTH AND SPEED...AT THESE NUMBERS, NOT EVEN THE *AVENGERS* CAN STOP THEM.
"CONTAINMENT ISN'T AN OPTION."
"THE ONLY THING WORKING IN OUR FAVOR IS THE NATURE OF THE CURSE ITSELF.
"IT'S ONLY EFFECTIVE ON *CANADIAN SOIL.*"
"THAT LEAVES US WITH **35** MILLION PEOPLE TO SAVE."

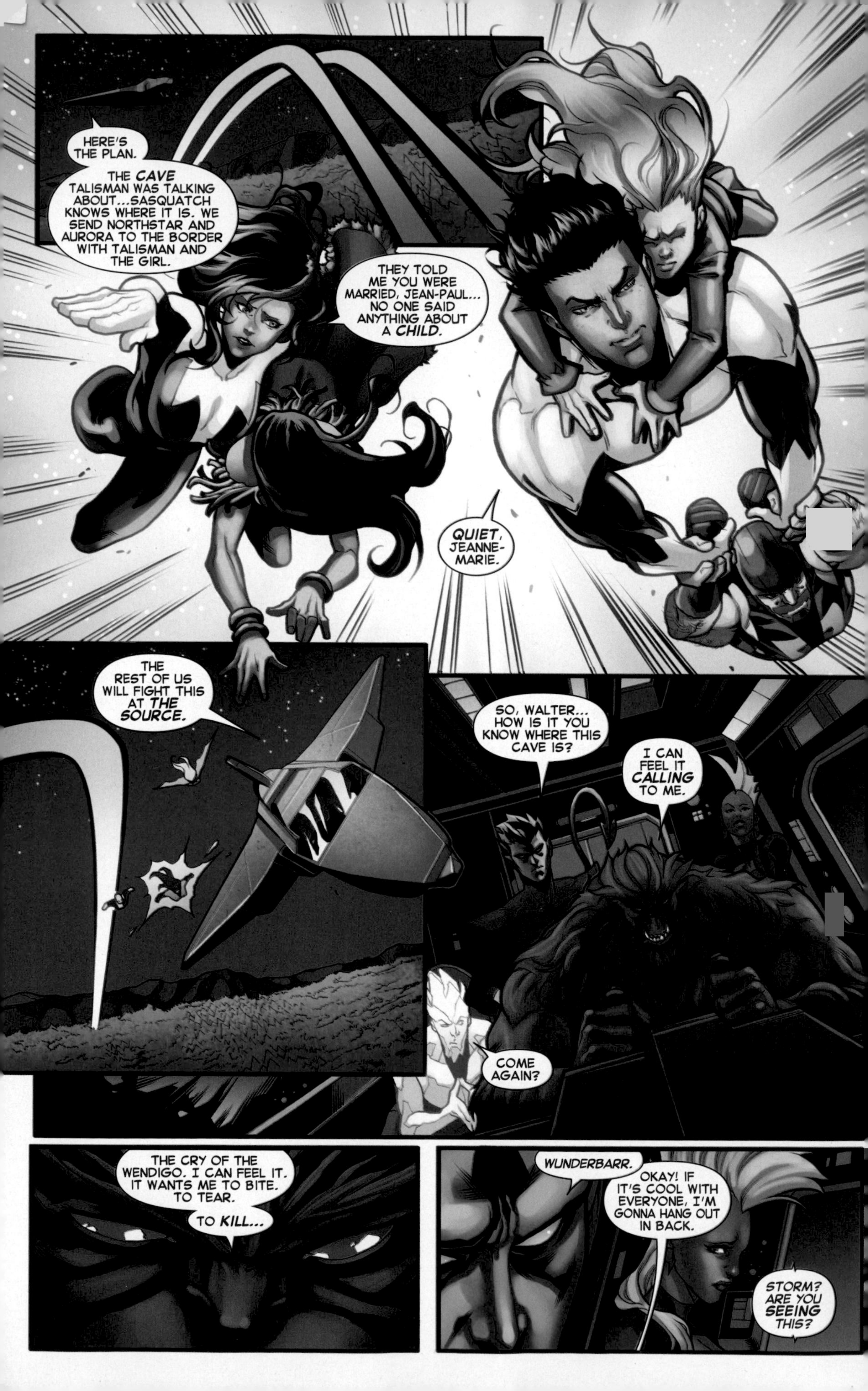
HERE'S THE PLAN.
THE CAVE TALISMAN WAS TALKING ABOUT...SASQUATCH KNOWS WHERE IT IS. WE SEND NORTHSTAR AND AURORA TO THE BORDER WITH TALISMAN AND THE GIRL.
THEY TOLD ME YOU WERE MARRIED, JEAN-PAUL... NO ONE SAID ANYTHING ABOUT A CHILD.
QUIET, JEANNE-MARIE.
THE REST OF US WILL FIGHT THIS AT THE SOURCE.
SO, WALTER... HOW IS IT YOU KNOW WHERE THIS CAVE IS?
I CAN FEEL IT CALLING TO ME.
COME AGAIN?
THE CRY OF THE WENDIGO. I CAN FEEL IT. IT WANTS ME TO BITE. TO TEAR.
TO KILL...
WUNDERBARR.
OKAY! IF IT'S COOL WITH EVERYONE, I'M GONNA HANG OUT IN BACK.
STORM? ARE YOU SEEING THIS?

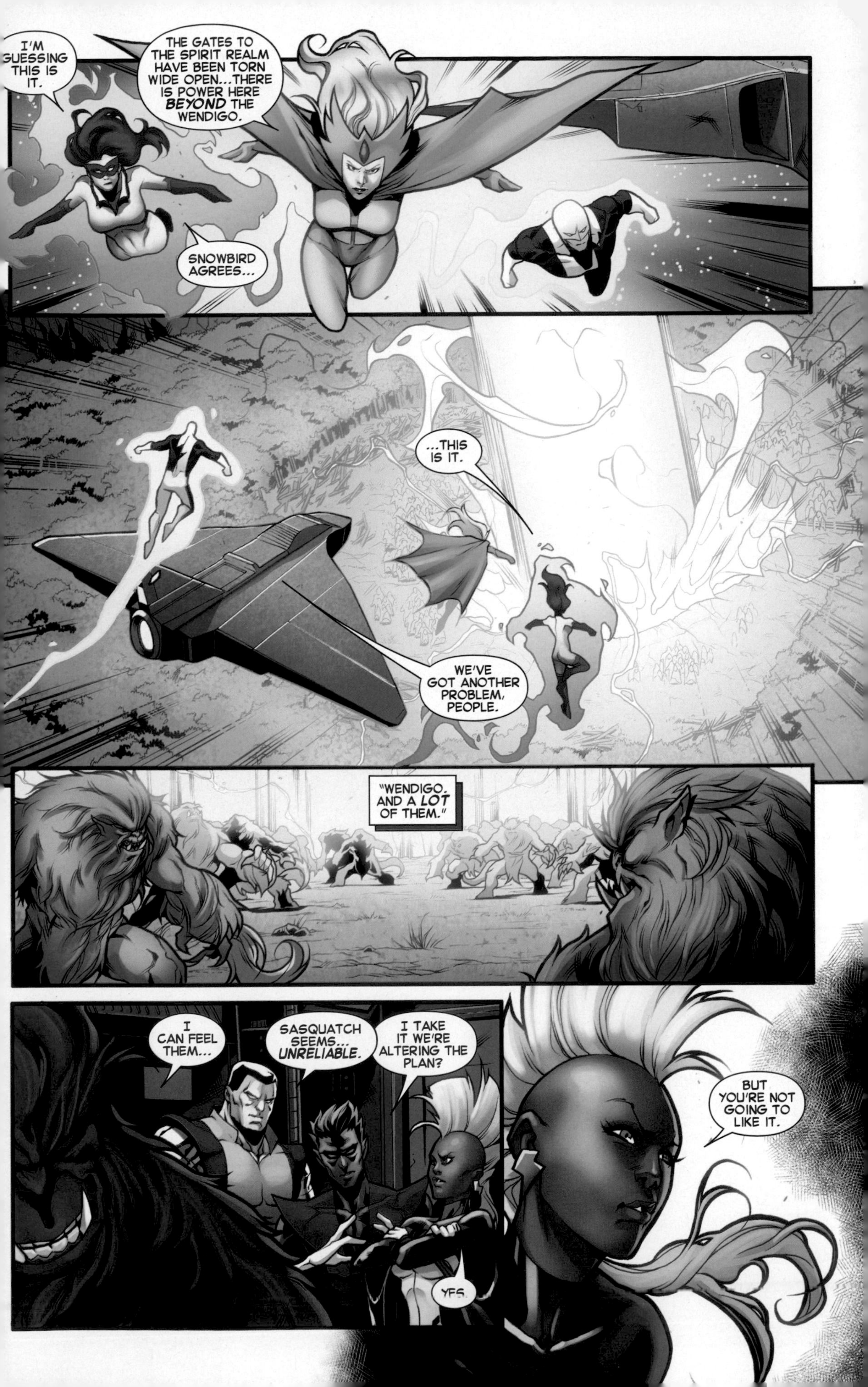
I'M GUESSING THIS IS IT.
THE GATES TO THE SPIRIT REALM HAVE BEEN TORN WIDE OPEN...THERE IS POWER HERE BEYOND THE WENDIGO.
SNOWBIRD AGREES...
...THIS IS IT.
WE'VE GOT ANOTHER PROBLEM, PEOPLE.
"WENDIGO. AND A LOT OF THEM."
I CAN FEEL THEM...
SASQUATCH SEEMS... UNRELIABLE.
I TAKE IT WE'RE ALTERING THE PLAN?
YES.
BUT YOU'RE NOT GOING TO LIKE IT.

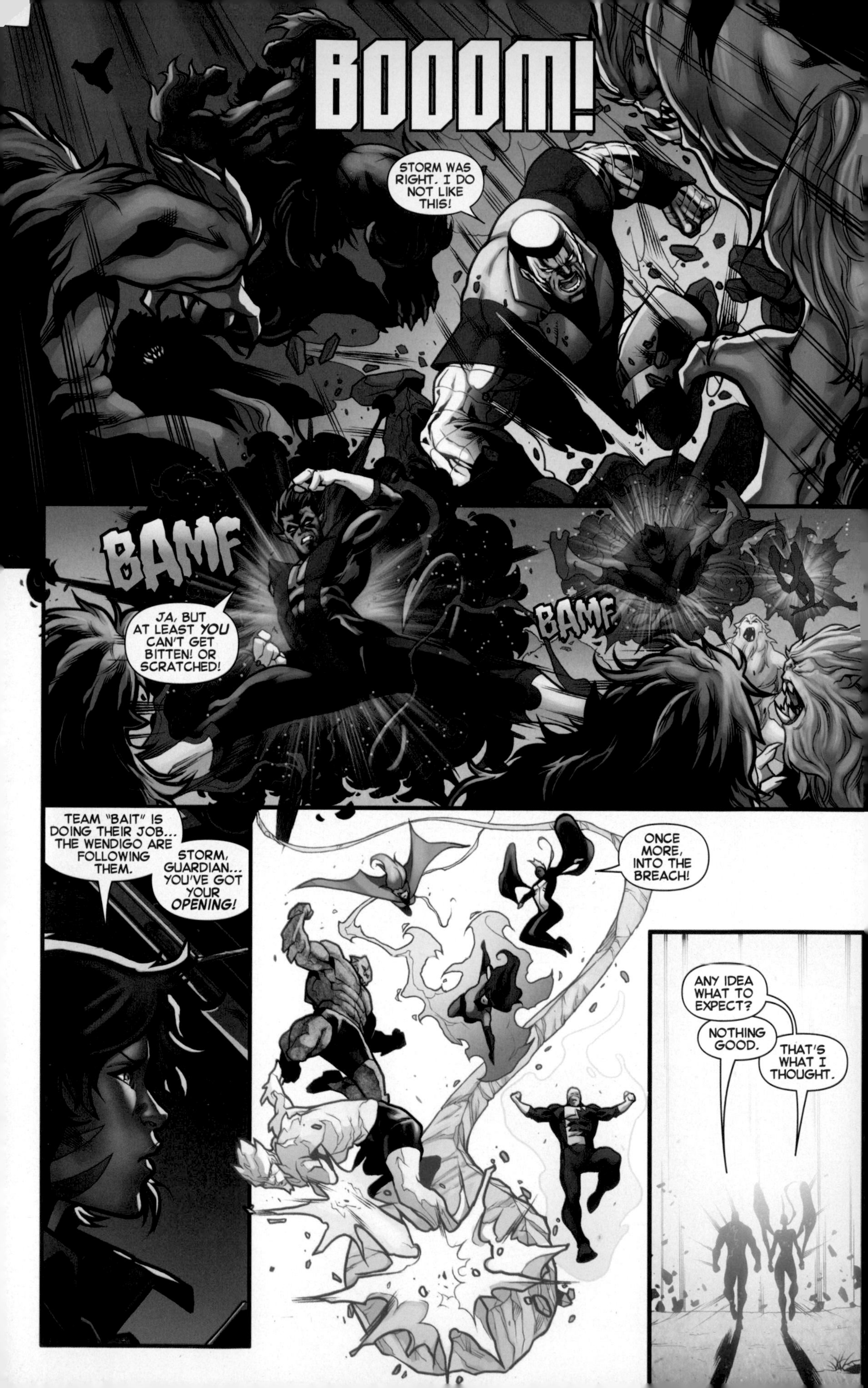
BOOOM!
STORM WAS RIGHT. I DO NOT LIKE THIS!
BAMF
JA, BUT AT LEAST YOU CAN'T GET BITTEN! OR SCRATCHED!
BAMF
TEAM "BAIT" IS DOING THEIR JOB... THE WENDIGO ARE FOLLOWING THEM.
STORM, GUARDIAN... YOU'VE GOT YOUR OPENING!
ONCE MORE, INTO THE BREACH!
ANY IDEA WHAT TO EXPECT?
NOTHING GOOD.
THAT'S WHAT I THOUGHT.

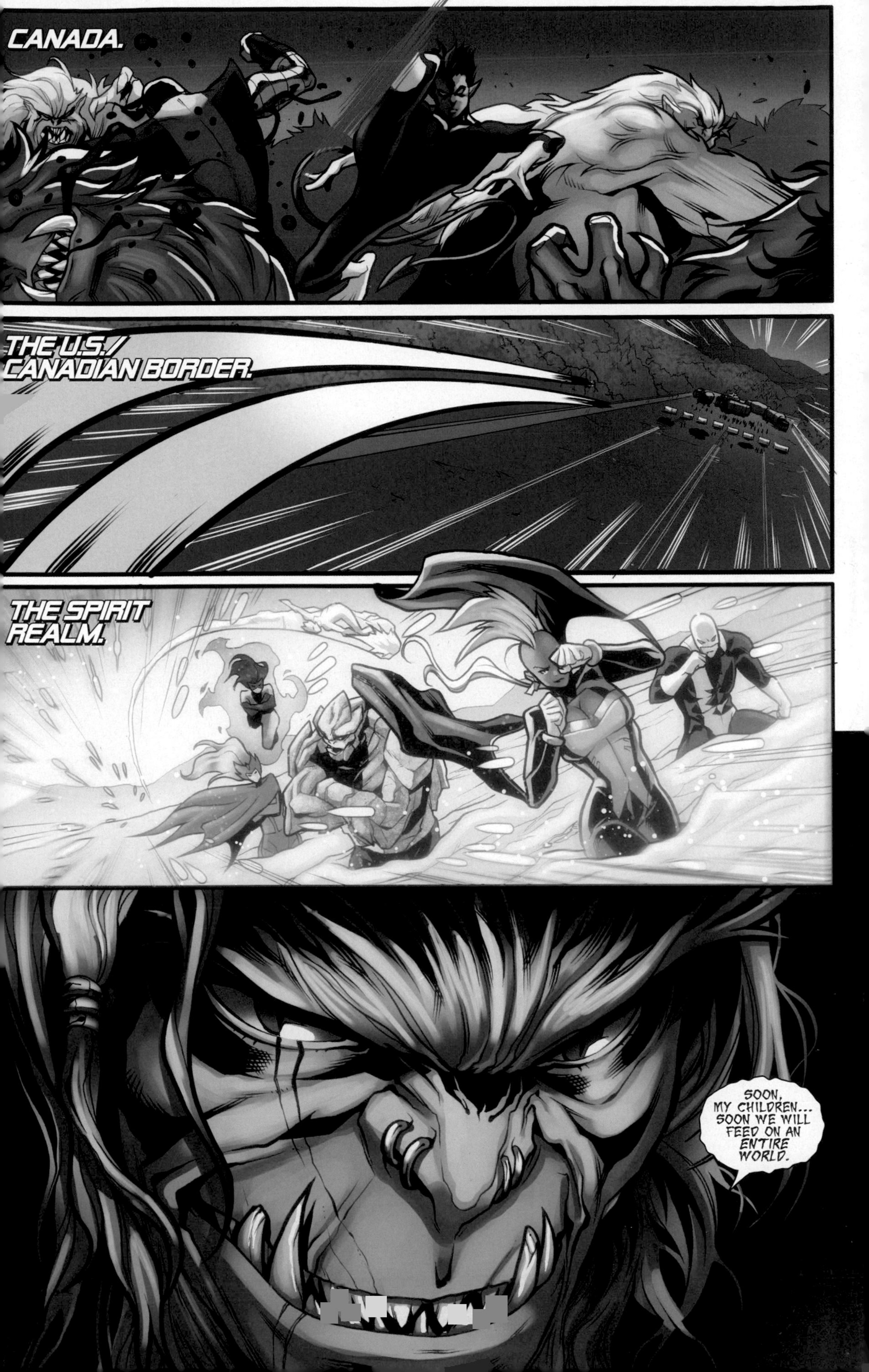
CANADA.
THE U.S./ CANADIAN BORDER.
THE SPIRIT REALM.
SOON, MY CHILDREN... SOON WE WILL FEED ON AN ENTIRE WORLD.

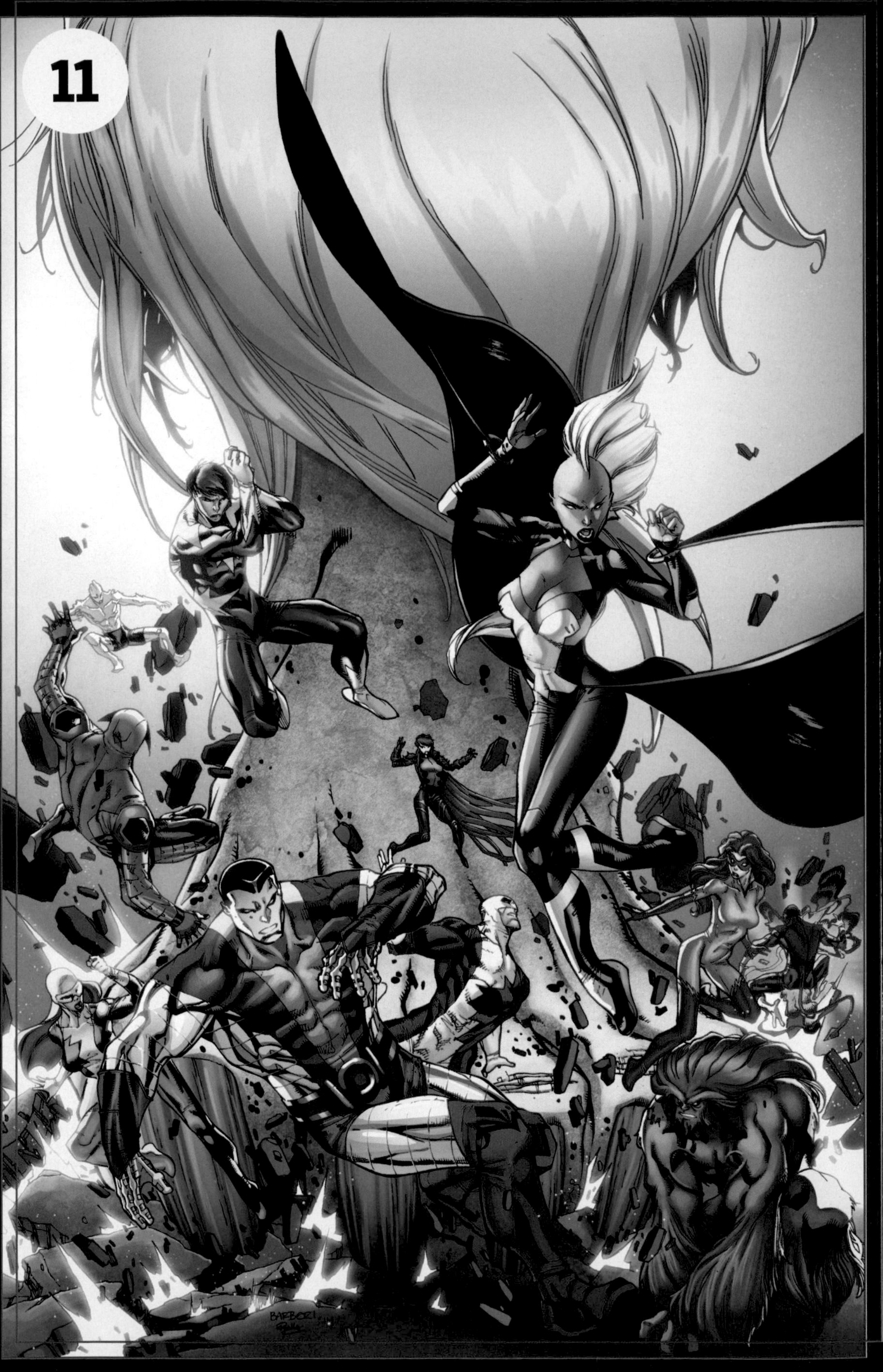
11

WORLD WAR WENDIGO! PART 4

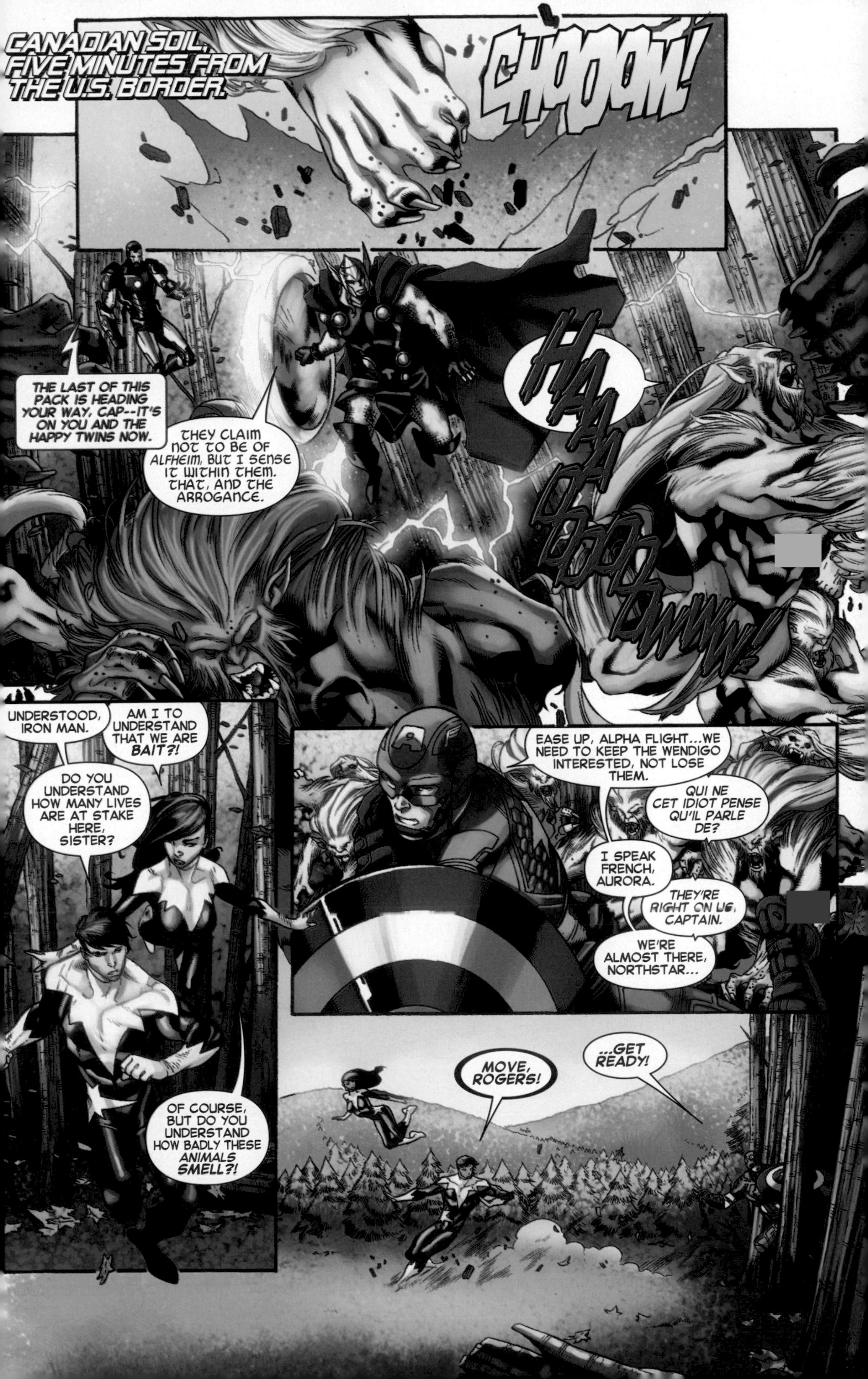
CANADIAN SOIL, FIVE MINUTES FROM THE U.S. BORDER.
CHOOOM!
THE LAST OF THIS PACK IS HEADING YOUR WAY, CAP--IT'S ON YOU AND THE HAPPY TWINS NOW.
THEY CLAIM NOT TO BE OF ALFHEIM, BUT I SENSE IT WITHIN THEM. THAT, AND THE ARROGANCE.
UNDERSTOOD, IRON MAN.
AM I TO UNDERSTAND THAT WE ARE BAIT?!
DO YOU UNDERSTAND HOW MANY LIVES ARE AT STAKE HERE, SISTER?
EASE UP, ALPHA FLIGHT...WE NEED TO KEEP THE WENDIGO INTERESTED, NOT LOSE THEM.
QUI NE CET IDIOT PENSE QU'IL PARLE DE?
I SPEAK FRENCH, AURORA.
THEY'RE RIGHT ON US, CAPTAIN.
WE'RE ALMOST THERE, NORTHSTAR...
OF COURSE, BUT DO YOU UNDERSTAND HOW BADLY THESE ANIMALS SMELL?!
MOVE, ROGERS!
...GET READY!

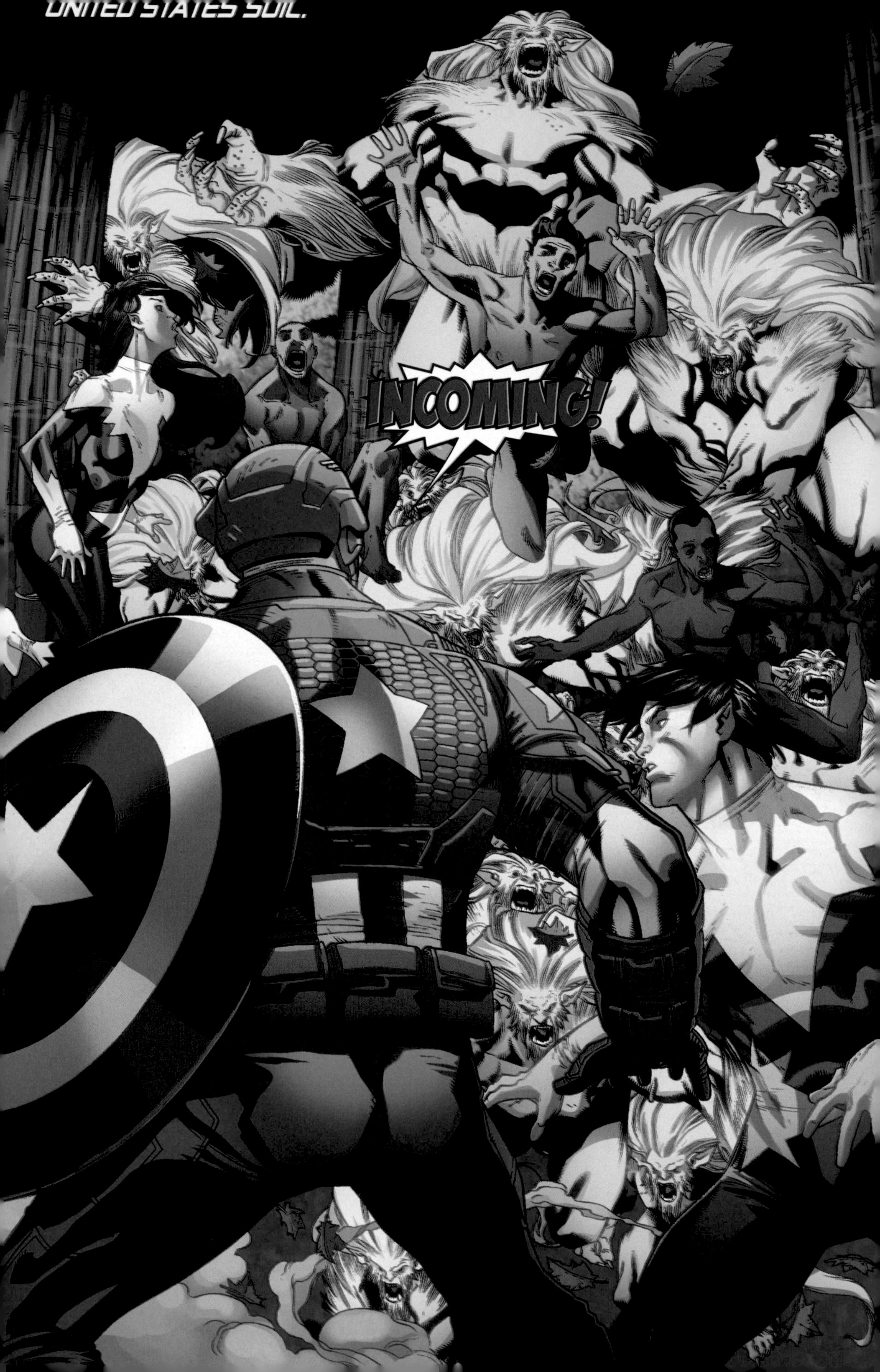
UNITED STATES SOIL.
INCOMING!

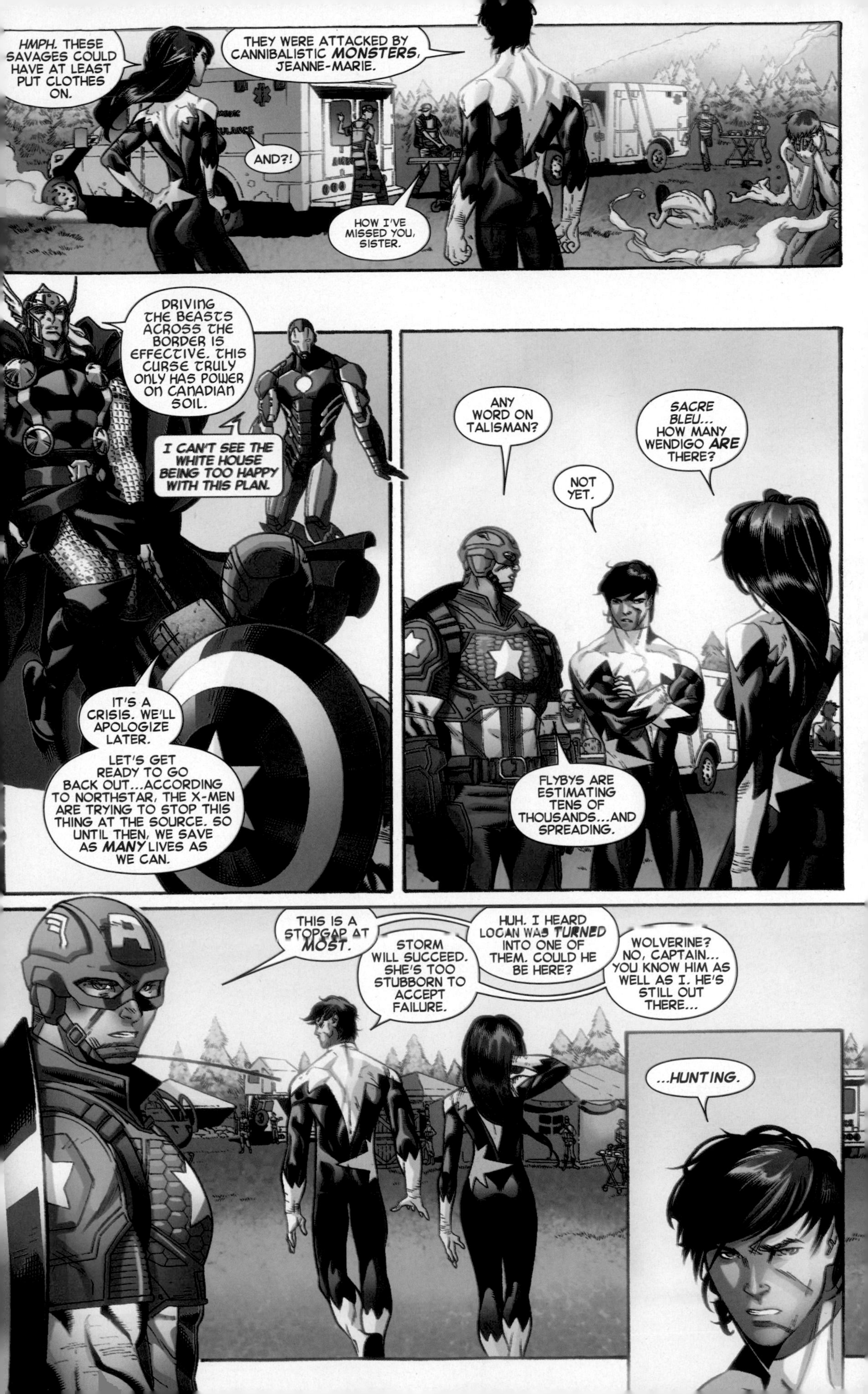
HMPH. THESE SAVAGES COULD HAVE AT LEAST PUT CLOTHES ON.
THEY WERE ATTACKED BY CANNIBALISTIC MONSTERS, JEANNE-MARIE.
AND?!
HOW I'VE MISSED YOU, SISTER.
DRIVING THE BEASTS ACROSS THE BORDER IS EFFECTIVE. THIS CURSE TRULY ONLY HAS POWER ON CANADIAN SOIL.
I CAN'T SEE THE WHITE HOUSE BEING TOO HAPPY WITH THIS PLAN.
IT'S A CRISIS. WE'LL APOLOGIZE LATER.
LET'S GET READY TO GO BACK OUT...ACCORDING TO NORTHSTAR, THE X-MEN ARE TRYING TO STOP THIS THING AT THE SOURCE. SO UNTIL THEN, WE SAVE AS MANY LIVES AS WE CAN.
ANY WORD ON TALISMAN?
NOT YET.
SACRE BLEU... HOW MANY WENDIGO ARE THERE?
FLYBYS ARE ESTIMATING TENS OF THOUSANDS...AND SPREADING.
THIS IS A STOPGAP AT MOST.
STORM WILL SUCCEED. SHE'S TOO STUBBORN TO ACCEPT FAILURE.
HUH. I HEARD LOGAN WAS TURNED INTO ONE OF THEM. COULD HE BE HERE?
WOLVERINE? NO, CAPTAIN... YOU KNOW HIM AS WELL AS I. HE'S STILL OUT THERE...
...HUNTING.

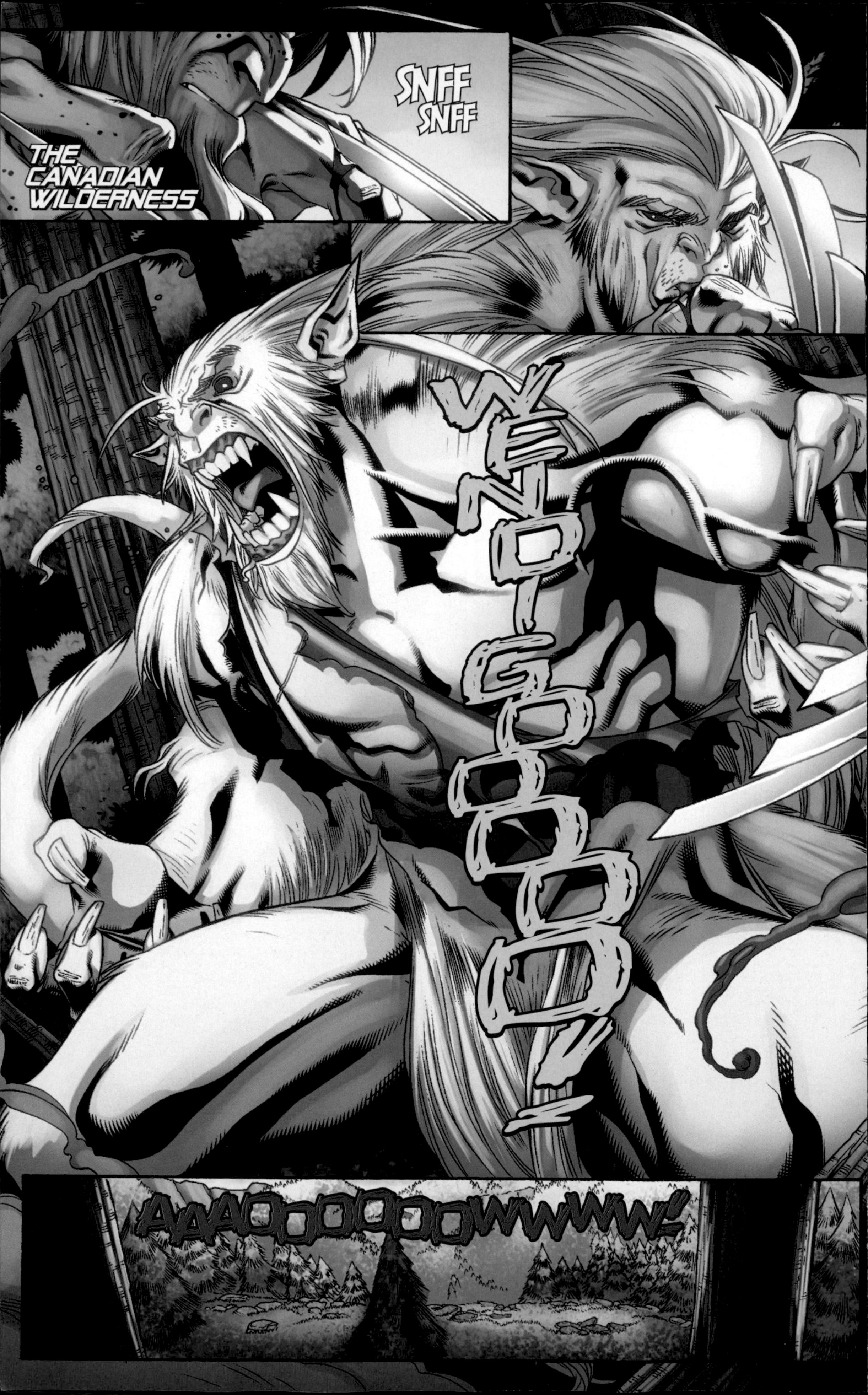
THE CANADIAN WILDERNESS
SNFF SNFF
WENDIGOOOOO!
AAAOOOOOOOWWWW!

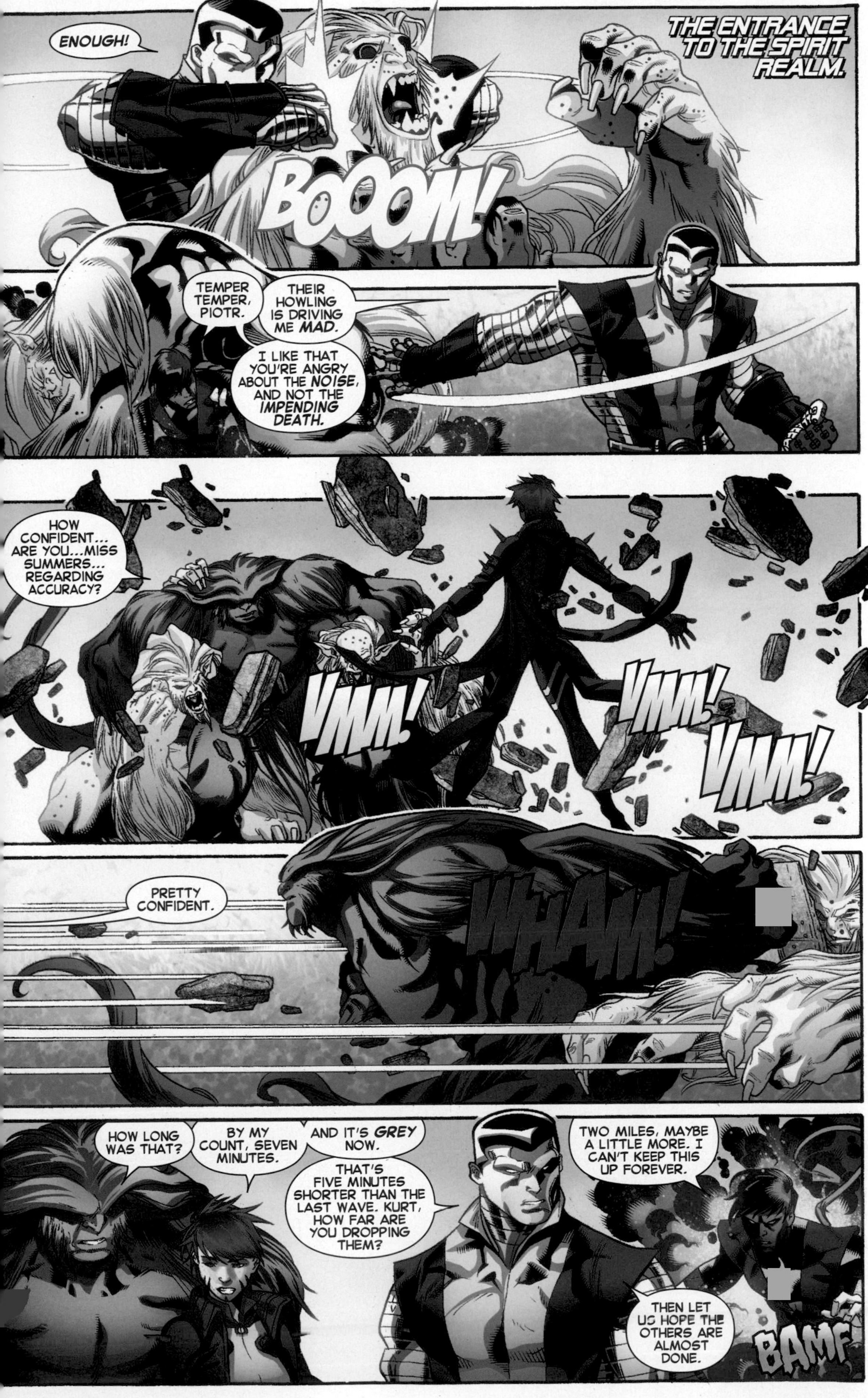

ENOUGH!
THE ENTRANCE TO THE SPIRIT REALM.
BOOOM!
TEMPER TEMPER, PIOTR.
THEIR HOWLING IS DRIVING ME MAD.
I LIKE THAT YOU'RE ANGRY ABOUT THE NOISE, AND NOT THE IMPENDING DEATH.
HOW CONFIDENT... ARE YOU...MISS SUMMERS... REGARDING ACCURACY?
VMM!
VMM!
VMM!
PRETTY CONFIDENT.
WHAM!
HOW LONG WAS THAT?
BY MY COUNT, SEVEN MINUTES.
AND IT'S GREY NOW.
THAT'S FIVE MINUTES SHORTER THAN THE LAST WAVE. KURT, HOW FAR ARE YOU DROPPING THEM?
TWO MILES, MAYBE A LITTLE MORE. I CAN'T KEEP THIS UP FOREVER.
THEN LET US HOPE THE OTHERS ARE ALMOST DONE.
BAMF

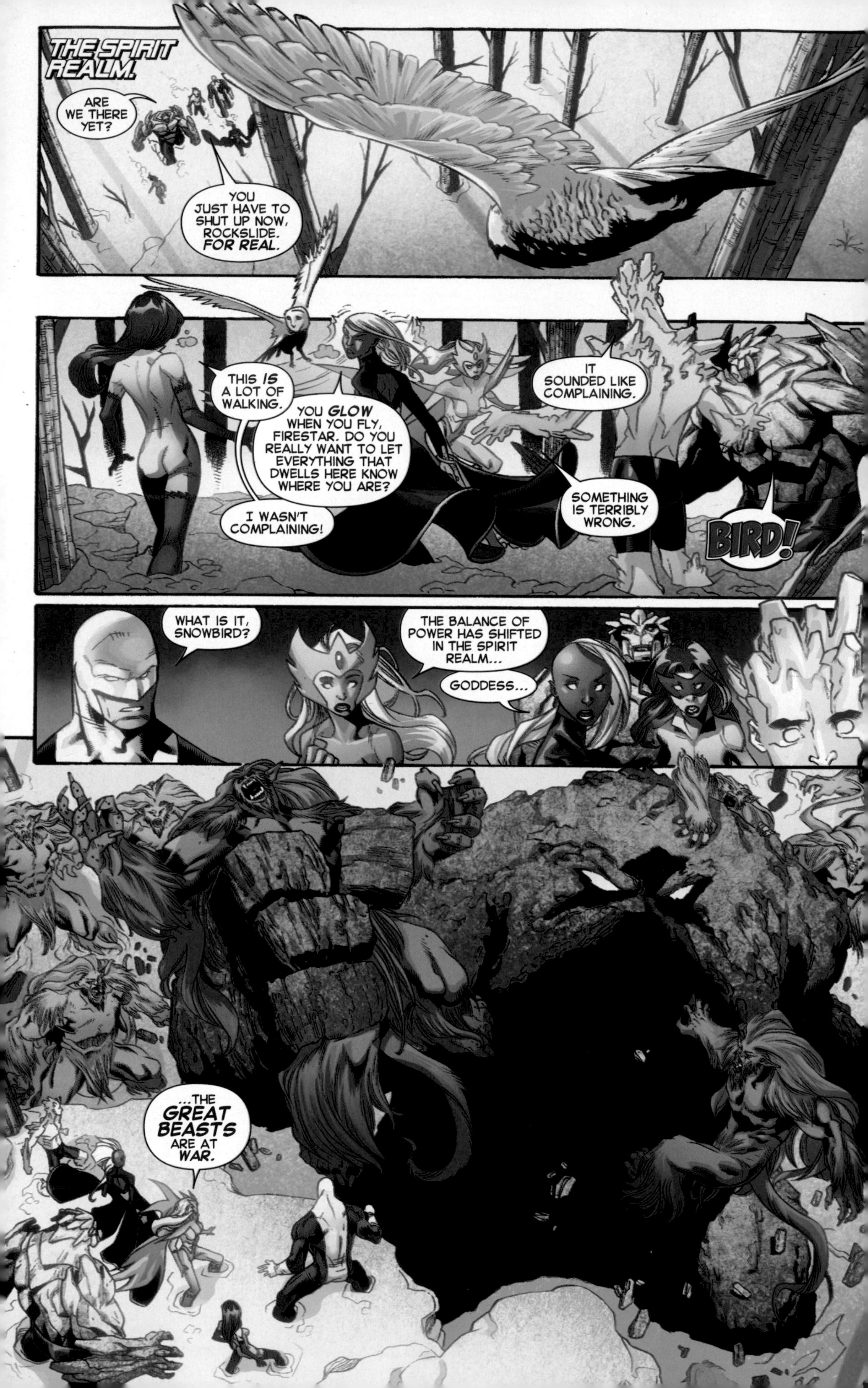
THE SPIRIT REALM.
ARE WE THERE YET?
YOU JUST HAVE TO SHUT UP NOW, ROCKSLIDE. FOR REAL.
THIS IS A LOT OF WALKING.
YOU GLOW WHEN YOU FLY, FIRESTAR. DO YOU REALLY WANT TO LET EVERYTHING THAT DWELLS HERE KNOW WHERE YOU ARE?
I WASN'T COMPLAINING!
IT SOUNDED LIKE COMPLAINING.
SOMETHING IS TERRIBLY WRONG.
BIRD!
WHAT IS IT, SNOWBIRD?
THE BALANCE OF POWER HAS SHIFTED IN THE SPIRIT REALM...
GODDESS...
...THE GREAT BEASTS ARE AT WAR.

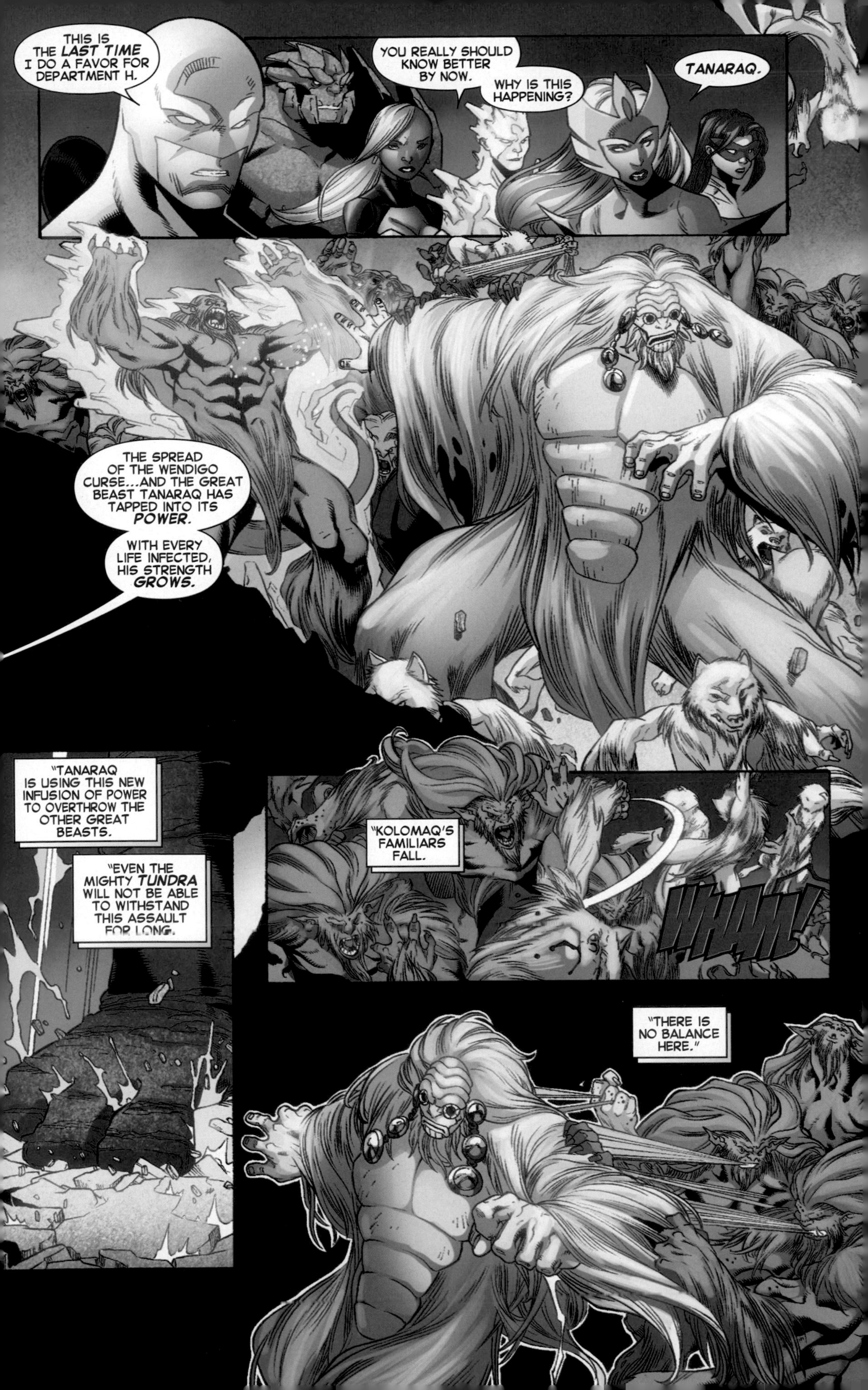
THIS IS THE LAST TIME I DO A FAVOR FOR DEPARTMENT H.
YOU REALLY SHOULD KNOW BETTER BY NOW.
WHY IS THIS HAPPENING?
TANARAQ.
THE SPREAD OF THE WENDIGO CURSE...AND THE GREAT BEAST TANARAQ HAS TAPPED INTO ITS POWER.
WITH EVERY LIFE INFECTED, HIS STRENGTH GROWS.
"TANARAQ IS USING THIS NEW INFUSION OF POWER TO OVERTHROW THE OTHER GREAT BEASTS.
"EVEN THE MIGHTY TUNDRA WILL NOT BE ABLE TO WITHSTAND THIS ASSAULT FOR LONG.
"KOLOMAQ'S FAMILIARS FALL.
WHAM!
"THERE IS NO BALANCE HERE."

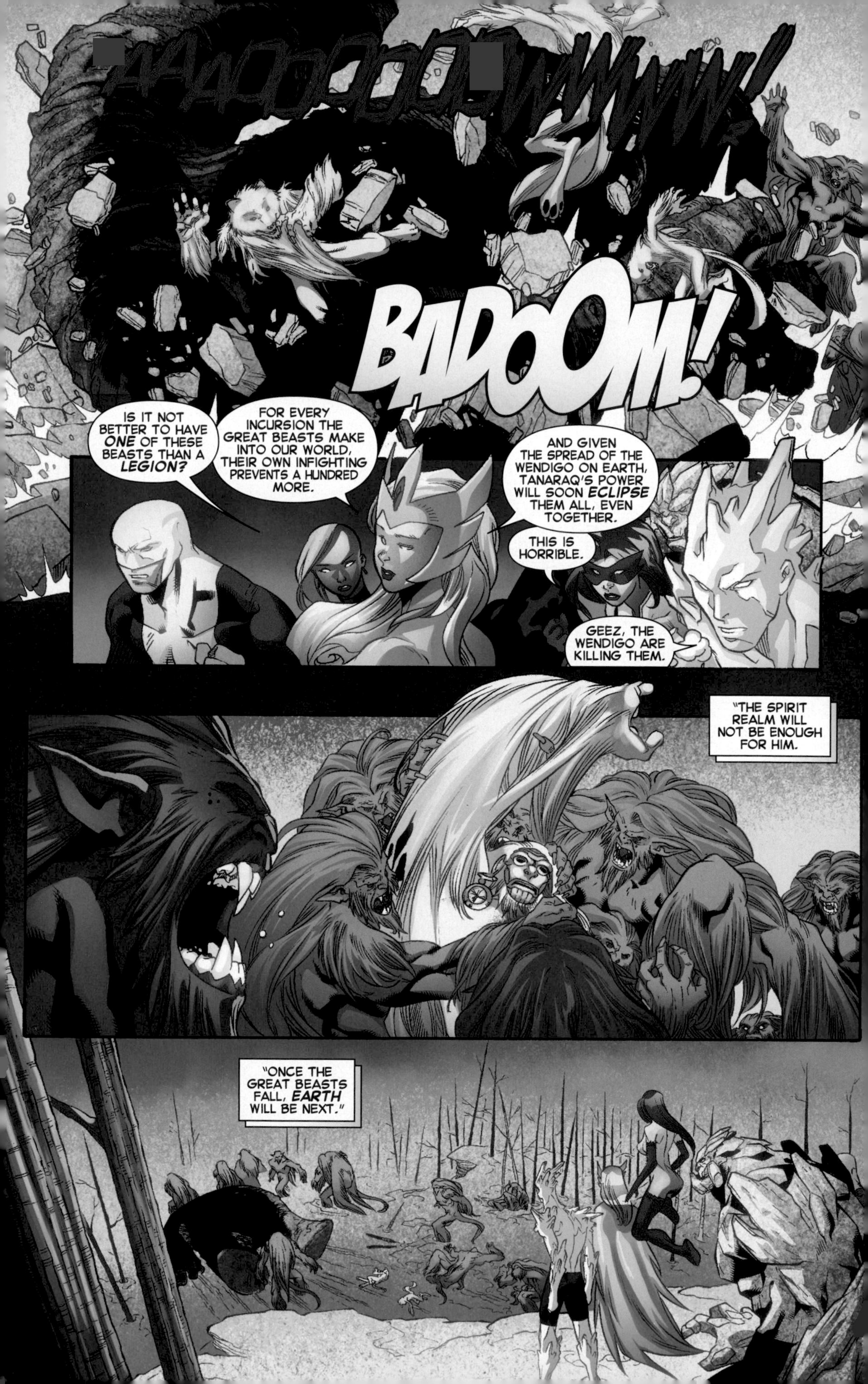
[redacted]AAAOOOOOO[redacted]WWWWWW!
BADOOM!
IS IT NOT BETTER TO HAVE ONE OF THESE BEASTS THAN A LEGION?
FOR EVERY INCURSION THE GREAT BEASTS MAKE INTO OUR WORLD, THEIR OWN INFIGHTING PREVENTS A HUNDRED MORE.
AND GIVEN THE SPREAD OF THE WENDIGO ON EARTH, TANARAQ'S POWER WILL SOON ECLIPSE THEM ALL, EVEN TOGETHER.
THIS IS HORRIBLE.
GEEZ, THE WENDIGO ARE KILLING THEM.
"THE SPIRIT REALM WILL NOT BE ENOUGH FOR HIM.
"ONCE THE GREAT BEASTS FALL, EARTH WILL BE NEXT."

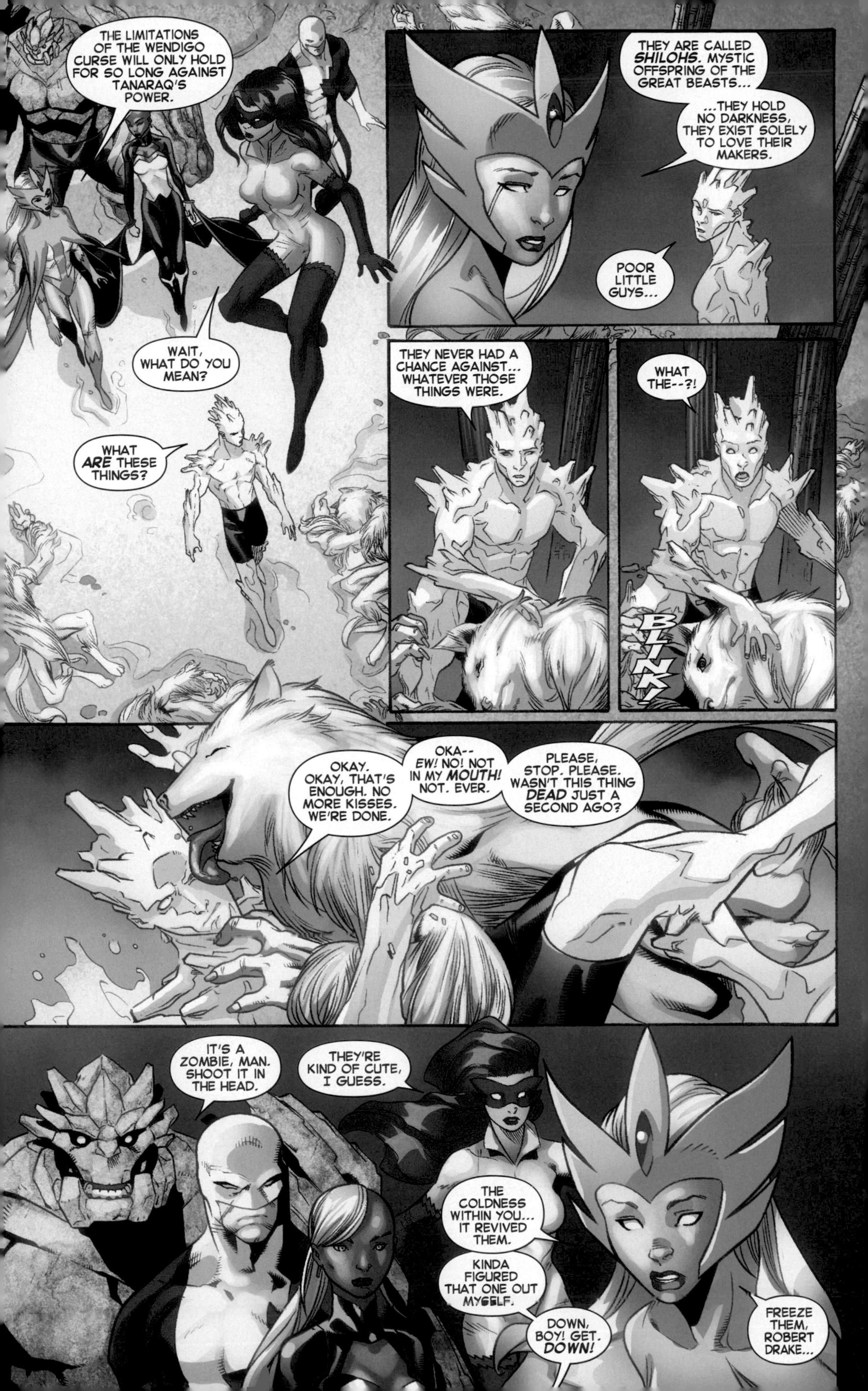
THE LIMITATIONS OF THE WENDIGO CURSE WILL ONLY HOLD FOR SO LONG AGAINST TANARAQ'S POWER.
WAIT, WHAT DO YOU MEAN?
WHAT *ARE* THESE THINGS?
THEY ARE CALLED *SHILOHS*. MYSTIC OFFSPRING OF THE GREAT BEASTS...
...THEY HOLD NO DARKNESS, THEY EXIST SOLELY TO LOVE THEIR MAKERS.
POOR LITTLE GUYS...
THEY NEVER HAD A CHANCE AGAINST... WHATEVER THOSE THINGS WERE.
WHAT THE--?!
BLINK!
OKAY. OKAY, THAT'S ENOUGH. NO MORE KISSES. WE'RE DONE.
OKA-- *EW!* NO! NOT IN MY *MOUTH!* NOT. EVER.
PLEASE, STOP. PLEASE. WASN'T THIS THING *DEAD* JUST A SECOND AGO?
IT'S A ZOMBIE, MAN. SHOOT IT IN THE HEAD.
THEY'RE KIND OF CUTE, I GUESS.
THE COLDNESS WITHIN YOU... IT REVIVED THEM.
KINDA FIGURED THAT ONE OUT MYSELF.
DOWN, BOY! GET. *DOWN!*
FREEZE THEM, ROBERT DRAKE...

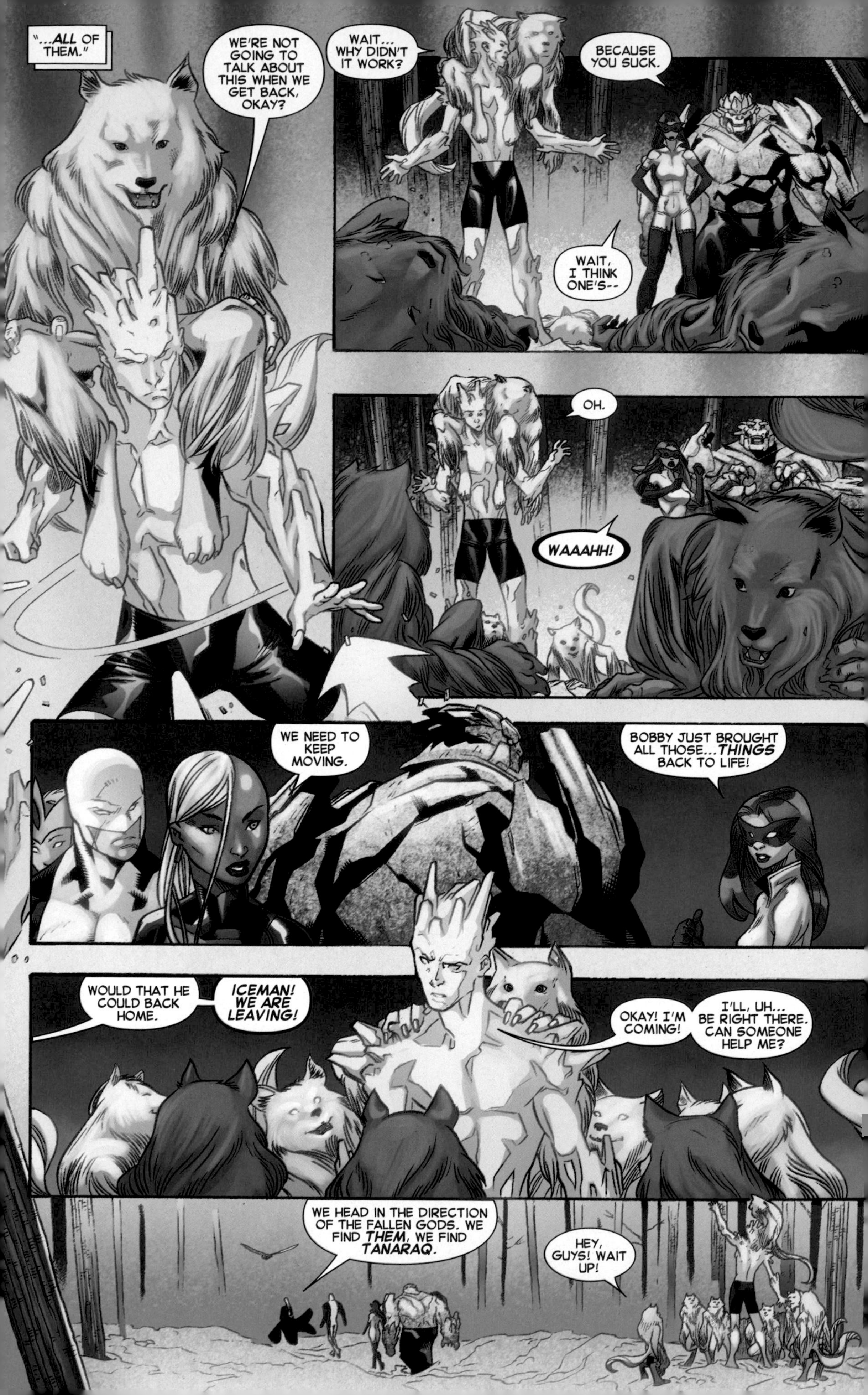
"...ALL OF THEM."
WE'RE NOT GOING TO TALK ABOUT THIS WHEN WE GET BACK, OKAY?
WAIT... WHY DIDN'T IT WORK?
BECAUSE YOU SUCK.
WAIT, I THINK ONE'S--
OH.
WAAAHH!
WE NEED TO KEEP MOVING.
BOBBY JUST BROUGHT ALL THOSE...THINGS BACK TO LIFE!
WOULD THAT HE COULD BACK HOME.
ICEMAN! WE ARE LEAVING!
OKAY! I'M COMING!
I'LL, UH... BE RIGHT THERE. CAN SOMEONE HELP ME?
WE HEAD IN THE DIRECTION OF THE FALLEN GODS. WE FIND THEM, WE FIND TANARAQ.
HEY, GUYS! WAIT UP!

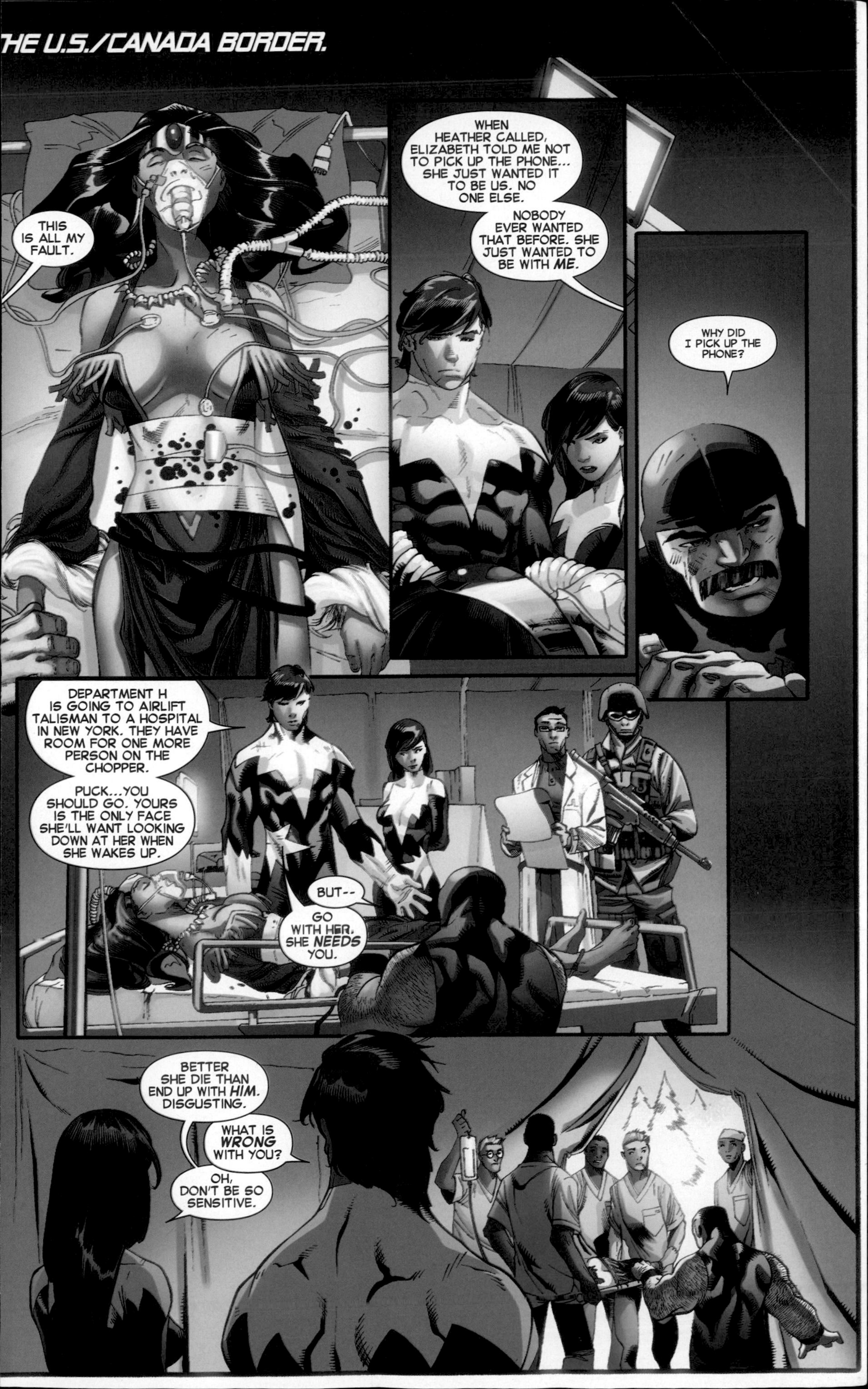
THE U.S./CANADA BORDER.
THIS IS ALL MY FAULT.
WHEN HEATHER CALLED, ELIZABETH TOLD ME NOT TO PICK UP THE PHONE... SHE JUST WANTED IT TO BE US. NO ONE ELSE.
NOBODY EVER WANTED THAT BEFORE. SHE JUST WANTED TO BE WITH ME.
WHY DID I PICK UP THE PHONE?
DEPARTMENT H IS GOING TO AIRLIFT TALISMAN TO A HOSPITAL IN NEW YORK. THEY HAVE ROOM FOR ONE MORE PERSON ON THE CHOPPER.
PUCK...YOU SHOULD GO. YOURS IS THE ONLY FACE SHE'LL WANT LOOKING DOWN AT HER WHEN SHE WAKES UP.
BUT--
GO WITH HER. SHE NEEDS YOU.
BETTER SHE DIE THAN END UP WITH HIM. DISGUSTING.
WHAT IS WRONG WITH YOU?
OH, DON'T BE SO SENSITIVE.

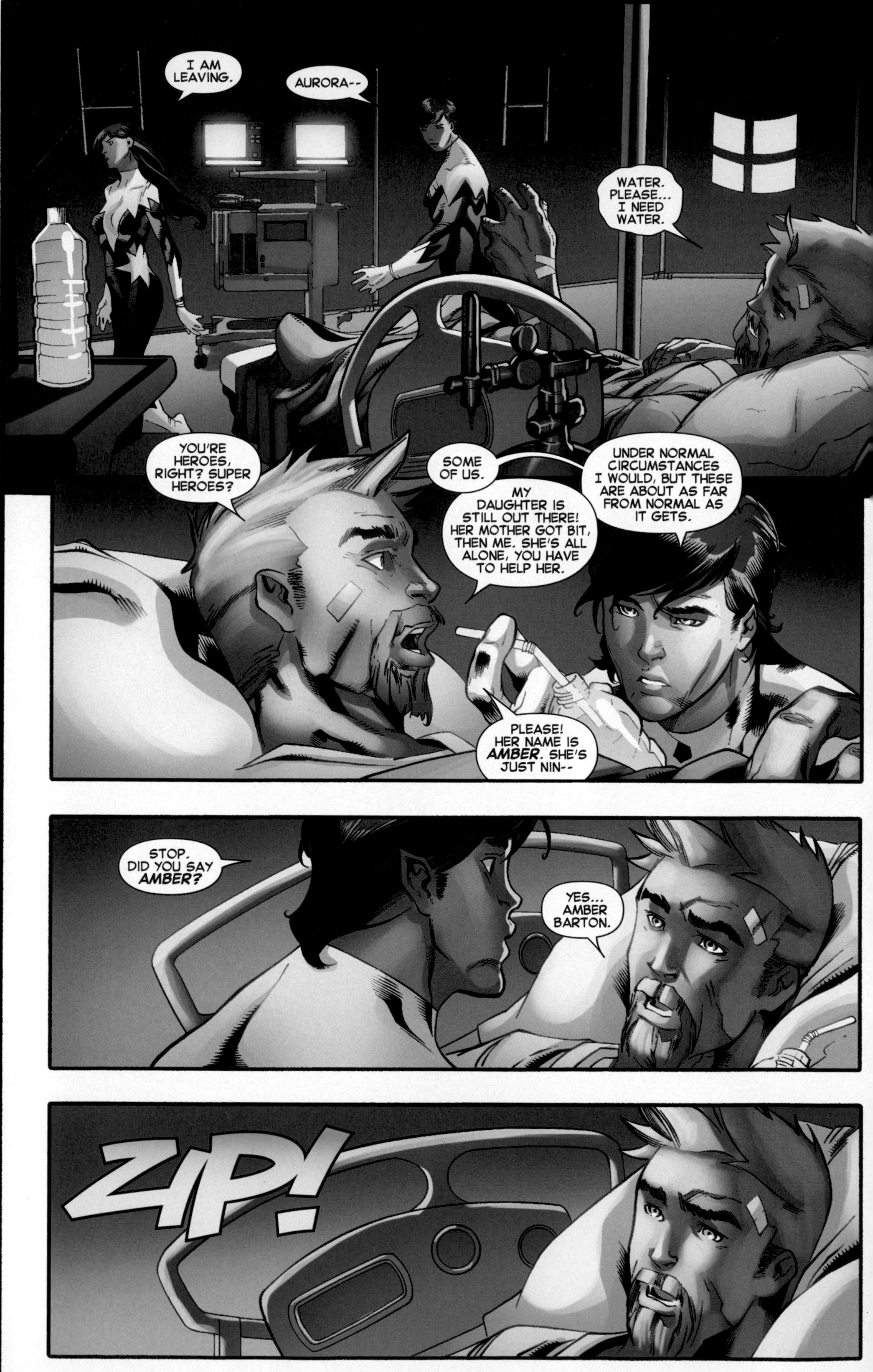
I AM LEAVING.
AURORA--
WATER. PLEASE... I NEED WATER.
YOU'RE HEROES, RIGHT? SUPER HEROES?
SOME OF US.
UNDER NORMAL CIRCUMSTANCES I WOULD, BUT THESE ARE ABOUT AS FAR FROM NORMAL AS IT GETS.
MY DAUGHTER IS STILL OUT THERE! HER MOTHER GOT BIT, THEN ME. SHE'S ALL ALONE, YOU HAVE TO HELP HER.
PLEASE! HER NAME IS *AMBER*. SHE'S JUST NIN--
STOP. DID YOU SAY *AMBER?*
YES... AMBER BARTON.
ZIP!

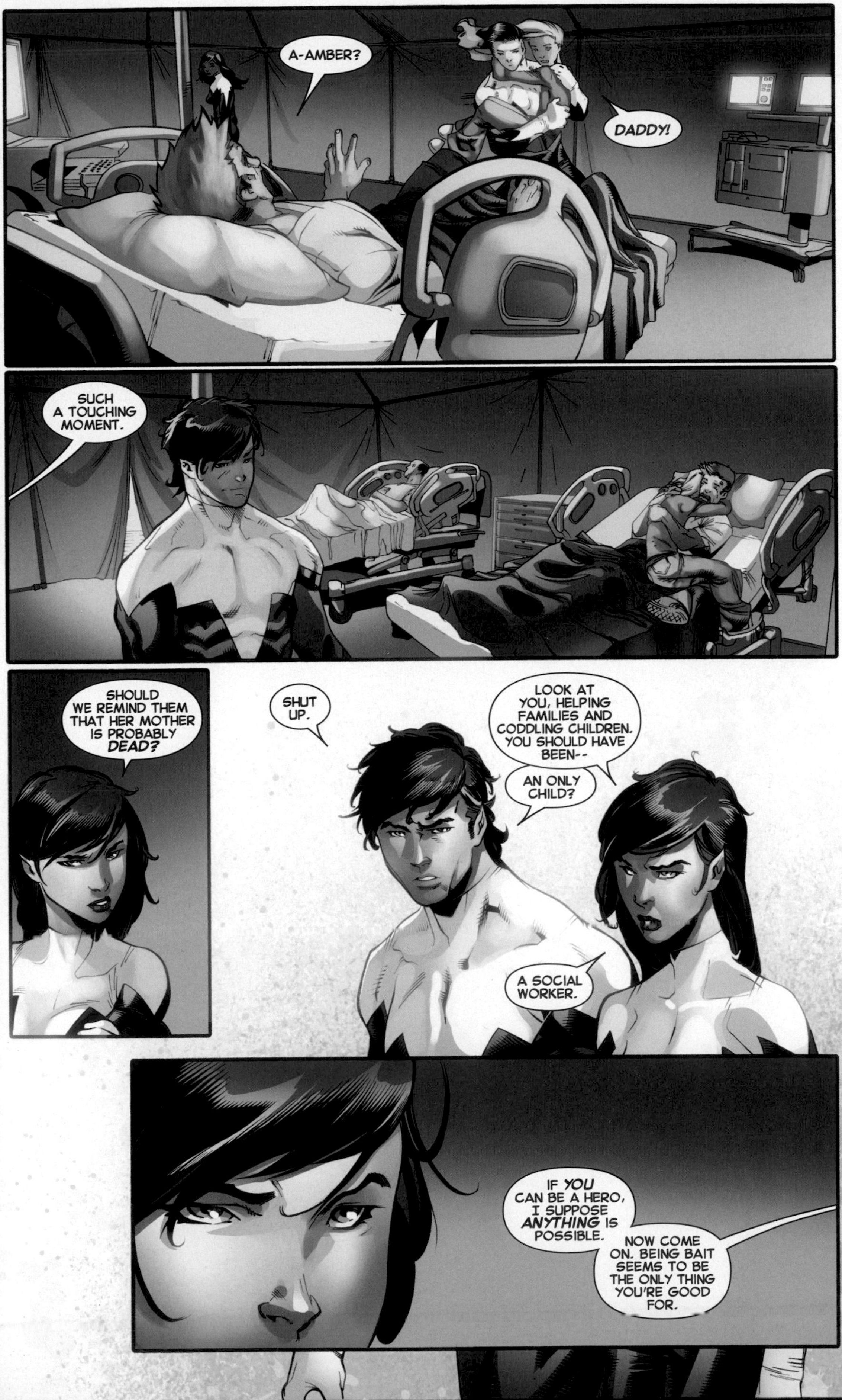

A-AMBER?
DADDY!
SUCH A TOUCHING MOMENT.
SHOULD WE REMIND THEM THAT HER MOTHER IS PROBABLY *DEAD?*
SHUT UP.
LOOK AT YOU, HELPING FAMILIES AND CODDLING CHILDREN. YOU SHOULD HAVE BEEN--
AN ONLY CHILD?
A SOCIAL WORKER.
IF *YOU* CAN BE A HERO, I SUPPOSE *ANYTHING* IS POSSIBLE.
NOW COME ON. BEING BAIT SEEMS TO BE THE ONLY THING YOU'RE GOOD FOR.

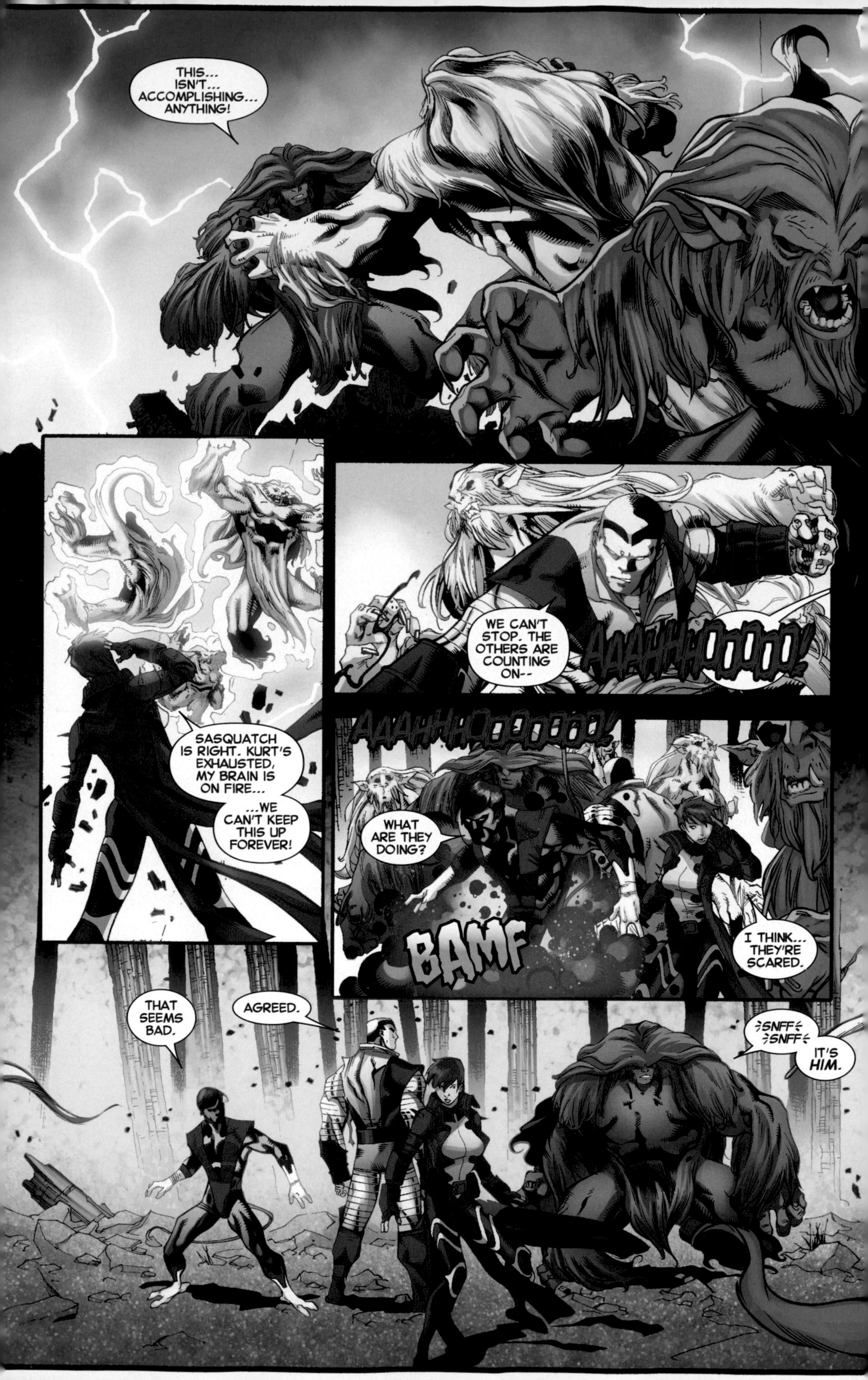

THIS... ISN'T... ACCOMPLISHING... ANYTHING!
SASQUATCH IS RIGHT. KURT'S EXHAUSTED, MY BRAIN IS ON FIRE...
...WE CAN'T KEEP THIS UP FOREVER!
WE CAN'T STOP. THE OTHERS ARE COUNTING ON--
AAAHHOOOOO!
AAAHHOOOOOOO!
WHAT ARE THEY DOING?
BAMF
I THINK... THEY'RE SCARED.
THAT SEEMS BAD.
AGREED.
SNFF SNFF
IT'S HIM.

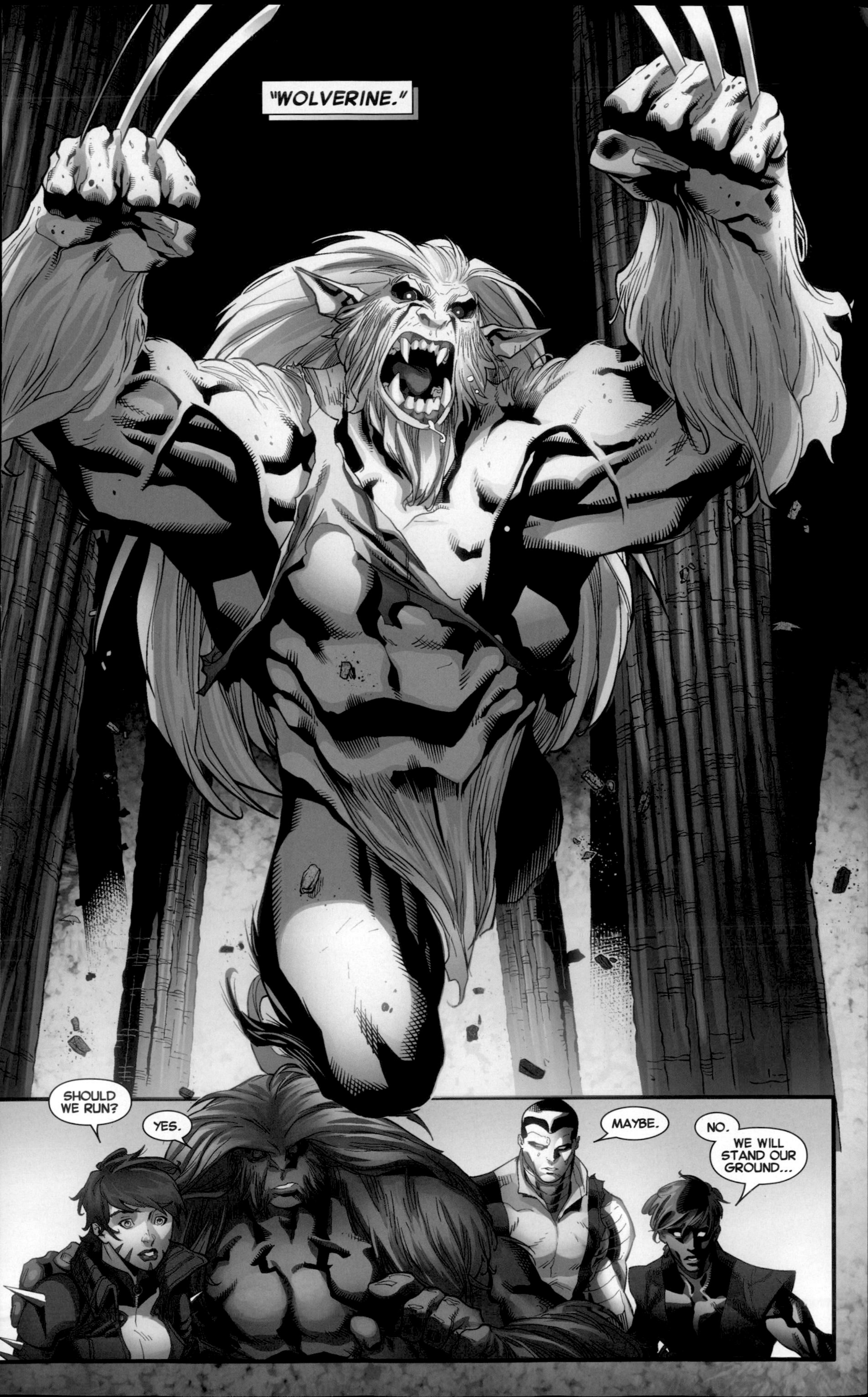
"WOLVERINE."
SHOULD WE RUN?
YES.
MAYBE.
NO. WE WILL STAND OUR GROUND...

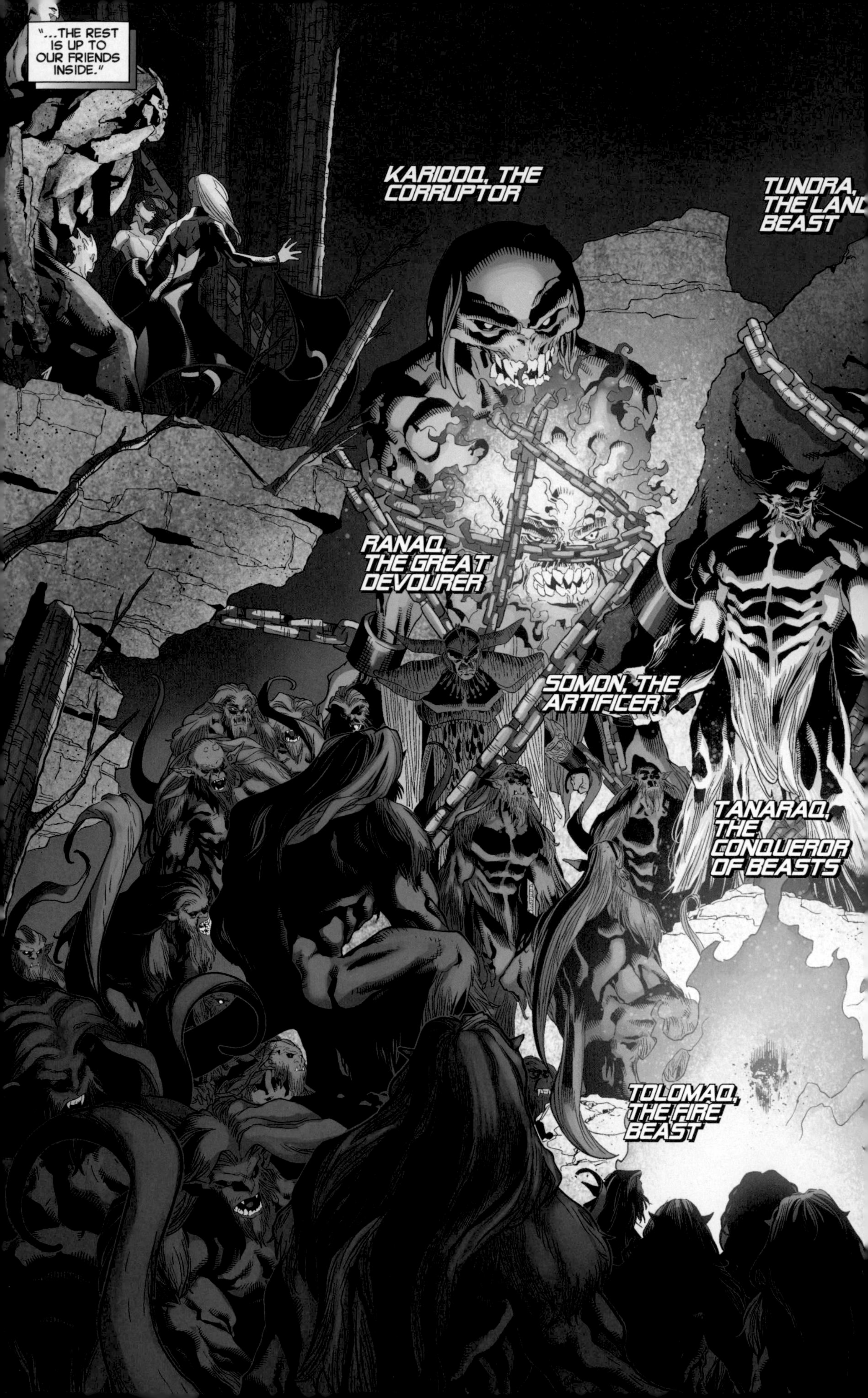
"...THE REST IS UP TO OUR FRIENDS INSIDE."
KARIOOQ, THE CORRUPTOR
TUNDRA, THE LAND BEAST
RANAQ, THE GREAT DEVOURER
SOMON, THE ARTIFICER
TANARAQ, THE CONQUEROR OF BEASTS
TOLOMAQ, THE FIRE BEAST

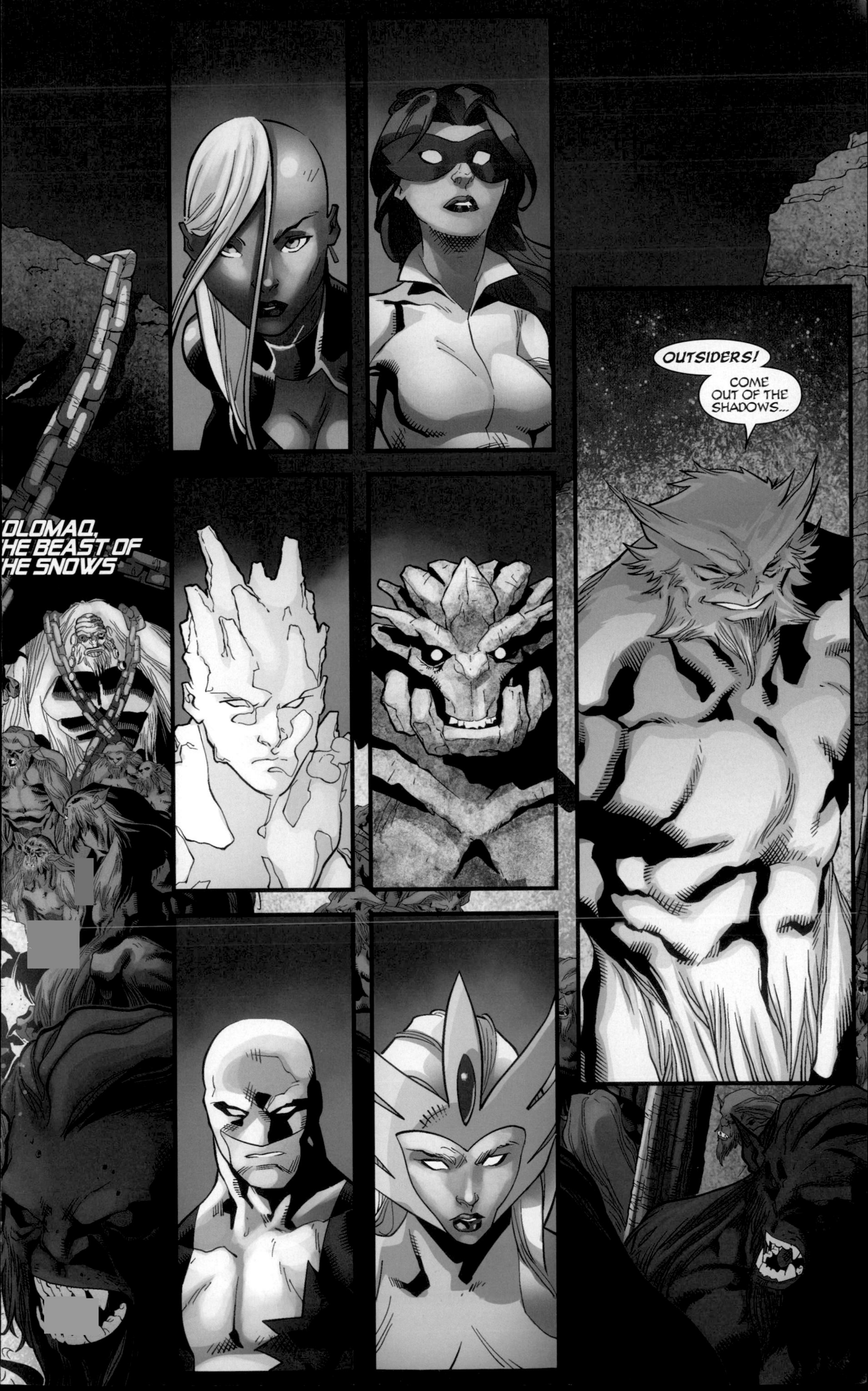
OLOMAQ,
HE BEAST OF
HE SNOWS
OUTSIDERS!
COME OUT OF THE SHADOWS...

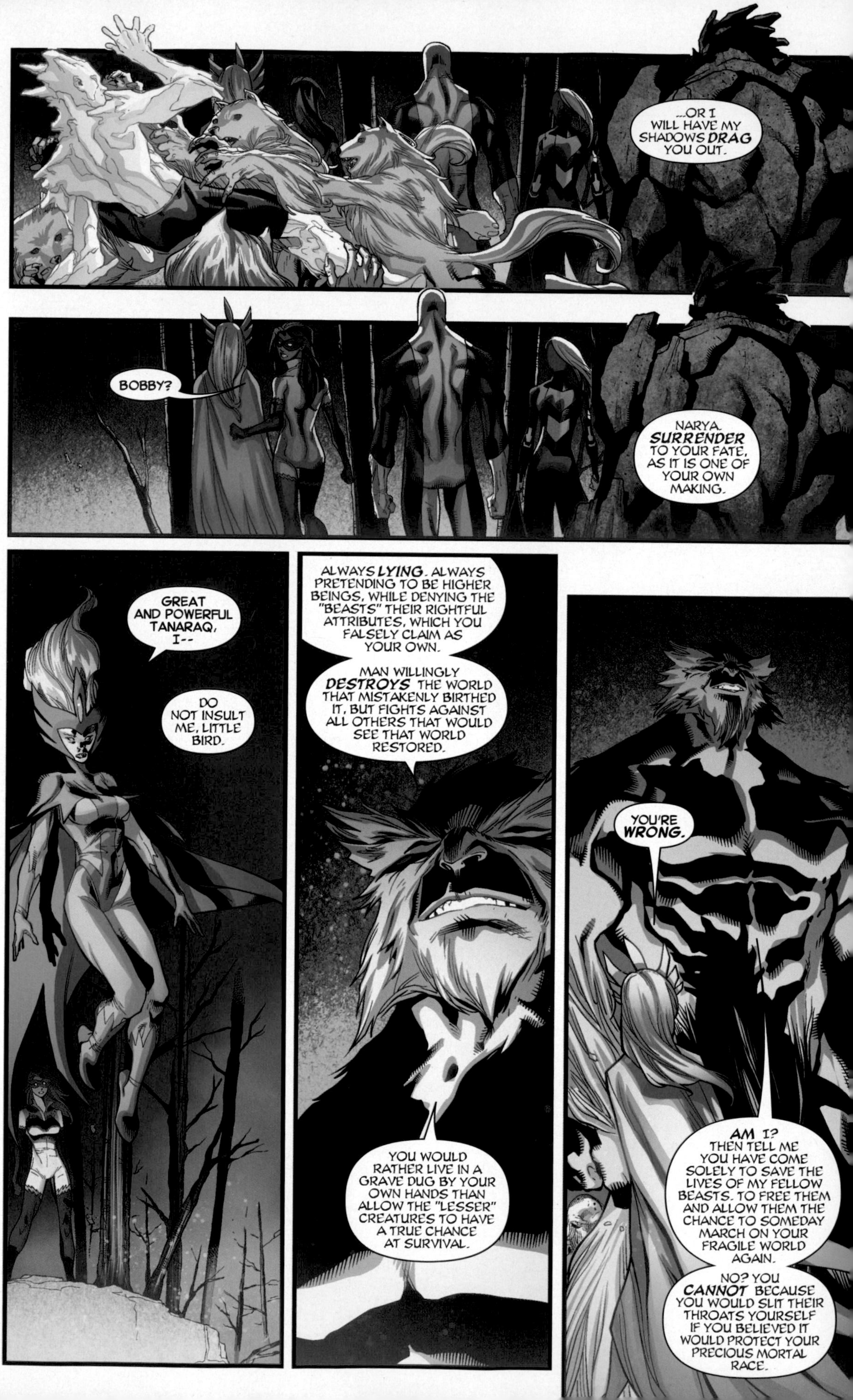
...OR I WILL HAVE MY SHADOWS DRAG YOU OUT.
BOBBY?
NARYA. SURRENDER TO YOUR FATE, AS IT IS ONE OF YOUR OWN MAKING.
GREAT AND POWERFUL TANARAQ, I--
DO NOT INSULT ME, LITTLE BIRD.
ALWAYS LYING. ALWAYS PRETENDING TO BE HIGHER BEINGS, WHILE DENYING THE "BEASTS" THEIR RIGHTFUL ATTRIBUTES, WHICH YOU FALSELY CLAIM AS YOUR OWN.
MAN WILLINGLY DESTROYS THE WORLD THAT MISTAKENLY BIRTHED IT, BUT FIGHTS AGAINST ALL OTHERS THAT WOULD SEE THAT WORLD RESTORED.
YOU WOULD RATHER LIVE IN A GRAVE DUG BY YOUR OWN HANDS THAN ALLOW THE "LESSER" CREATURES TO HAVE A TRUE CHANCE AT SURVIVAL.
YOU'RE WRONG.
AM I? THEN TELL ME YOU HAVE COME SOLELY TO SAVE THE LIVES OF MY FELLOW BEASTS. TO FREE THEM AND ALLOW THEM THE CHANCE TO SOMEDAY MARCH ON YOUR FRAGILE WORLD AGAIN.
NO? YOU CANNOT BECAUSE YOU WOULD SLIT THEIR THROATS YOURSELF IF YOU BELIEVED IT WOULD PROTECT YOUR PRECIOUS MORTAL RACE.

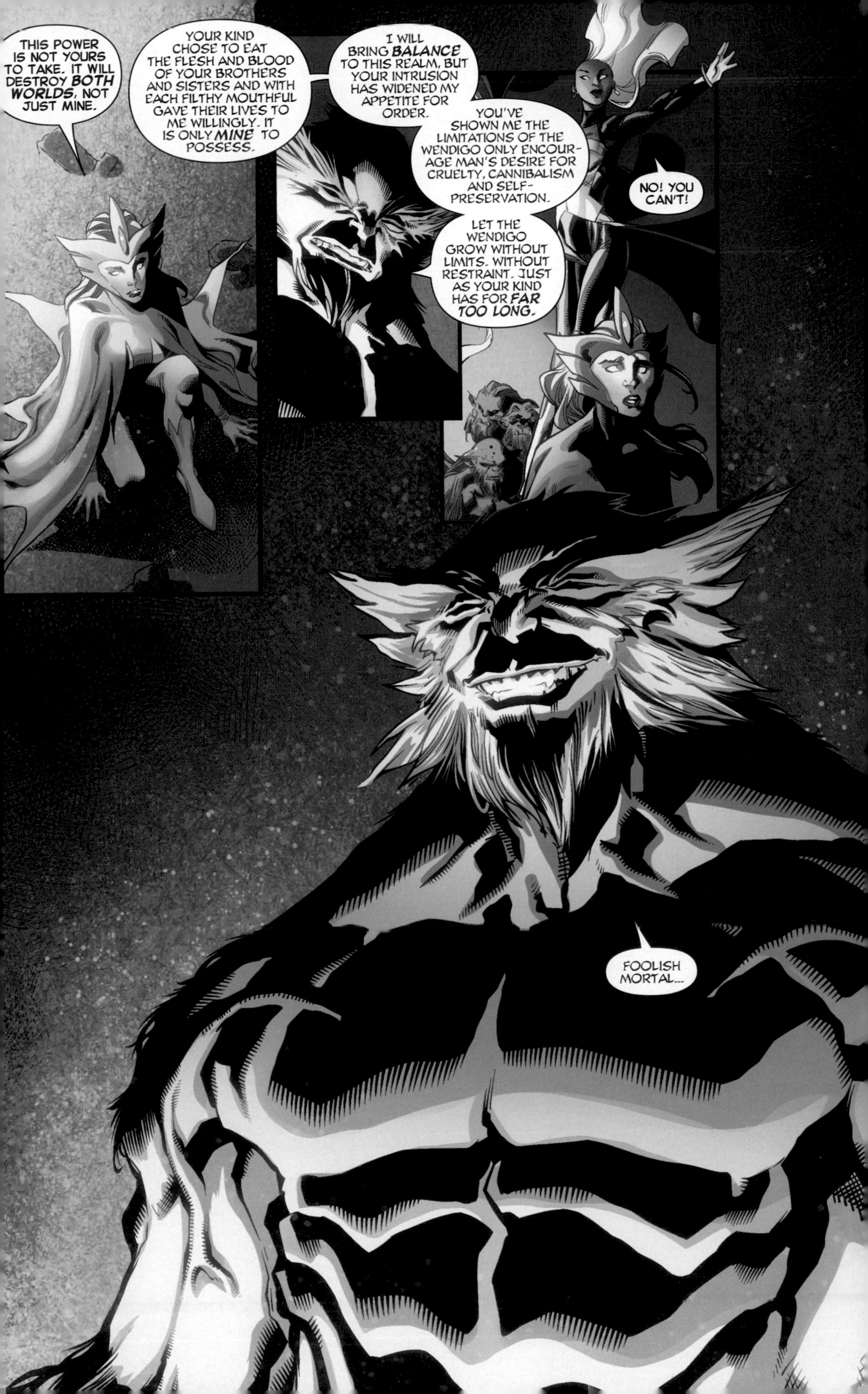
THIS POWER IS NOT YOURS TO TAKE. IT WILL DESTROY BOTH WORLDS, NOT JUST MINE.
YOUR KIND CHOSE TO EAT THE FLESH AND BLOOD OF YOUR BROTHERS AND SISTERS AND WITH EACH FILTHY MOUTHFUL GAVE THEIR LIVES TO ME WILLINGLY. IT IS ONLY MINE TO POSSESS.
I WILL BRING BALANCE TO THIS REALM, BUT YOUR INTRUSION HAS WIDENED MY APPETITE FOR ORDER.
YOU'VE SHOWN ME THE LIMITATIONS OF THE WENDIGO ONLY ENCOURAGE MAN'S DESIRE FOR CRUELTY, CANNIBALISM AND SELF-PRESERVATION.
LET THE WENDIGO GROW WITHOUT LIMITS. WITHOUT RESTRAINT. JUST AS YOUR KIND HAS FOR FAR TOO LONG.
NO! YOU CAN'T!
FOOLISH MORTAL...

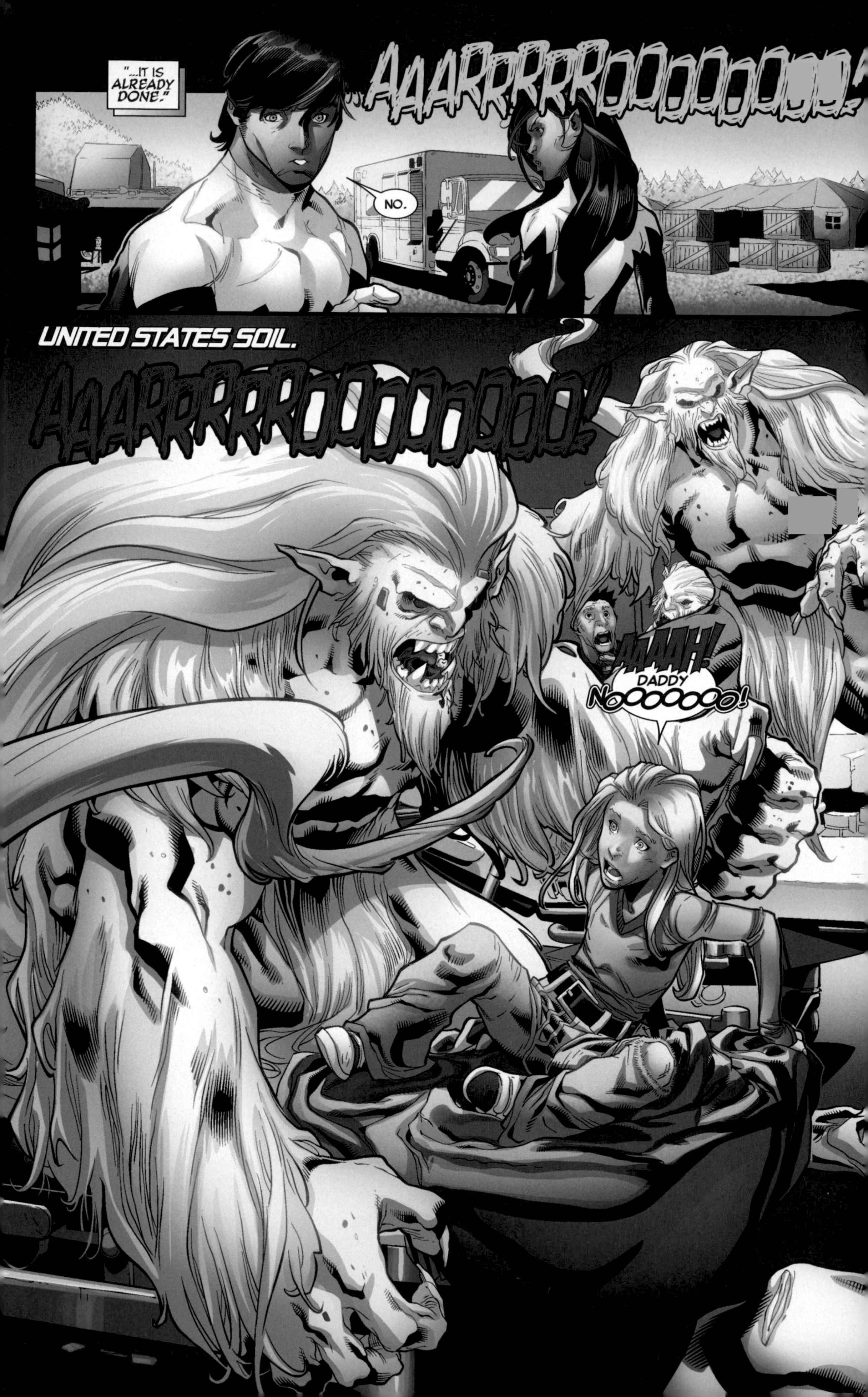

"...IT IS ALREADY DONE."
AAARRRRROOOOOOOOO!
NO.
UNITED STATES SOIL.
AAARRRRROOOOOOOOO!
AAAAH!
DADDY NOOOOOOOO!

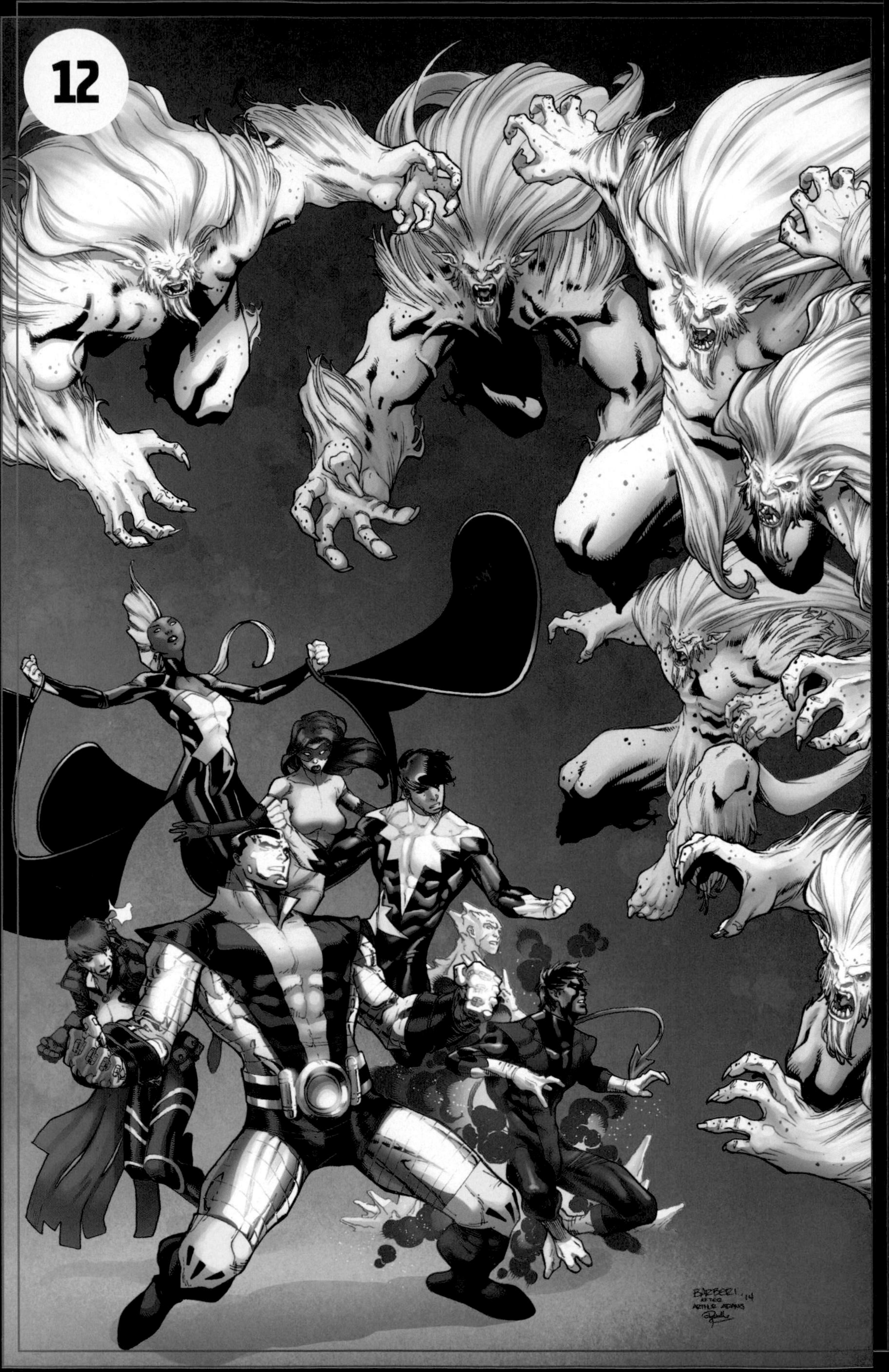
12

WORLD WAR WENDIGO! PART 5

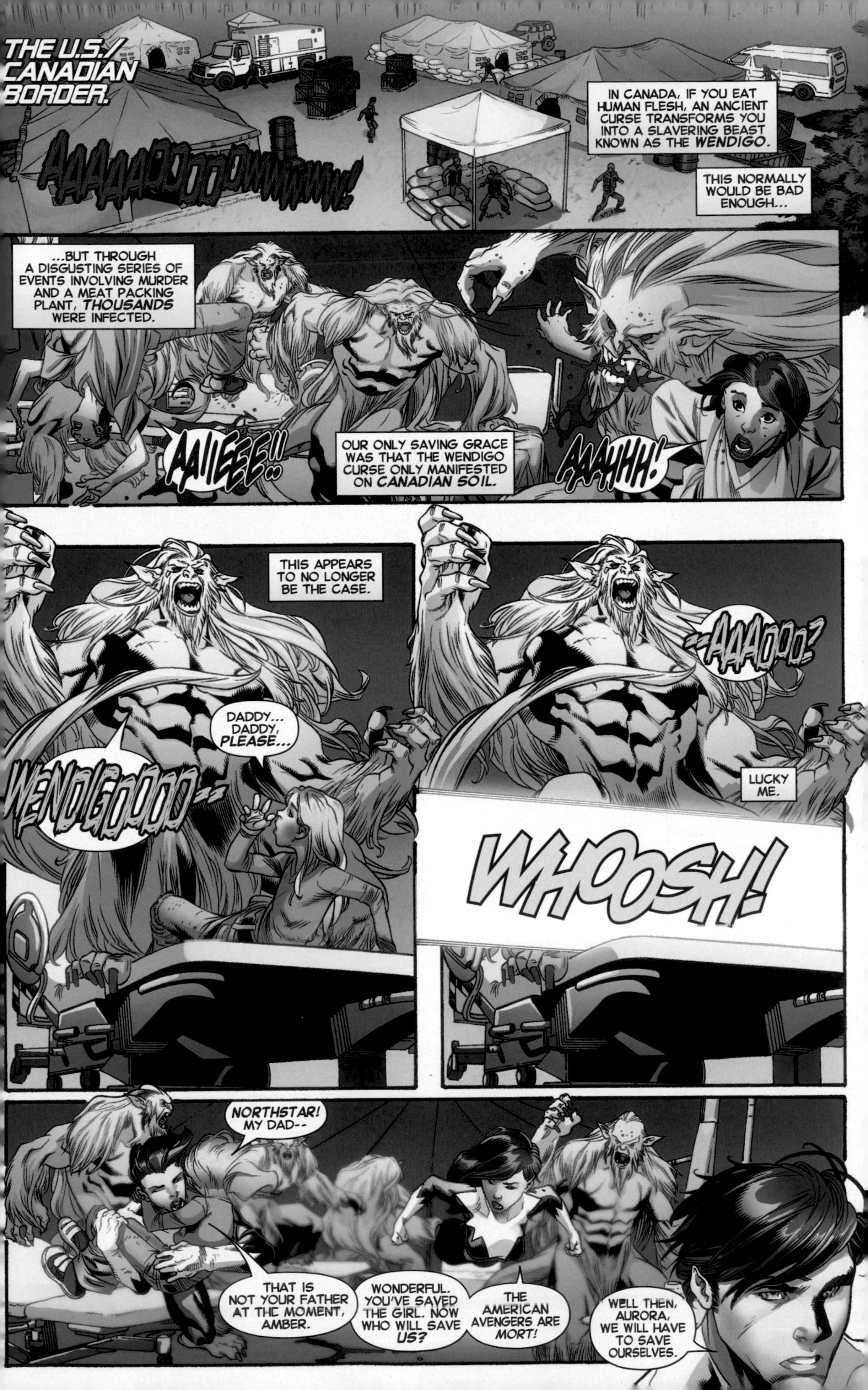
THE U.S./ CANADIAN BORDER.
AAAAAOOOOOWWWWW!
IN CANADA, IF YOU EAT HUMAN FLESH, AN ANCIENT CURSE TRANSFORMS YOU INTO A SLAVERING BEAST KNOWN AS THE WENDIGO.
THIS NORMALLY WOULD BE BAD ENOUGH...
...BUT THROUGH A DISGUSTING SERIES OF EVENTS INVOLVING MURDER AND A MEAT PACKING PLANT, THOUSANDS WERE INFECTED.
AAIIEEE!!
OUR ONLY SAVING GRACE WAS THAT THE WENDIGO CURSE ONLY MANIFESTED ON CANADIAN SOIL.
AAAHHH!
THIS APPEARS TO NO LONGER BE THE CASE.
DADDY... DADDY, PLEASE...
WENDIGOOOO--
--AAAOOO?
LUCKY ME.
WHOOSH!
NORTHSTAR! MY DAD--
THAT IS NOT YOUR FATHER AT THE MOMENT, AMBER.
WONDERFUL. YOU'VE SAVED THE GIRL. NOW WHO WILL SAVE US?
THE AMERICAN AVENGERS ARE MORT!
WELL THEN, AURORA, WE WILL HAVE TO SAVE OURSELVES.

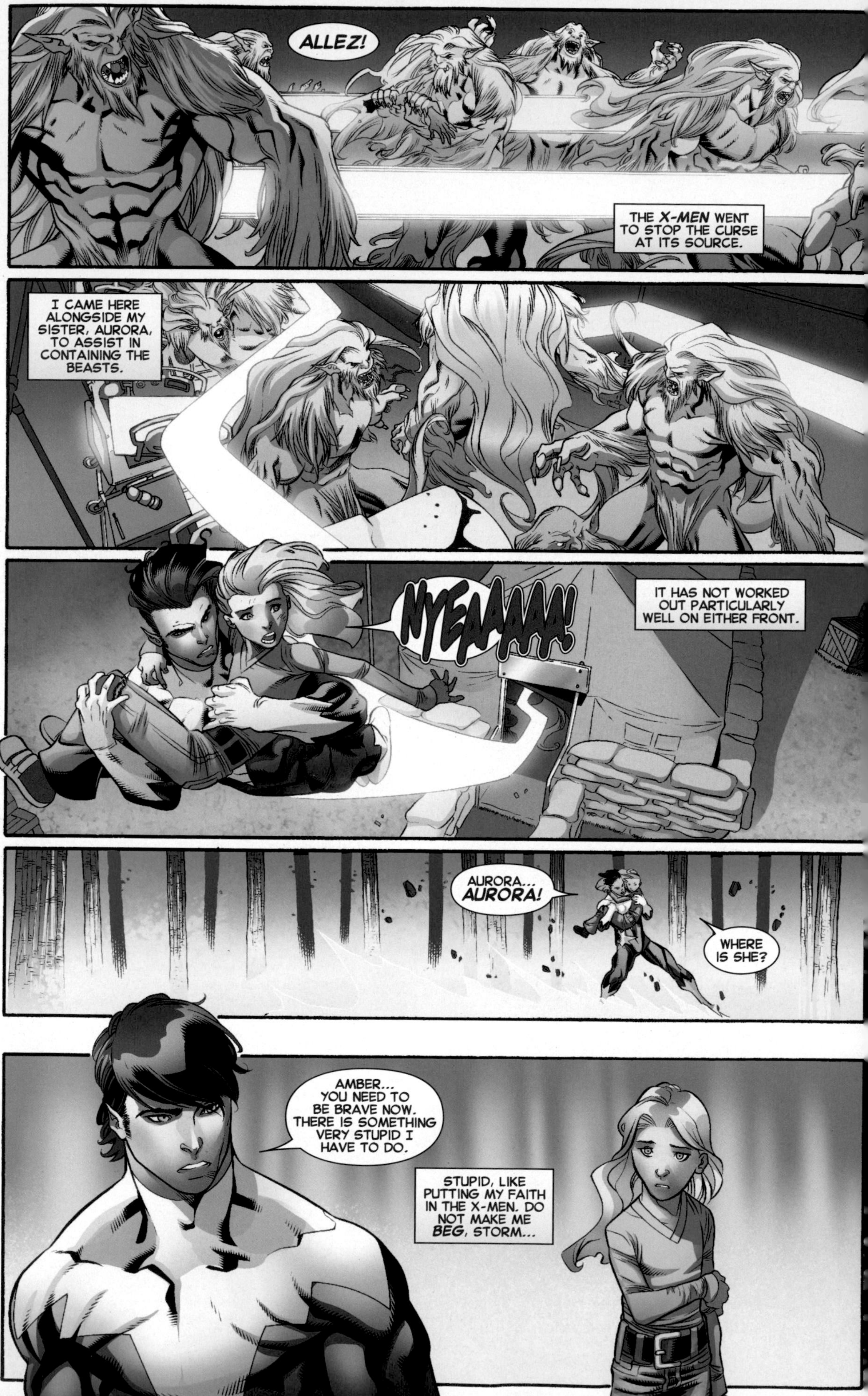
ALLEZ!
THE X-MEN WENT TO STOP THE CURSE AT ITS SOURCE.
I CAME HERE ALONGSIDE MY SISTER, AURORA, TO ASSIST IN CONTAINING THE BEASTS.
NYEAAAAA!
IT HAS NOT WORKED OUT PARTICULARLY WELL ON EITHER FRONT.
AURORA... AURORA!
WHERE IS SHE?
AMBER... YOU NEED TO BE BRAVE NOW. THERE IS SOMETHING VERY STUPID I HAVE TO DO.
STUPID, LIKE PUTTING MY FAITH IN THE X-MEN. DO NOT MAKE ME BEG, STORM...

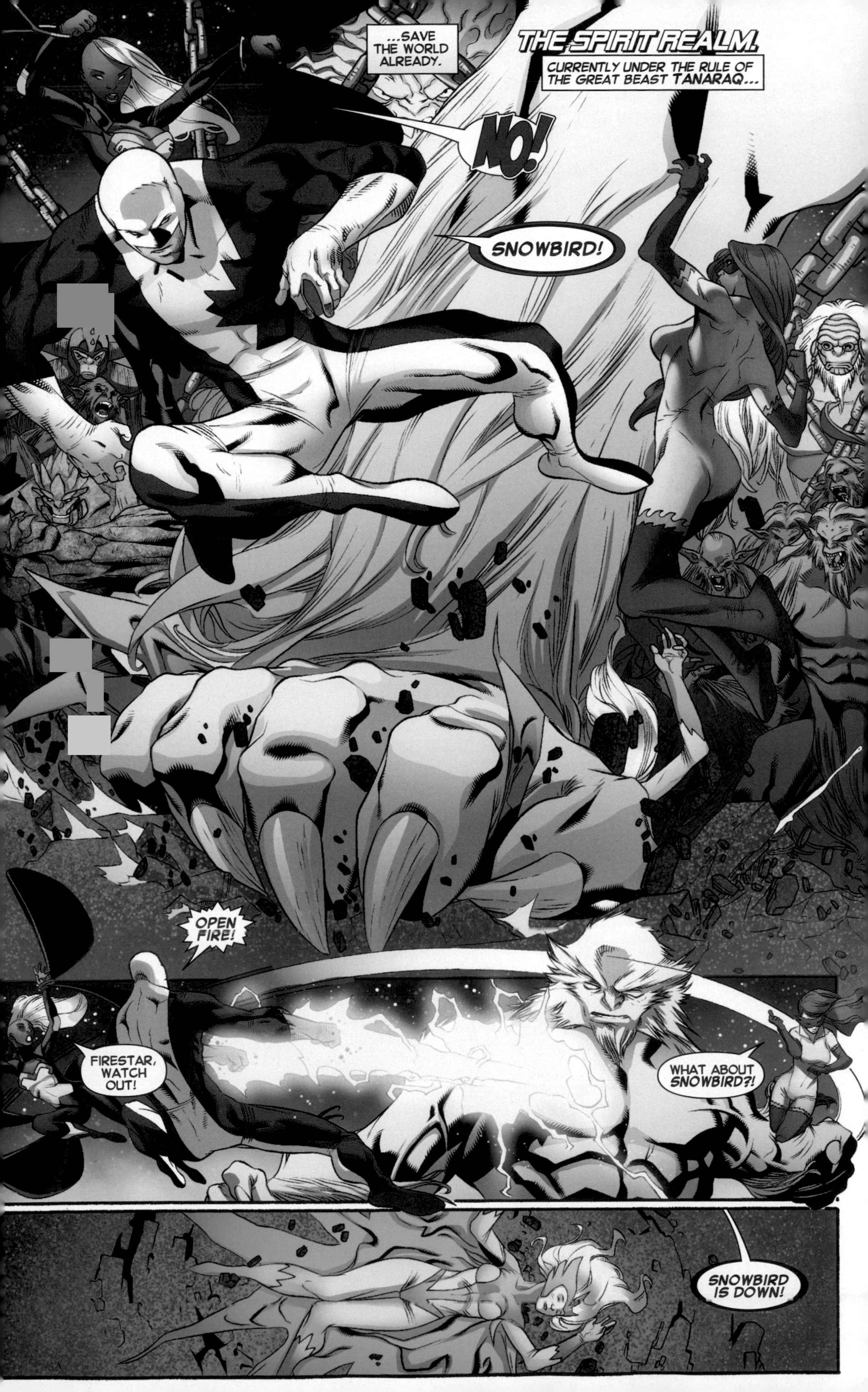
...SAVE THE WORLD ALREADY.
THE SPIRIT REALM.
CURRENTLY UNDER THE RULE OF THE GREAT BEAST TANARAQ...
NO!
SNOWBIRD!
OPEN FIRE!
FIRESTAR, WATCH OUT!
WHAT ABOUT SNOWBIRD?!
SNOWBIRD IS DOWN!

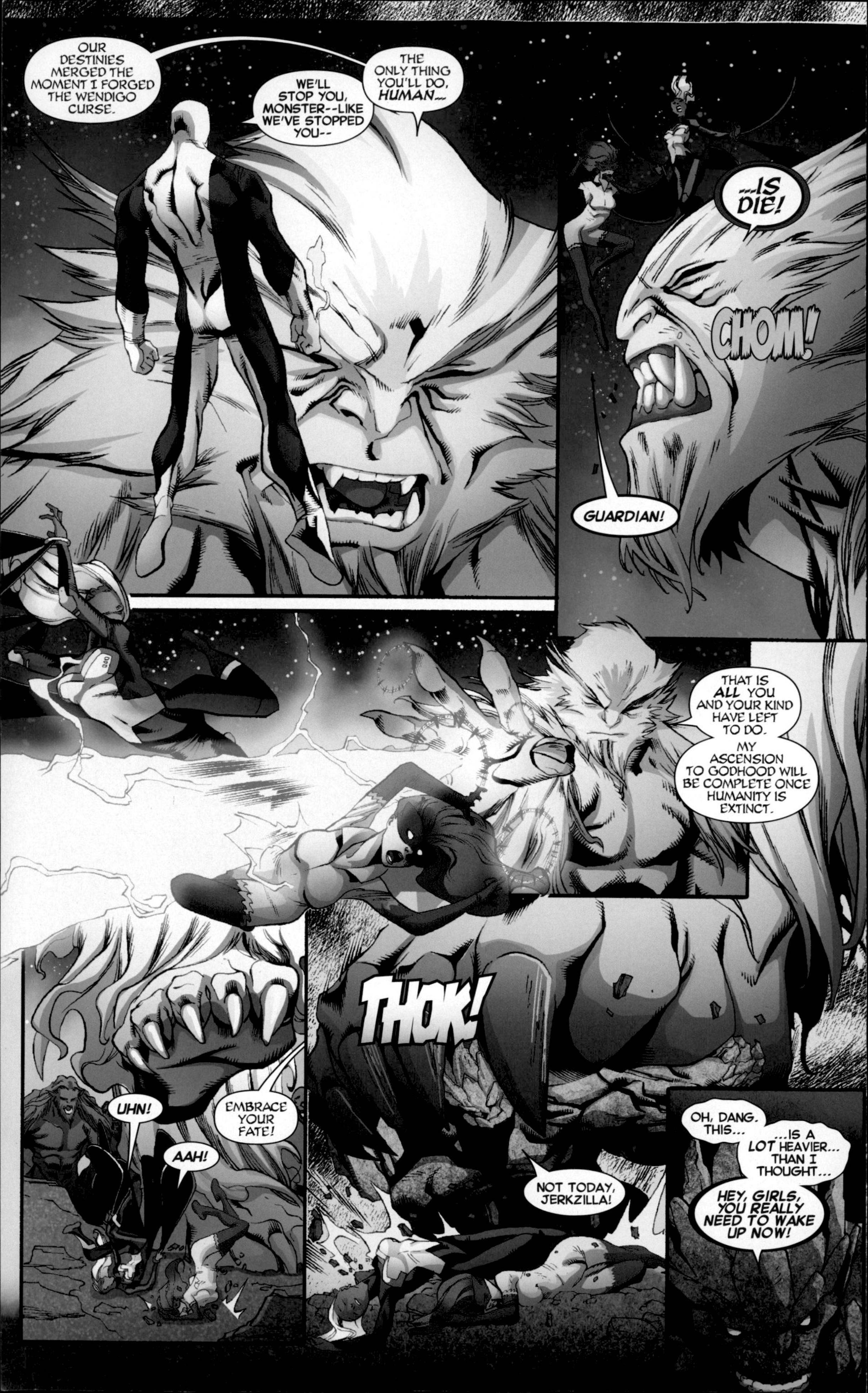

OUR DESTINIES MERGED THE MOMENT I FORGED THE WENDIGO CURSE.
WE'LL STOP YOU, MONSTER--LIKE WE'VE STOPPED YOU--
THE ONLY THING YOU'LL DO, HUMAN...
...IS DIE!
CHOM!
GUARDIAN!
THAT IS ALL YOU AND YOUR KIND HAVE LEFT TO DO.
MY ASCENSION TO GODHOOD WILL BE COMPLETE ONCE HUMANITY IS EXTINCT.
UHN!
EMBRACE YOUR FATE!
AAH!
THOK!
NOT TODAY, JERKZILLA!
OH, DANG. THIS...
...IS A LOT HEAVIER... THAN I THOUGHT...
HEY, GIRLS, YOU REALLY NEED TO WAKE UP NOW!

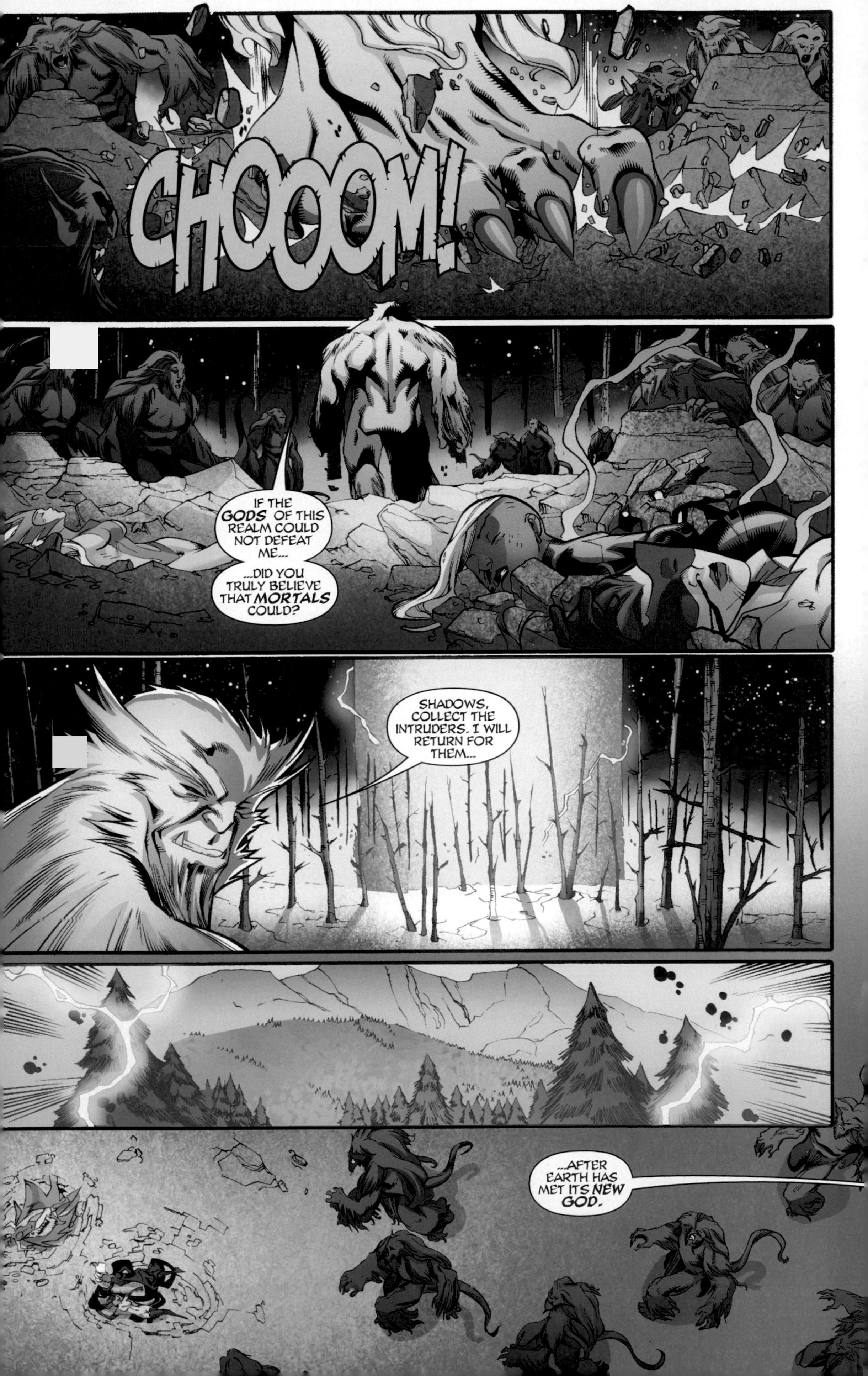
CHOOOM!
IF THE GODS OF THIS REALM COULD NOT DEFEAT ME...
...DID YOU TRULY BELIEVE THAT MORTALS COULD?
SHADOWS, COLLECT THE INTRUDERS. I WILL RETURN FOR THEM...
...AFTER EARTH HAS MET ITS NEW GOD.

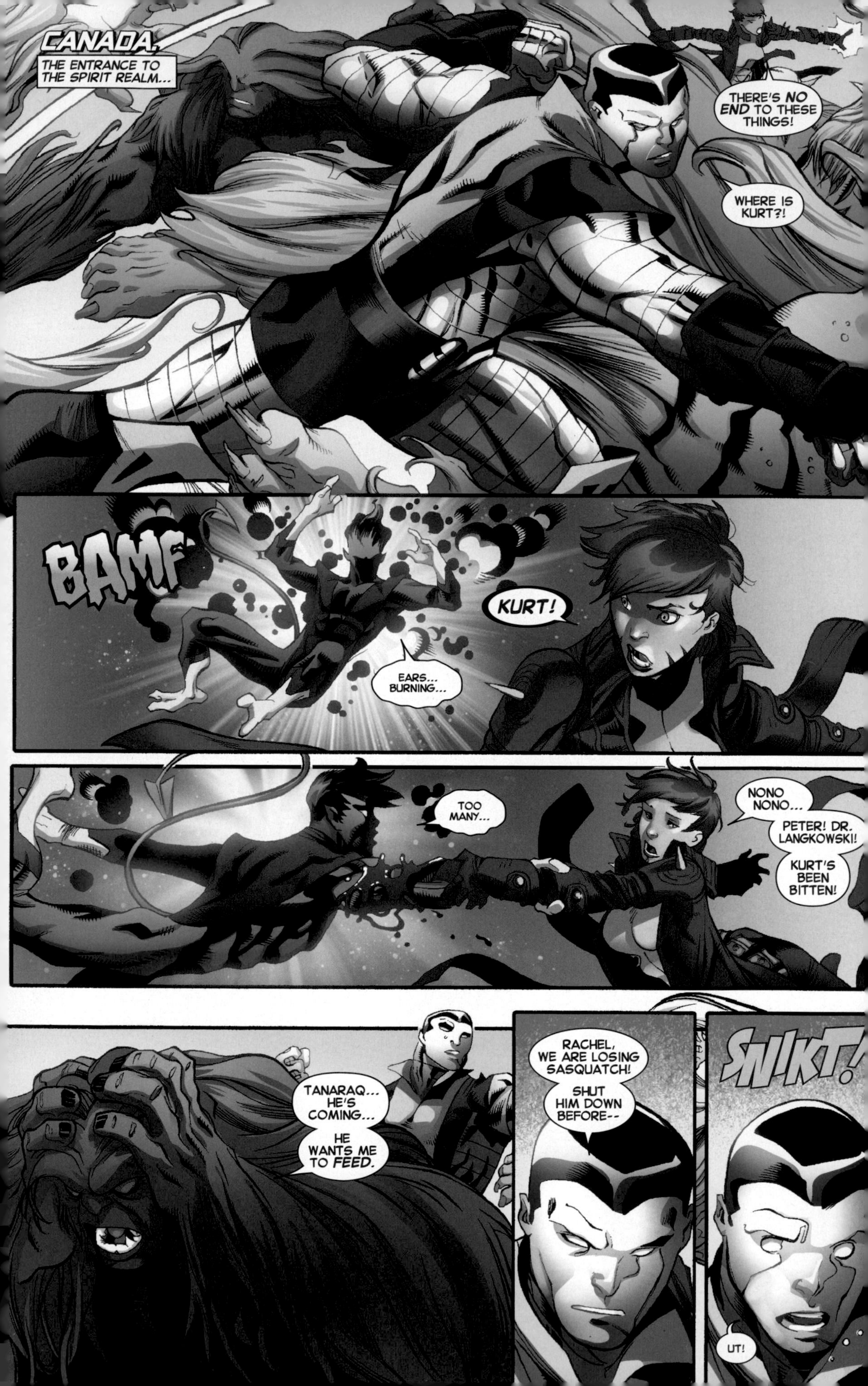
CANADA.
THE ENTRANCE TO THE SPIRIT REALM...
THERE'S NO END TO THESE THINGS!
WHERE IS KURT?!
BAMF
KURT!
EARS... BURNING...
TOO MANY...
NONO NONO...
PETER! DR. LANGKOWSKI!
KURT'S BEEN BITTEN!
TANARAQ... HE'S COMING...
HE WANTS ME TO FEED.
RACHEL, WE ARE LOSING SASQUATCH!
SHUT HIM DOWN BEFORE--
SNIKT!
UT!

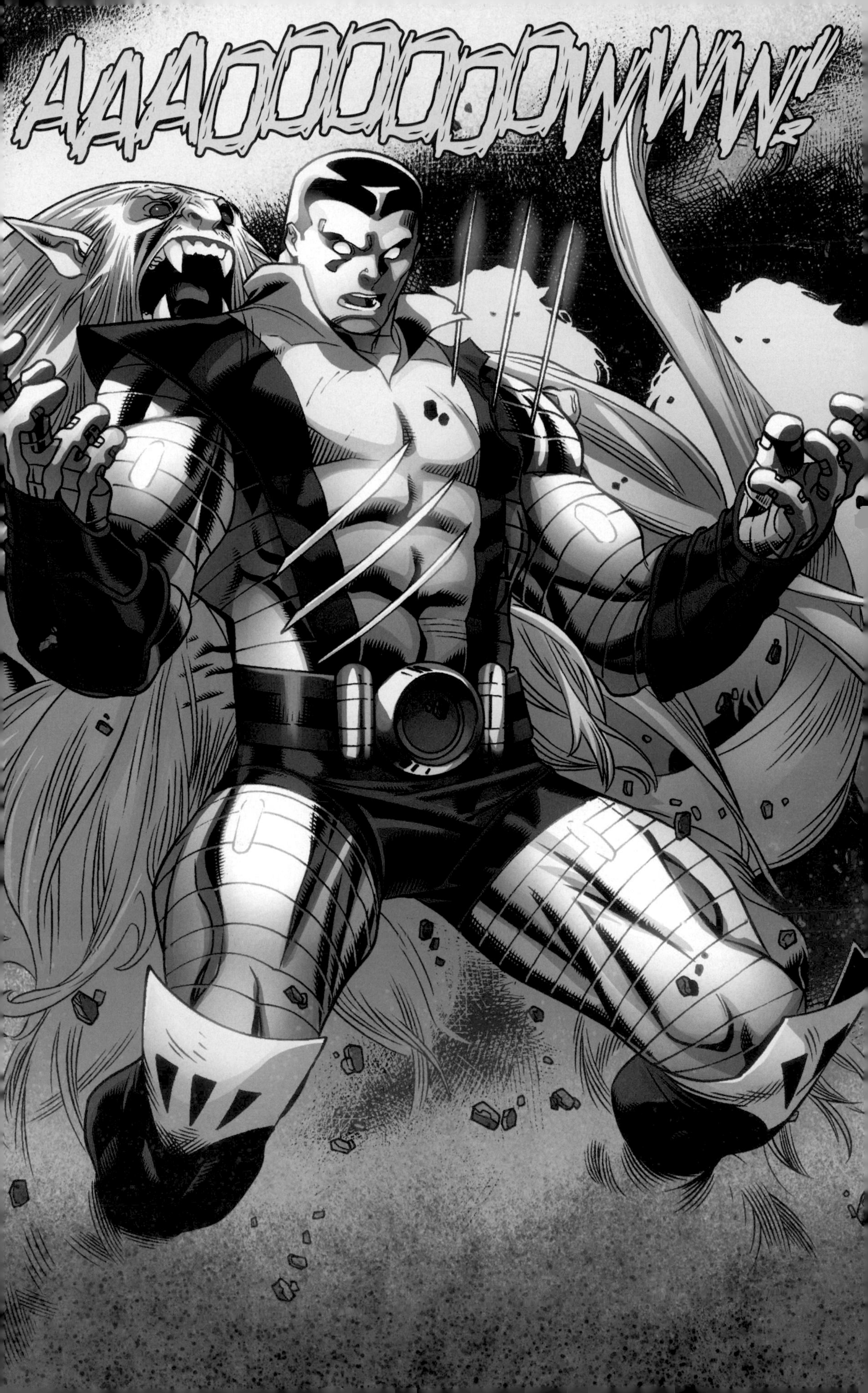
AAAOOOOOOOWWW!

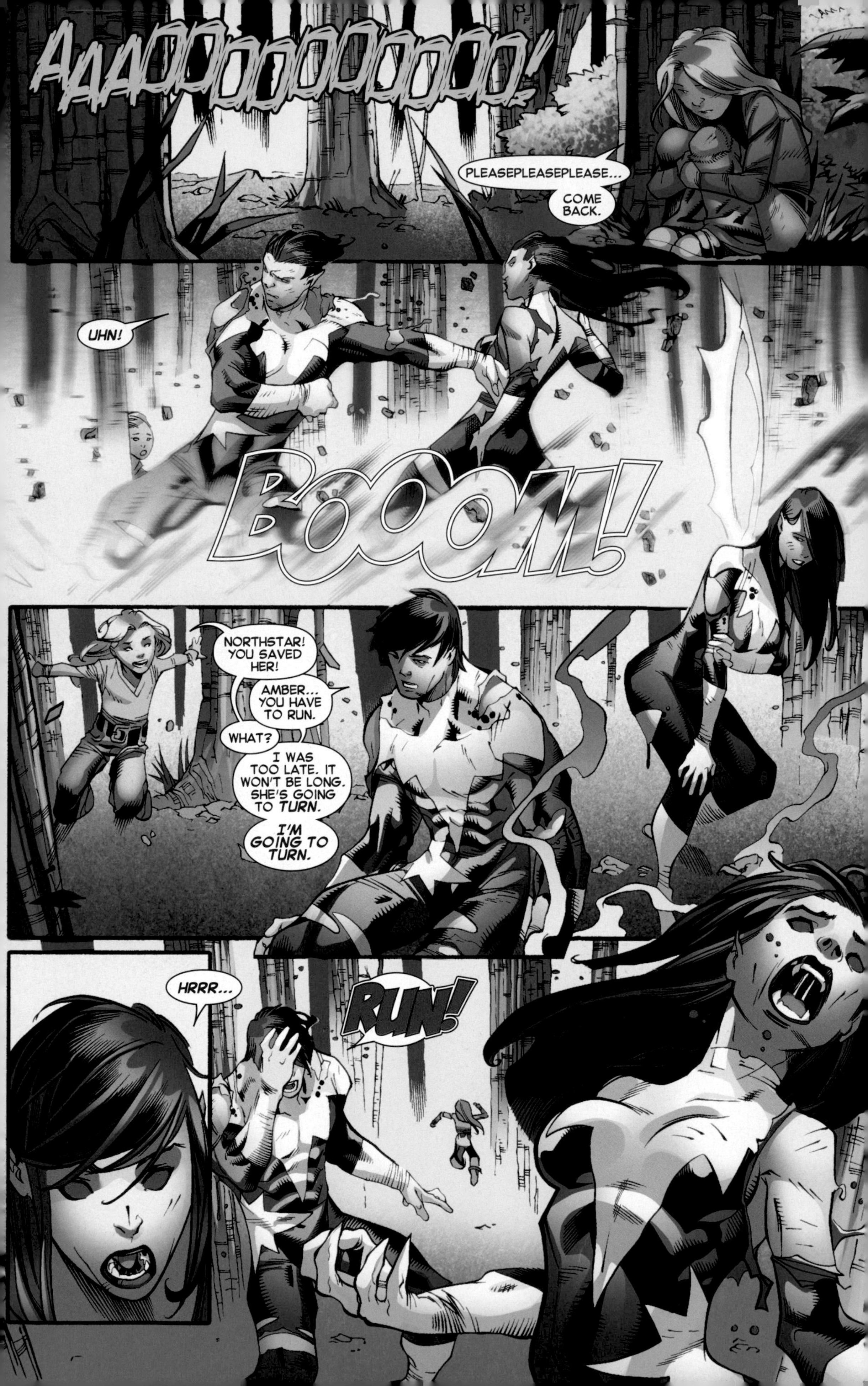
AAAOOOOOOOOOOO!
PLEASEPLEASEPLEASE...
COME BACK.
UHN!
BOOOM!
NORTHSTAR! YOU SAVED HER!
AMBER... YOU HAVE TO RUN.
WHAT?
I WAS TOO LATE. IT WON'T BE LONG. SHE'S GOING TO *TURN*.
I'M GOING TO TURN.
HRRR...
RUN!

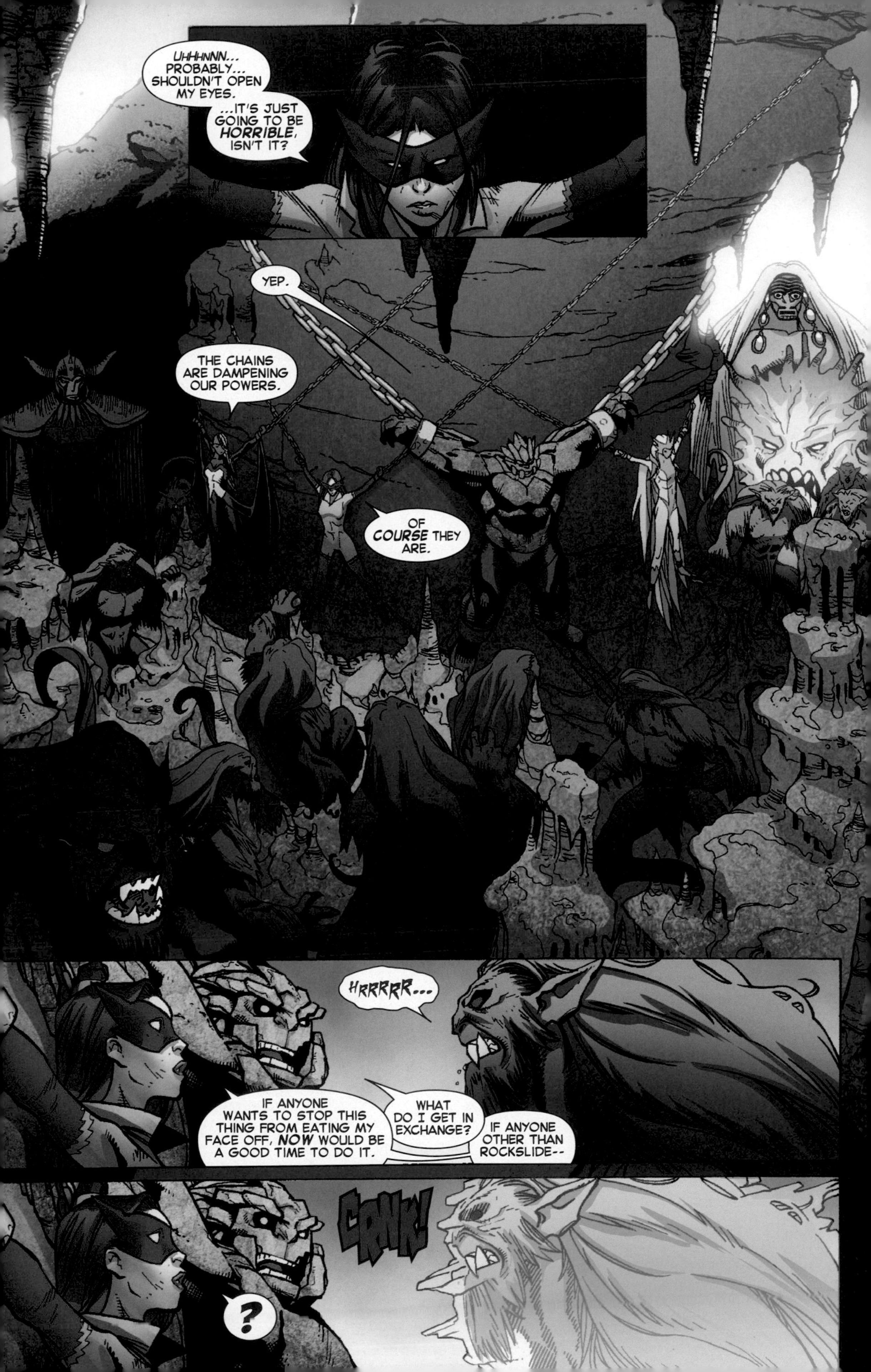
UHHHNNN... PROBABLY... SHOULDN'T OPEN MY EYES.
...IT'S JUST GOING TO BE HORRIBLE, ISN'T IT?
YEP.
THE CHAINS ARE DAMPENING OUR POWERS.
OF COURSE THEY ARE.
HRRRRR...
IF ANYONE WANTS TO STOP THIS THING FROM EATING MY FACE OFF, NOW WOULD BE A GOOD TIME TO DO IT.
WHAT DO I GET IN EXCHANGE?
IF ANYONE OTHER THAN ROCKSLIDE--
CRNK!
?

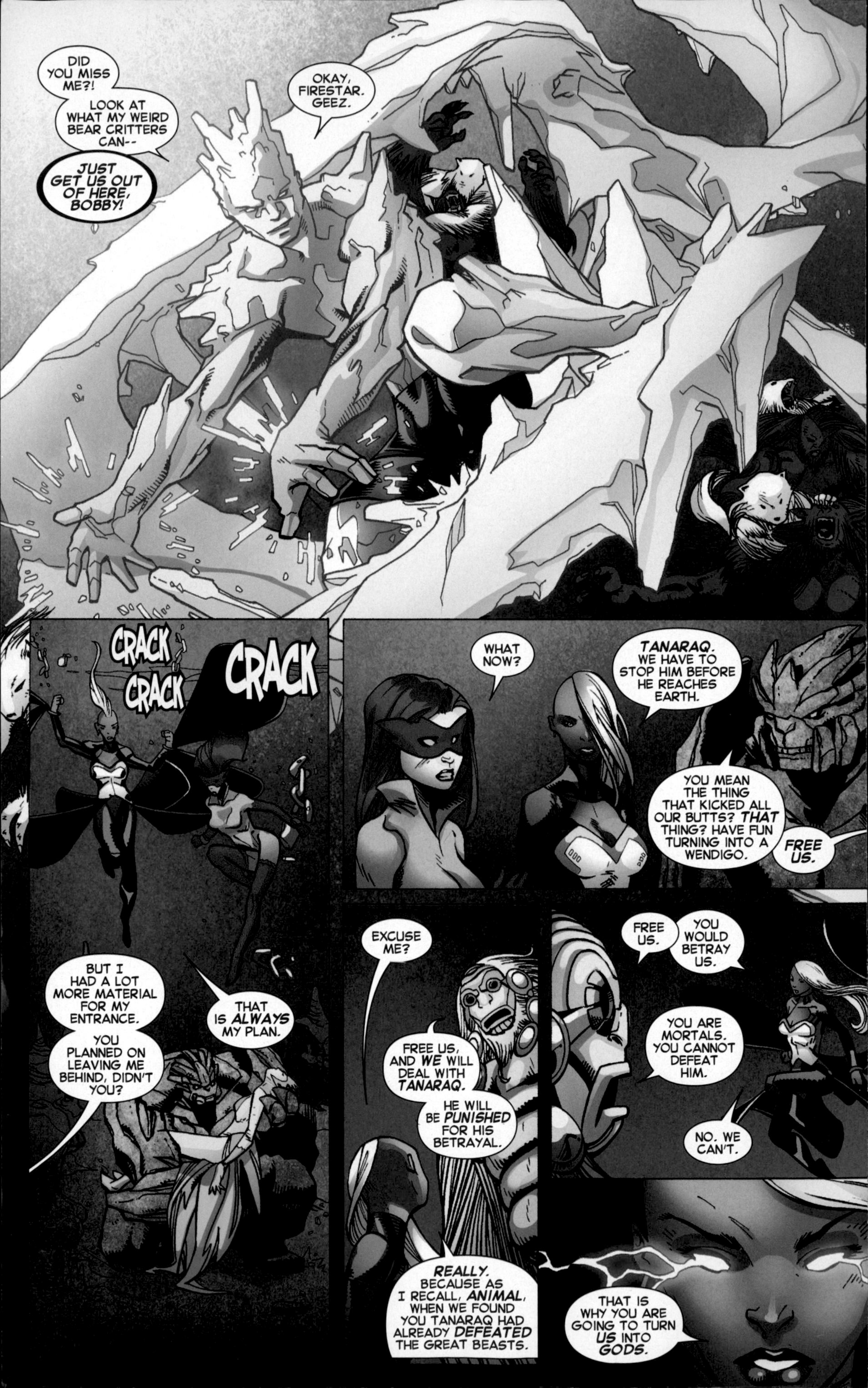
DID YOU MISS ME?! LOOK AT WHAT MY WEIRD BEAR CRITTERS CAN--
JUST GET US OUT OF HERE, BOBBY!
OKAY, FIRESTAR. GEEZ.
CRACK
CRACK
CRACK
BUT I HAD A LOT MORE MATERIAL FOR MY ENTRANCE.
YOU PLANNED ON LEAVING ME BEHIND, DIDN'T YOU?
THAT IS ALWAYS MY PLAN.
WHAT NOW?
TANARAQ. WE HAVE TO STOP HIM BEFORE HE REACHES EARTH.
YOU MEAN THE THING THAT KICKED ALL OUR BUTTS? THAT THING? HAVE FUN TURNING INTO A WENDIGO.
FREE US.
EXCUSE ME?
FREE US, AND WE WILL DEAL WITH TANARAQ.
HE WILL BE PUNISHED FOR HIS BETRAYAL.
FREE US.
YOU WOULD BETRAY US.
YOU ARE MORTALS. YOU CANNOT DEFEAT HIM.
NO. WE CAN'T.
REALLY. BECAUSE AS I RECALL, ANIMAL, WHEN WE FOUND YOU TANARAQ HAD ALREADY DEFEATED THE GREAT BEASTS.
THAT IS WHY YOU ARE GOING TO TURN US INTO GODS.

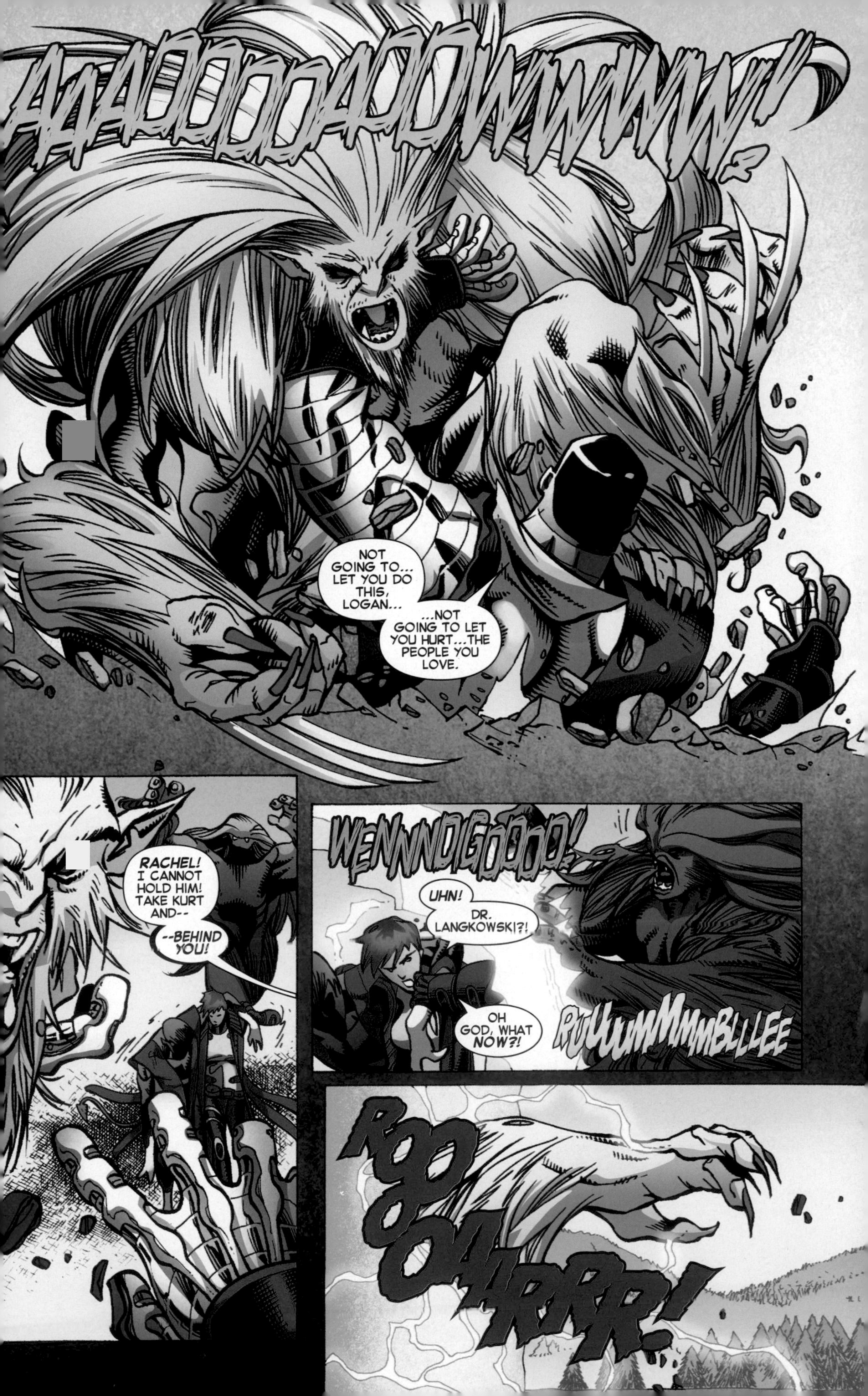
AAAOOOOAOOWWWWW!
NOT GOING TO... LET YOU DO THIS, LOGAN...
...NOT GOING TO LET YOU HURT...THE PEOPLE YOU LOVE.
RACHEL! I CANNOT HOLD HIM! TAKE KURT AND--
--BEHIND YOU!
WENNNDIGOOOO!
UHN!
DR. LANGKOWSKI?!
OH GOD, WHAT NOW?!
RUUUMMMMBLLLEE
ROOOOAHRRR!

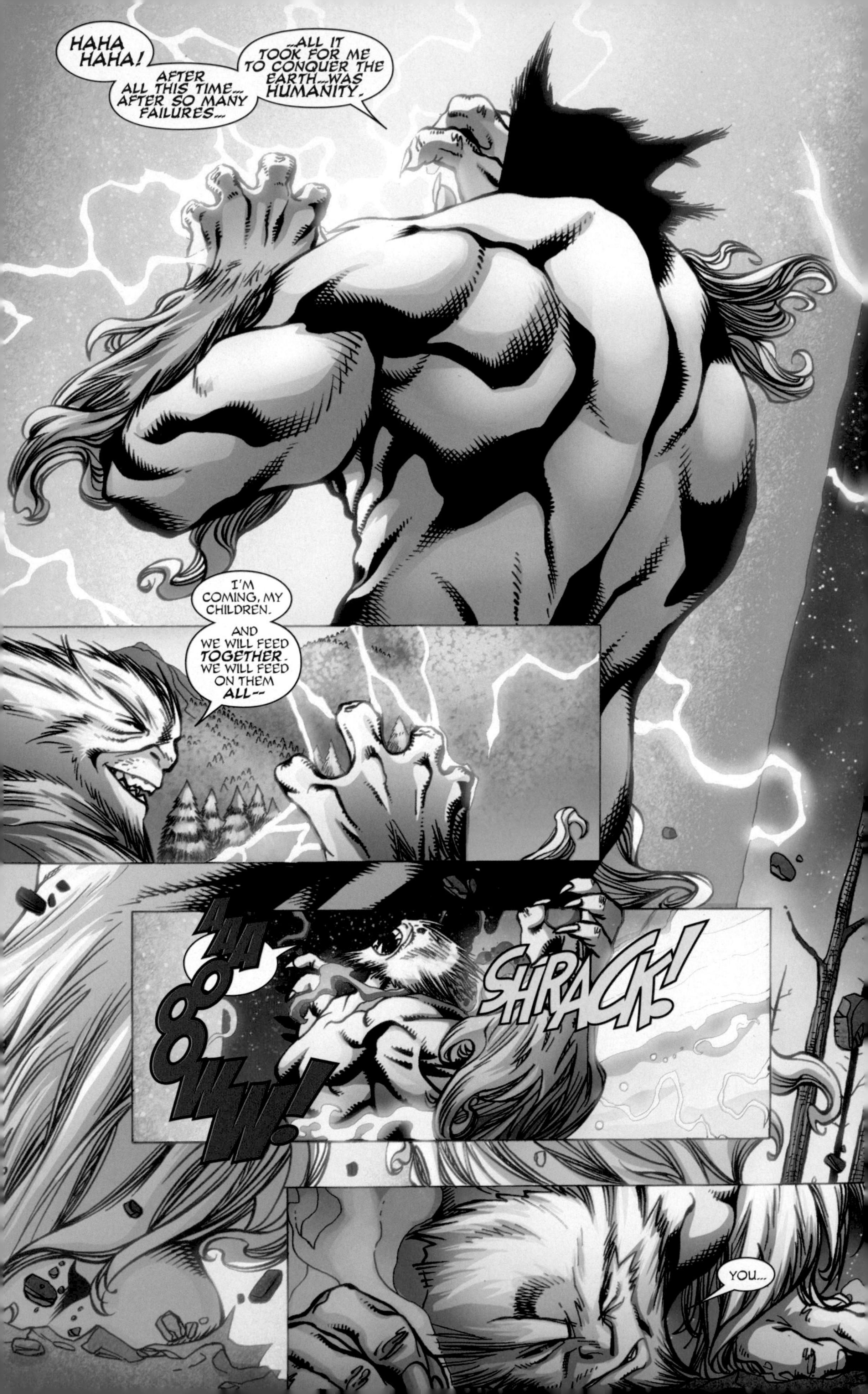
HAHA HAHA!
AFTER ALL THIS TIME... AFTER SO MANY FAILURES...
...ALL IT TOOK FOR ME TO CONQUER THE EARTH...WAS HUMANITY.
I'M COMING, MY CHILDREN.
AND WE WILL FEED TOGETHER. WE WILL FEED ON THEM ALL--
AAAOOOWW!
SHRACK!
YOU...

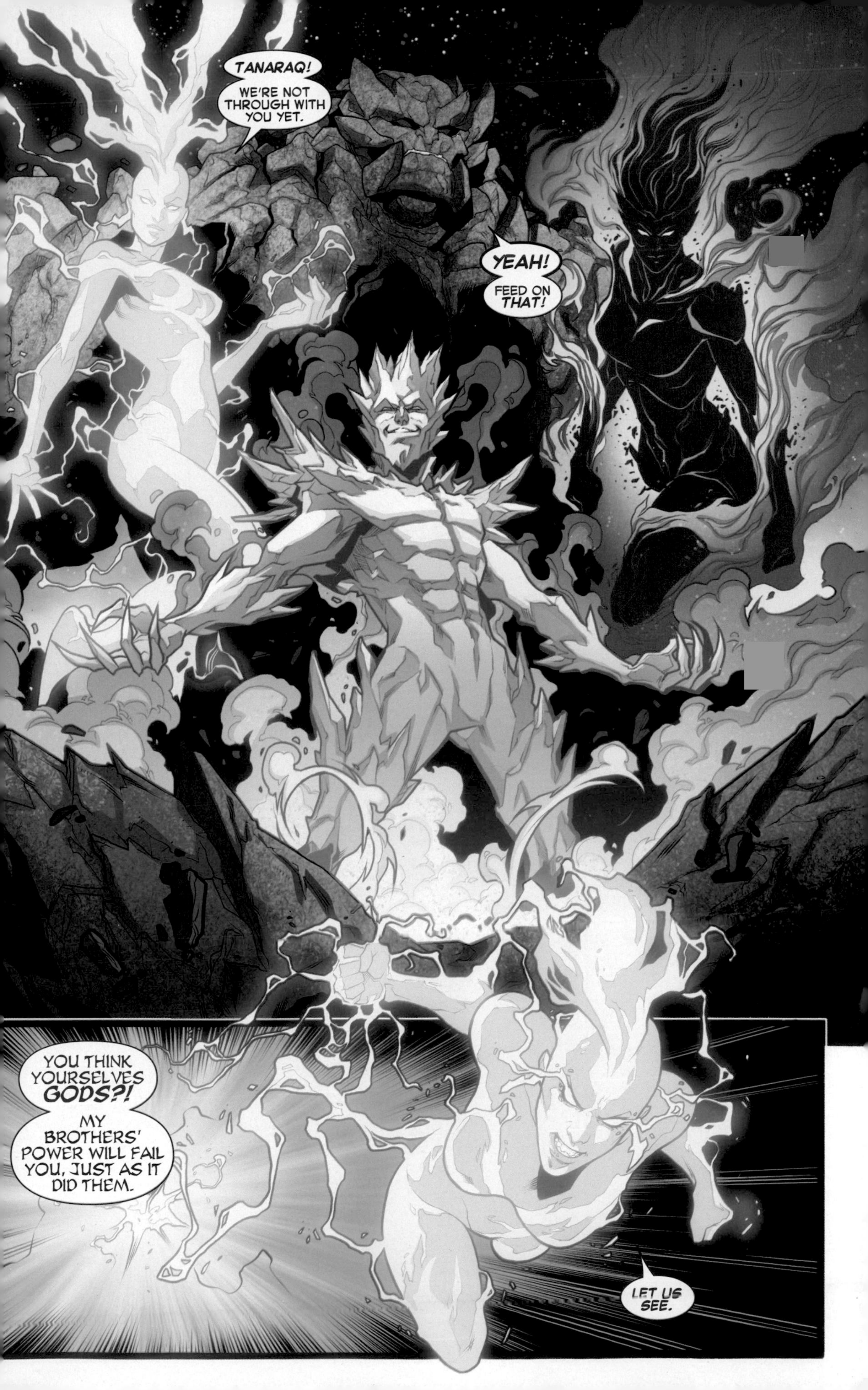
TANARAQ! WE'RE NOT THROUGH WITH YOU YET.
YEAH! FEED ON THAT!
YOU THINK YOURSELVES GODS?!
MY BROTHERS' POWER WILL FAIL YOU, JUST AS IT DID THEM.
LET US SEE.

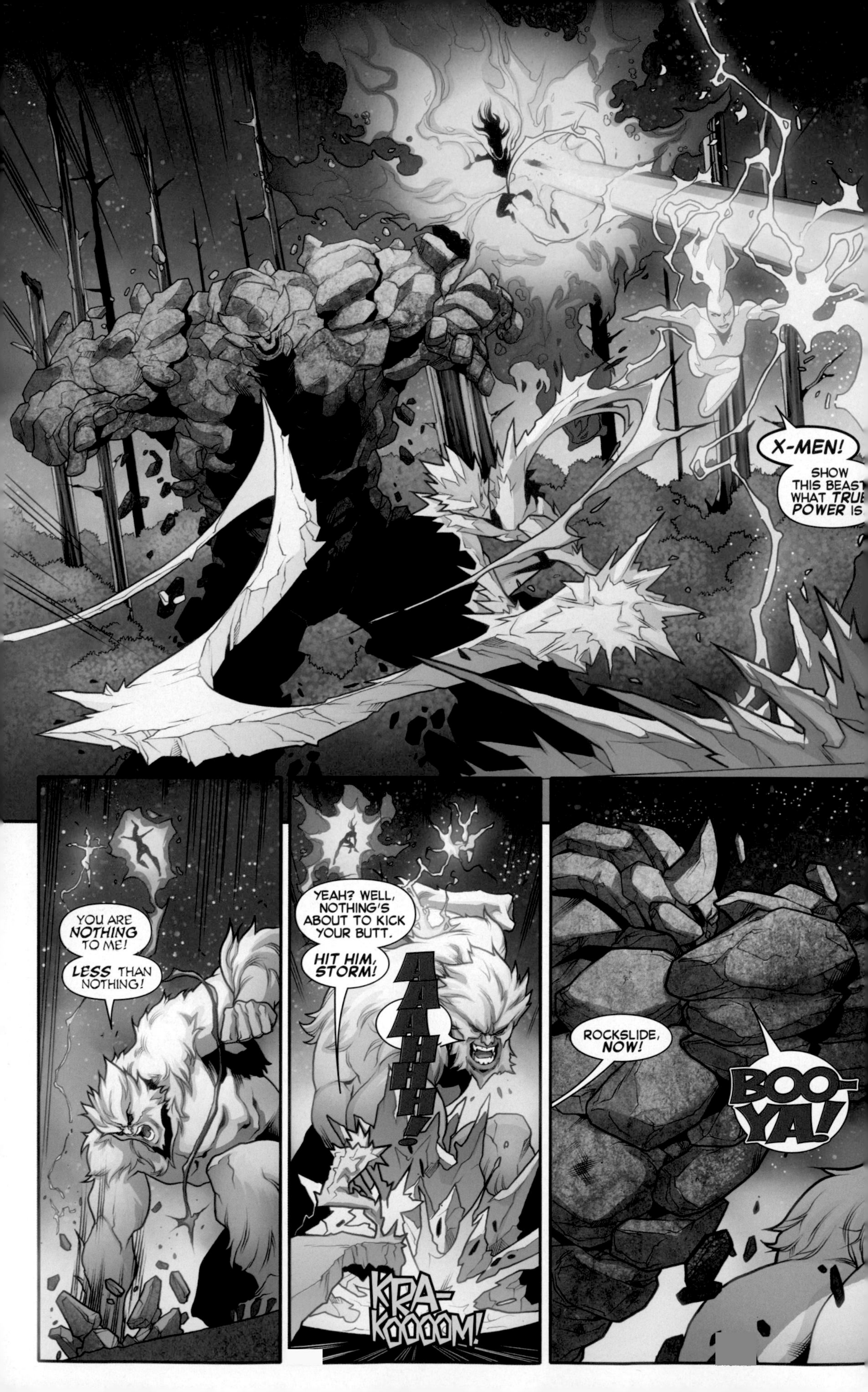
X-MEN!
SHOW THIS BEAST WHAT TRUE POWER IS
YOU ARE NOTHING TO ME!
LESS THAN NOTHING!
YEAH? WELL, NOTHING'S ABOUT TO KICK YOUR BUTT.
HIT HIM, STORM!
AAAHHHHH!
KRA-KOOOOM!
ROCKSLIDE, NOW!
BOO-YA!

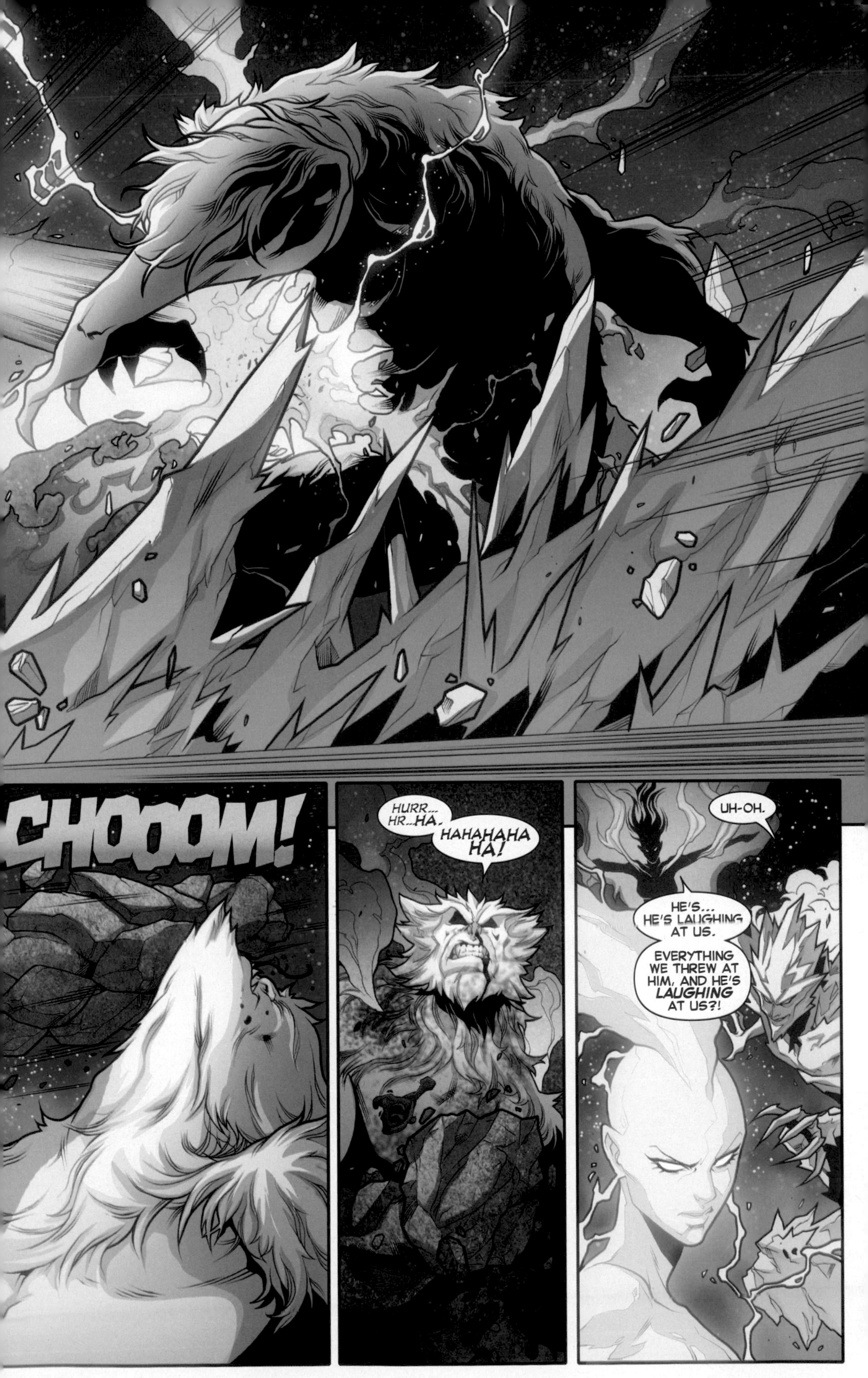
CHOOOM!
HURR... HR...HA.
HAHAHAHA HA!
UH-OH.
HE'S... HE'S LAUGHING AT US.
EVERYTHING WE THREW AT HIM, AND HE'S LAUGHING AT US?!

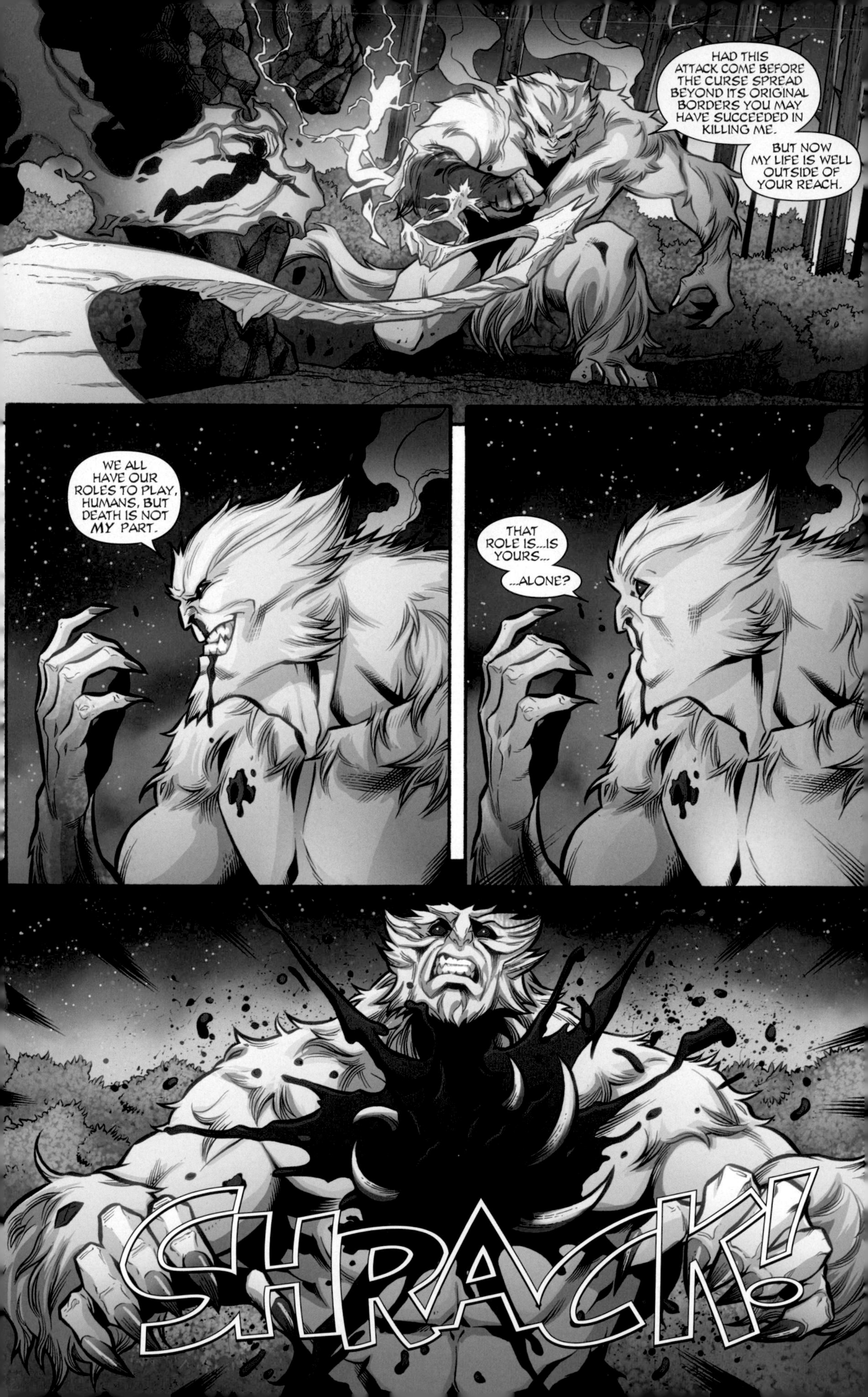
HAD THIS ATTACK COME BEFORE THE CURSE SPREAD BEYOND ITS ORIGINAL BORDERS YOU MAY HAVE SUCCEEDED IN KILLING ME.
BUT NOW MY LIFE IS WELL OUTSIDE OF YOUR REACH.
WE ALL HAVE OUR ROLES TO PLAY, HUMANS, BUT DEATH IS NOT MY PART.
THAT ROLE IS...IS YOURS...
...ALONE?
SHRACK!

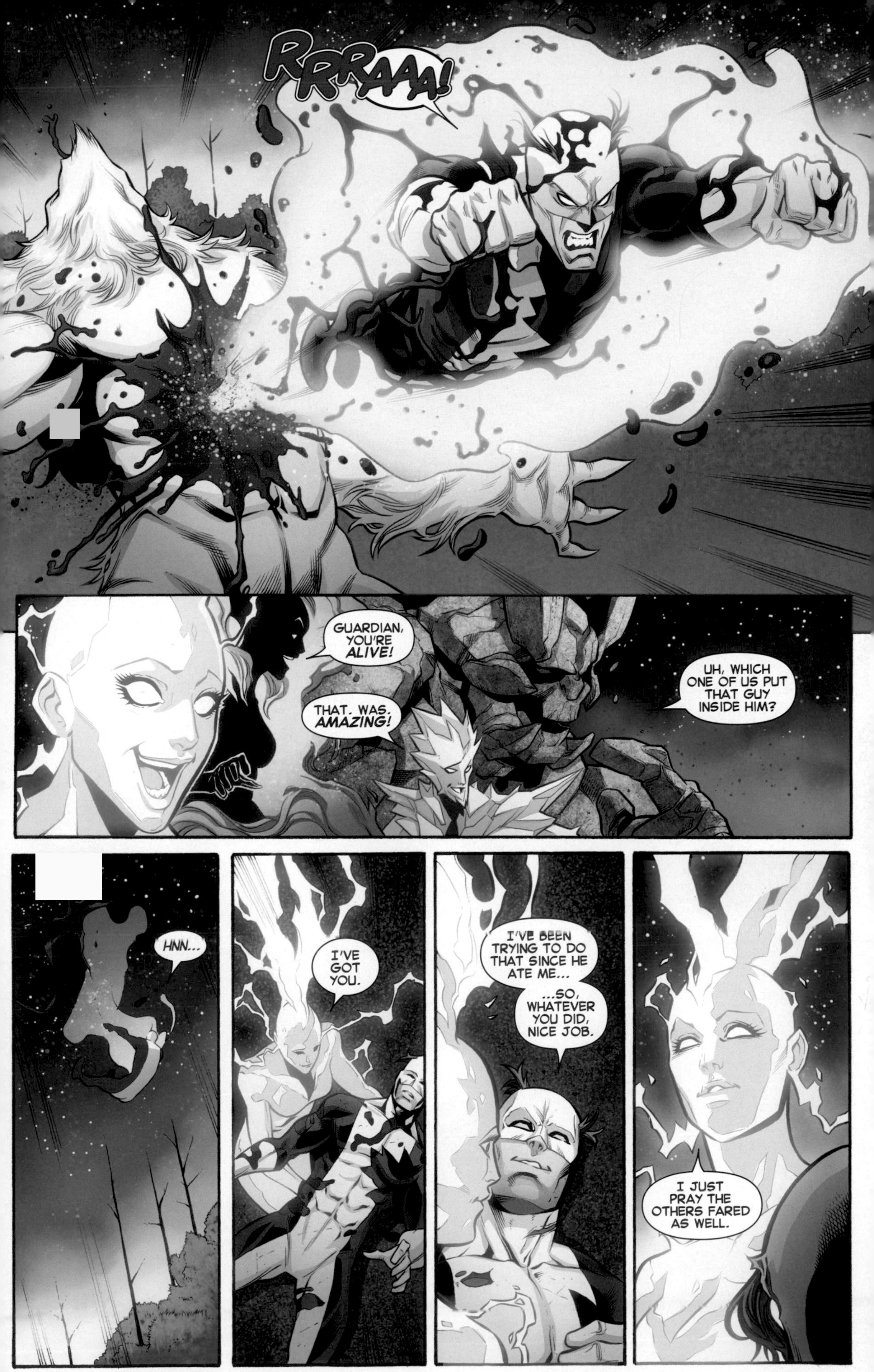
RRRAAA!
GUARDIAN, YOU'RE ALIVE!
THAT. WAS. AMAZING!
UH, WHICH ONE OF US PUT THAT GUY INSIDE HIM?
HNN...
I'VE GOT YOU.
I'VE BEEN TRYING TO DO THAT SINCE HE ATE ME...
...SO, WHATEVER YOU DID, NICE JOB.
I JUST PRAY THE OTHERS FARED AS WELL.

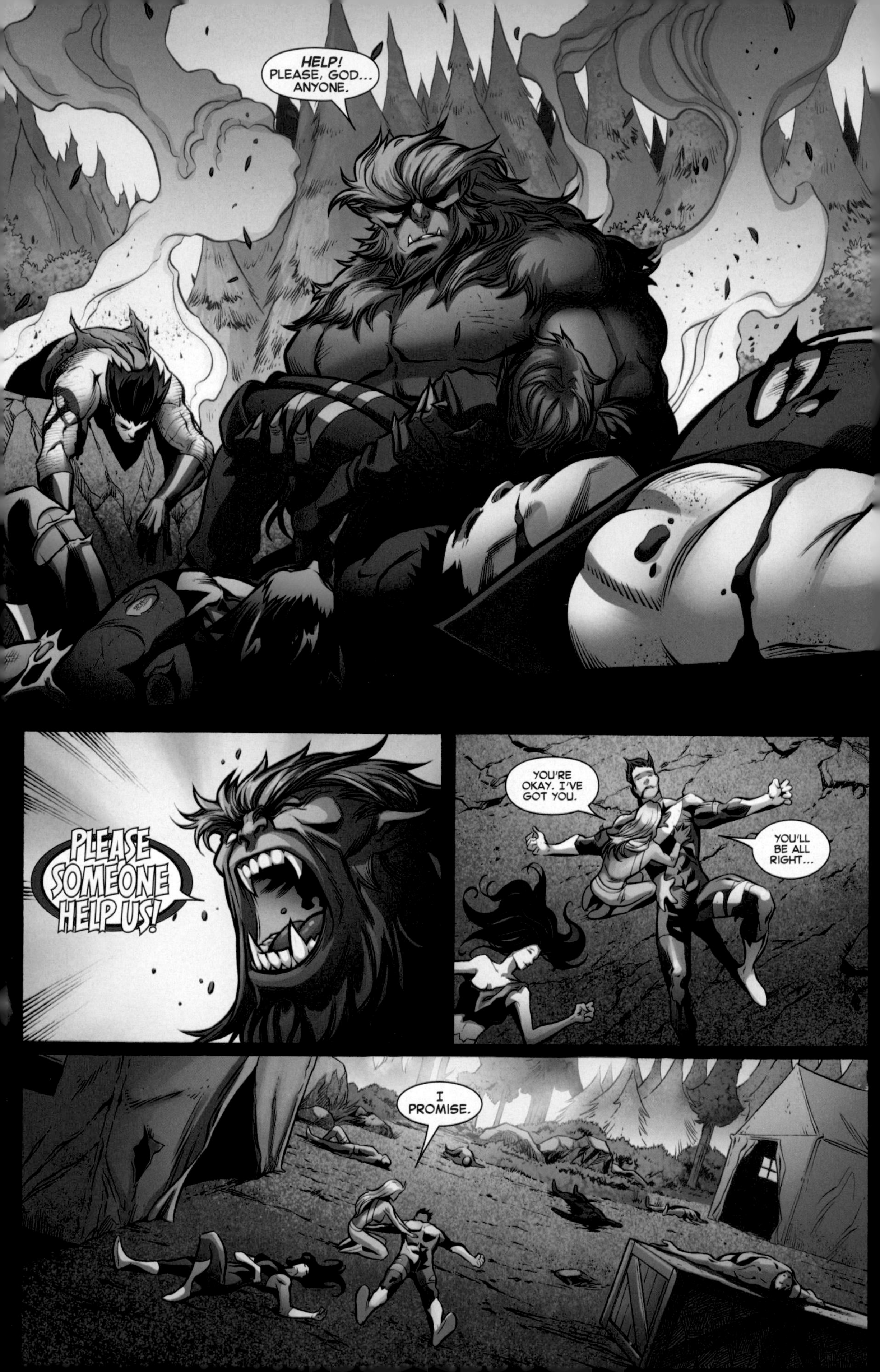
HELP! PLEASE, GOD... ANYONE.
PLEASE SOMEONE HELP US!
YOU'RE OKAY. I'VE GOT YOU.
YOU'LL BE ALL RIGHT...
I PROMISE.

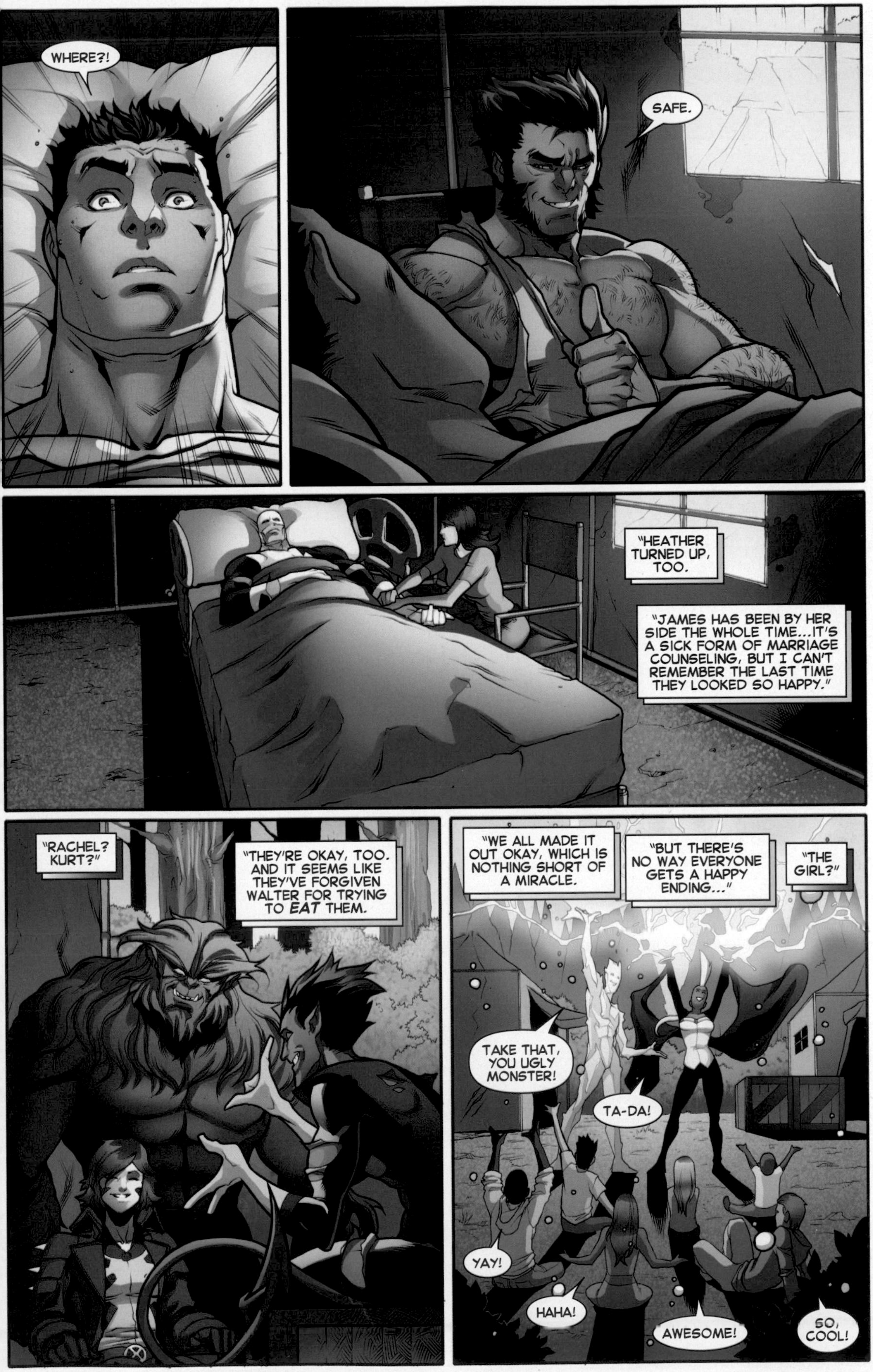
WHERE?!
SAFE.
"HEATHER TURNED UP, TOO.
"JAMES HAS BEEN BY HER SIDE THE WHOLE TIME...IT'S A SICK FORM OF MARRIAGE COUNSELING, BUT I CAN'T REMEMBER THE LAST TIME THEY LOOKED SO HAPPY."
"RACHEL? KURT?"
"THEY'RE OKAY, TOO. AND IT SEEMS LIKE THEY'VE FORGIVEN WALTER FOR TRYING TO EAT THEM.
"WE ALL MADE IT OUT OKAY, WHICH IS NOTHING SHORT OF A MIRACLE.
"BUT THERE'S NO WAY EVERYONE GETS A HAPPY ENDING..."
"THE GIRL?"
TAKE THAT, YOU UGLY MONSTER!
TA-DA!
YAY!
HAHA!
AWESOME!
SO, COOL!

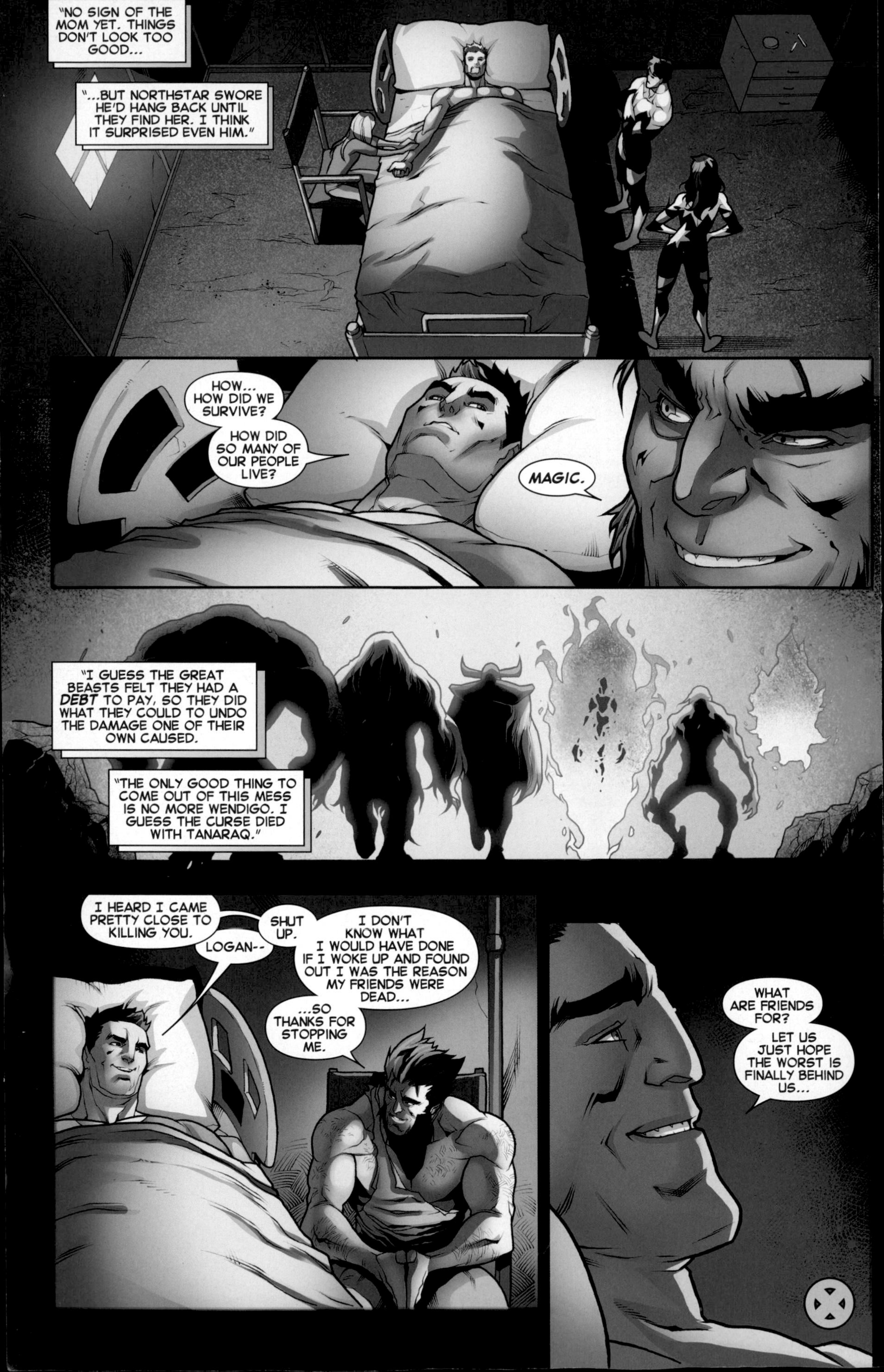

"NO SIGN OF THE MOM YET. THINGS DON'T LOOK TOO GOOD...
"...BUT NORTHSTAR SWORE HE'D HANG BACK UNTIL THEY FIND HER. I THINK IT SURPRISED EVEN HIM."
HOW... HOW DID WE SURVIVE?
HOW DID SO MANY OF OUR PEOPLE LIVE?
MAGIC.
"I GUESS THE GREAT BEASTS FELT THEY HAD A DEBT TO PAY, SO THEY DID WHAT THEY COULD TO UNDO THE DAMAGE ONE OF THEIR OWN CAUSED.
"THE ONLY GOOD THING TO COME OUT OF THIS MESS IS NO MORE WENDIGO. I GUESS THE CURSE DIED WITH TANARAQ."
I HEARD I CAME PRETTY CLOSE TO KILLING YOU.
LOGAN--
SHUT UP.
I DON'T KNOW WHAT I WOULD HAVE DONE IF I WOKE UP AND FOUND OUT I WAS THE REASON MY FRIENDS WERE DEAD...
...SO THANKS FOR STOPPING ME.
WHAT ARE FRIENDS FOR?
LET US JUST HOPE THE WORST IS FINALLY BEHIND US...

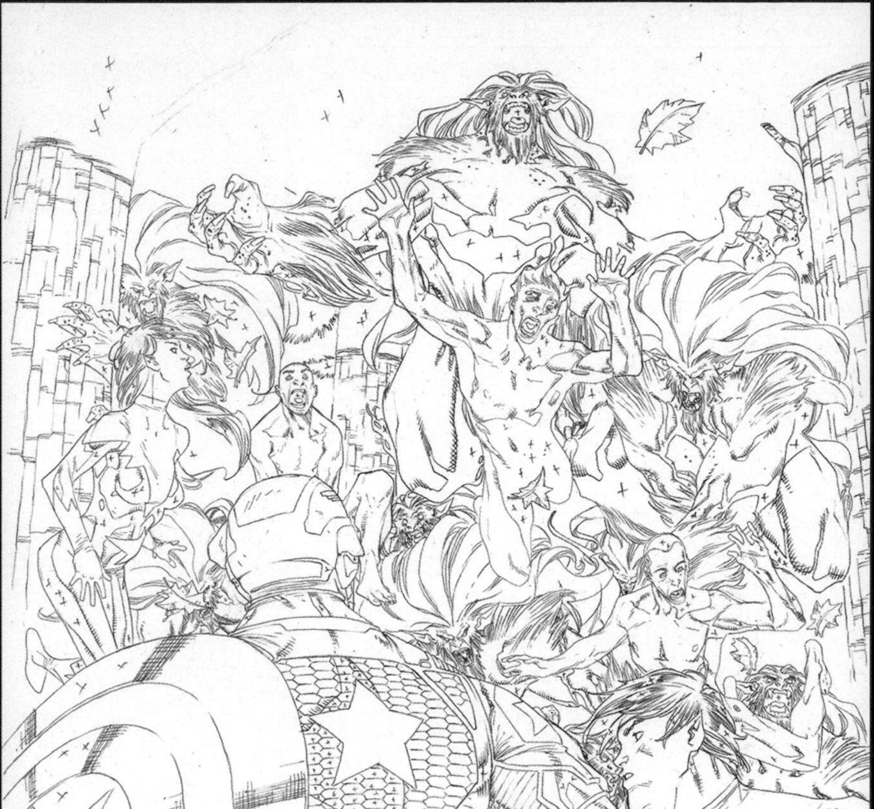

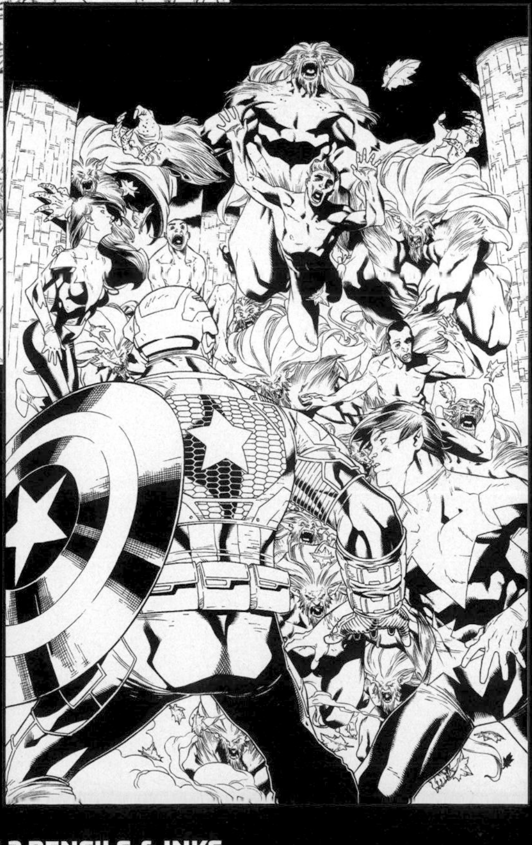

AMAZING X-MEN #11, PAGE 2 PENCILS & INKS
BY CARLO BARBERI & WALDEN WONG

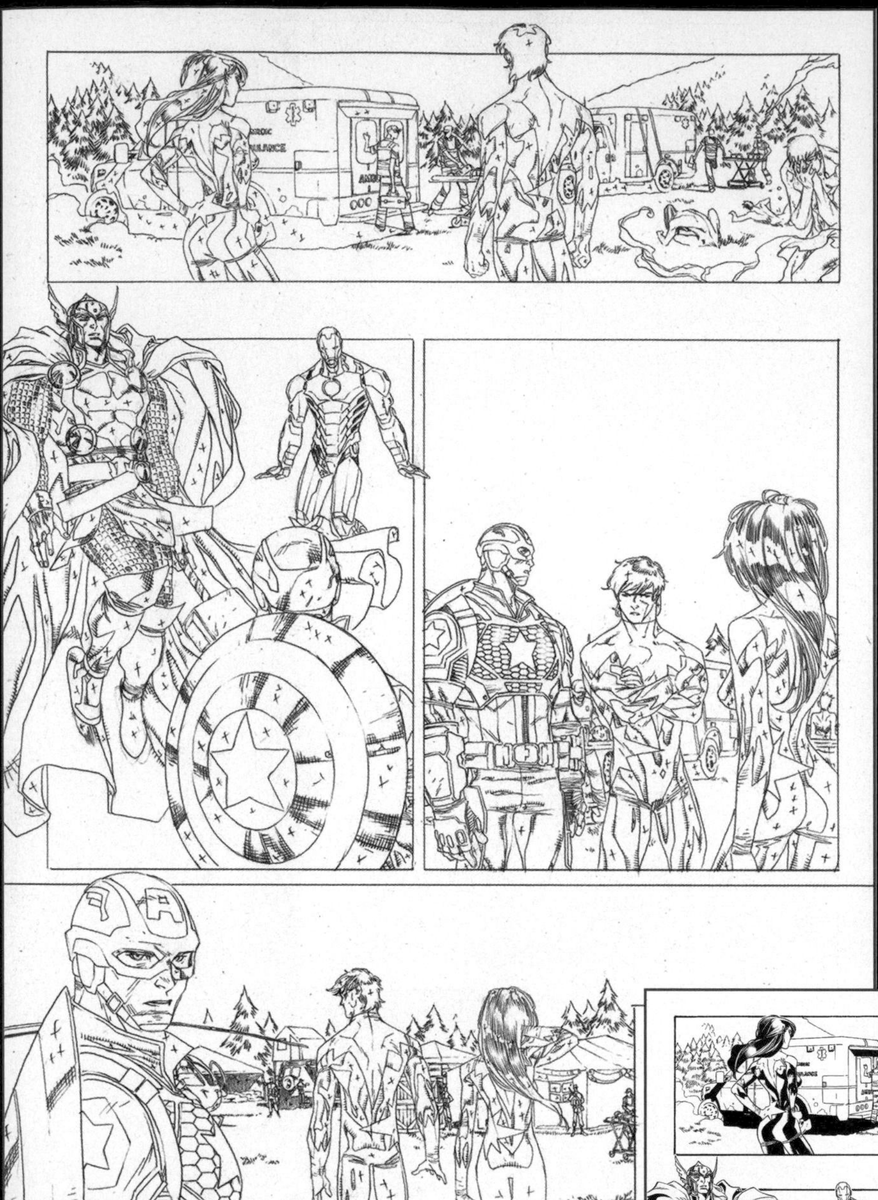

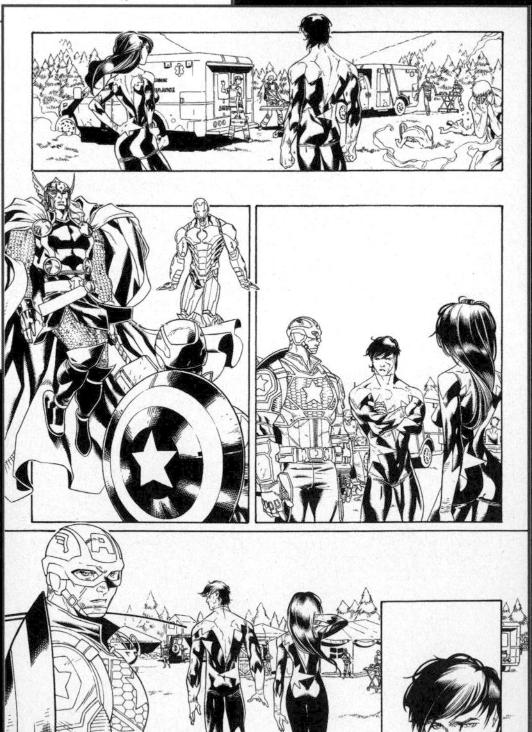

AMAZING X-MEN #11, PAGE 3 PENCILS & INKS
BY CARLO BARBERI & WALDEN WONG

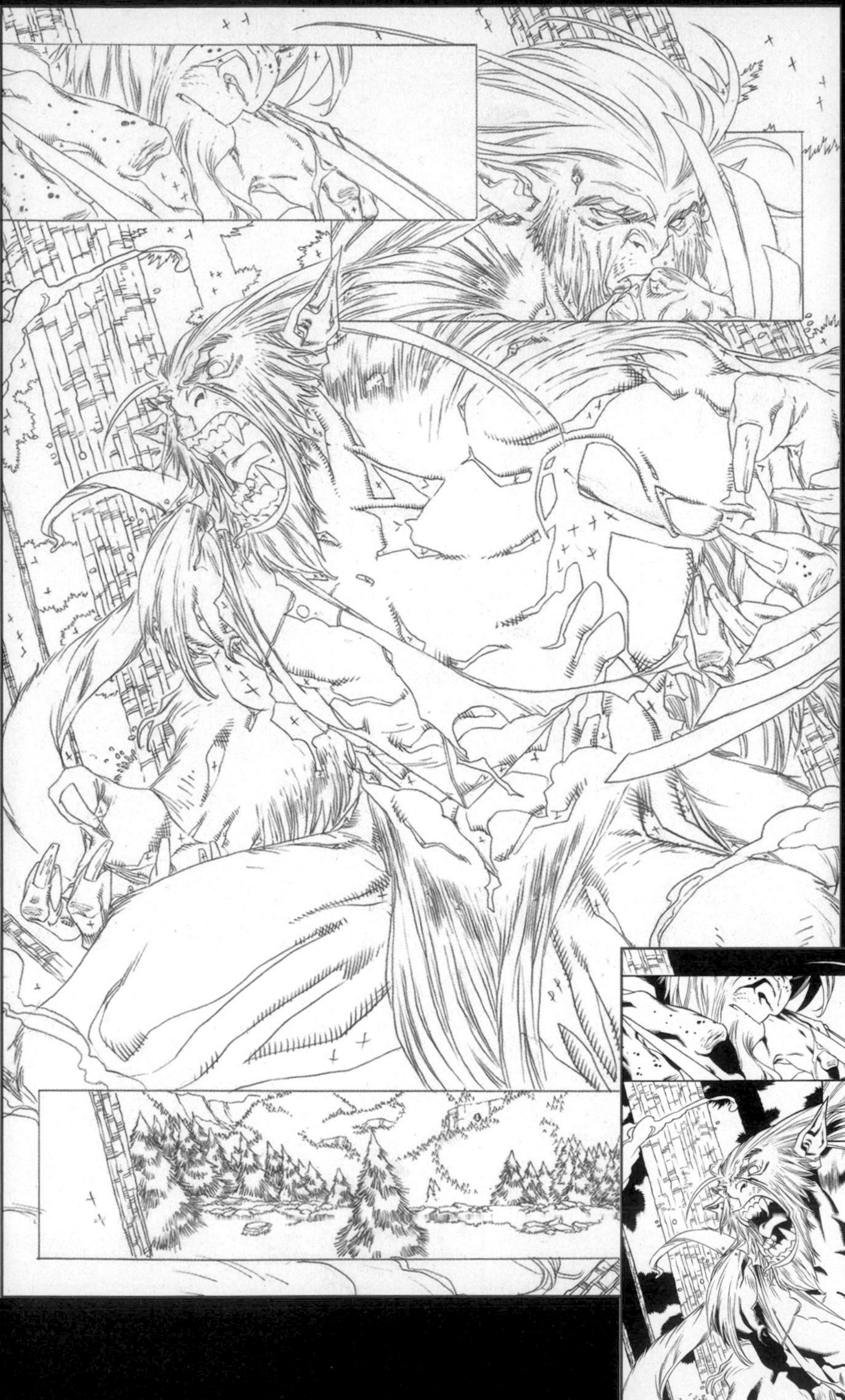

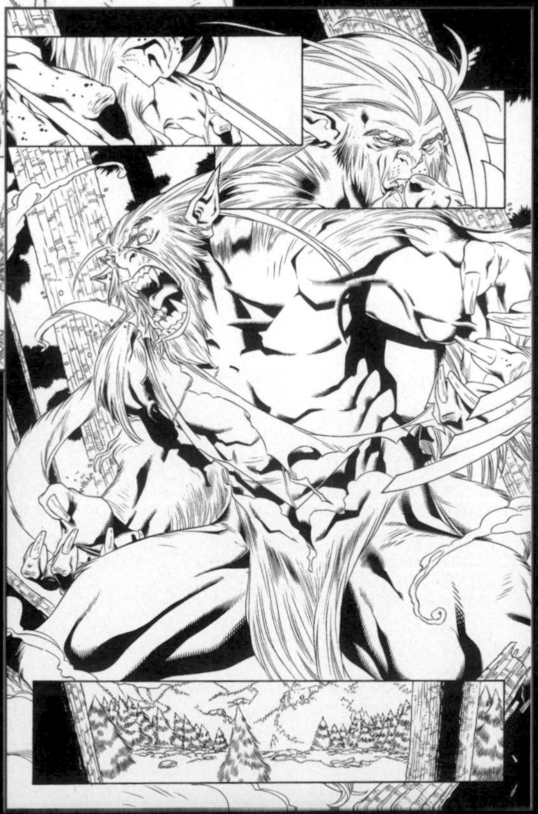

AMAZING X-MEN #11, PAGE 4 PENCILS & INKS
BY CARLO BARBERI & WALDEN WONG

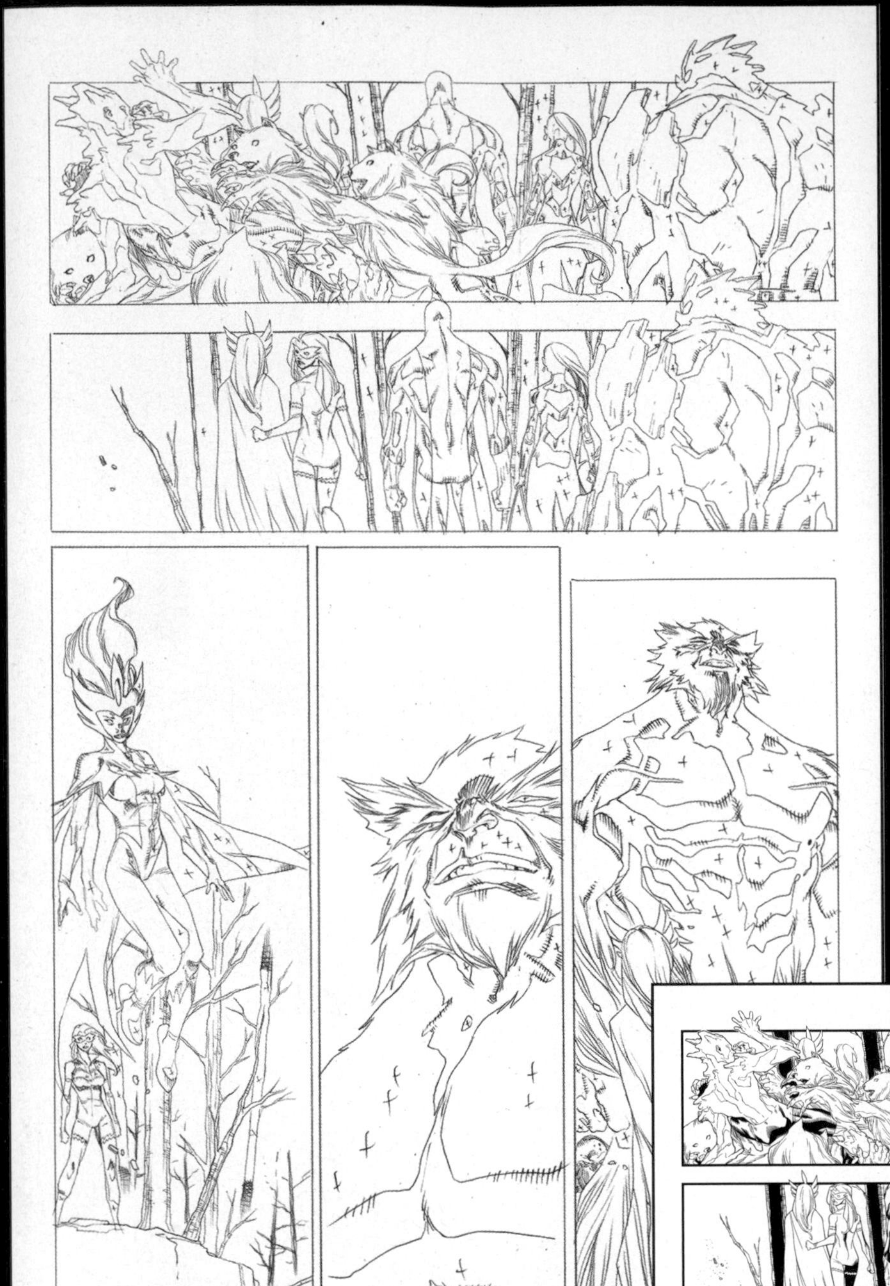

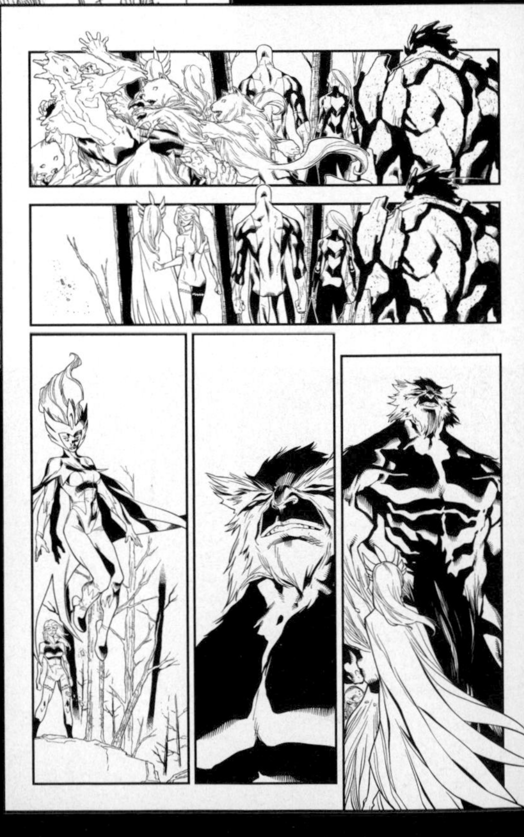

AMAZING X-MEN #11, PAGE 18 PENCILS & INKS
BY CARLO BARBERI & JUAN VLASCO

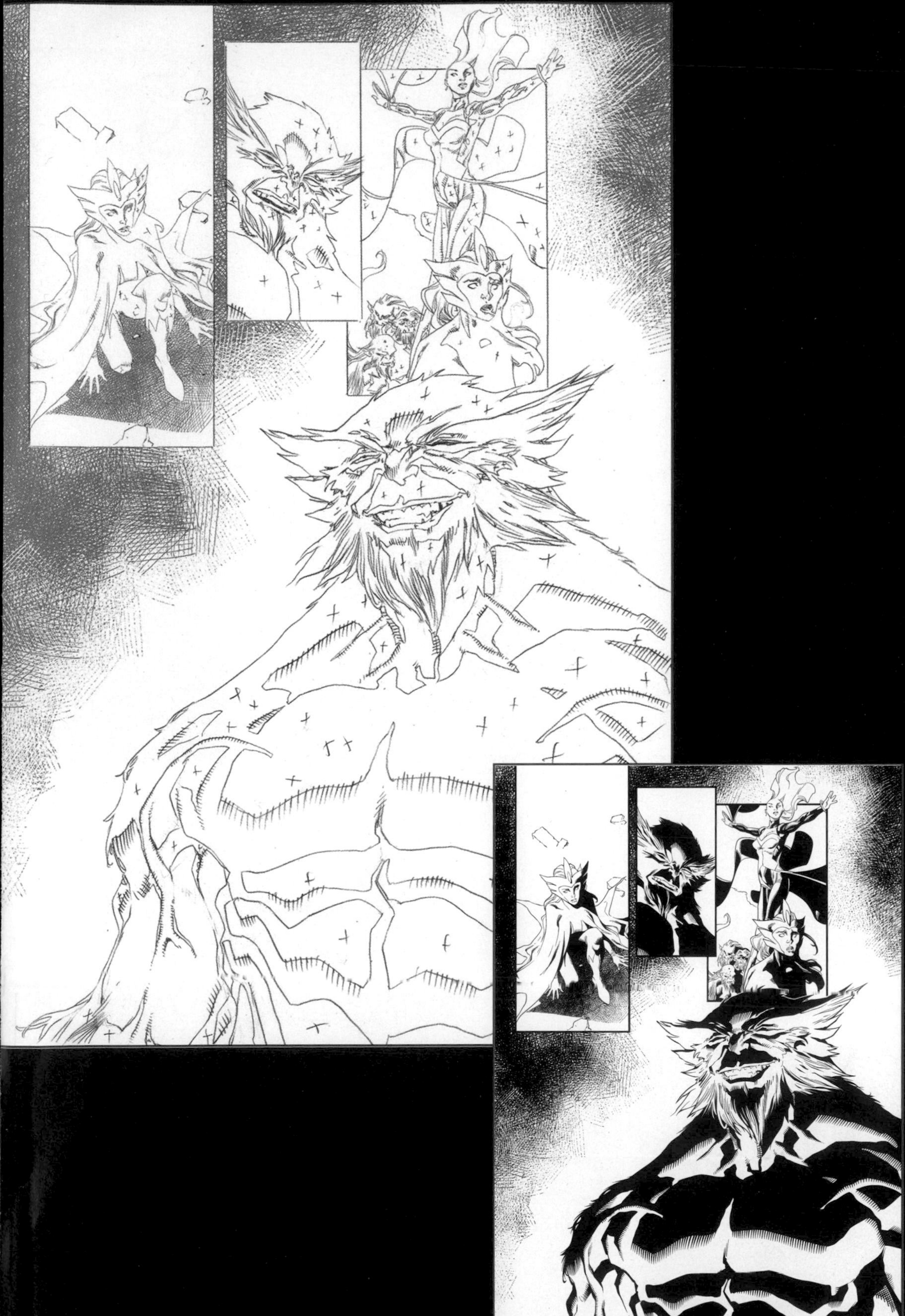

AMAZING X-MEN #11, PAGE 19 PENCILS & INKS
BY CARLO BARBERI & JUAN VLASCO

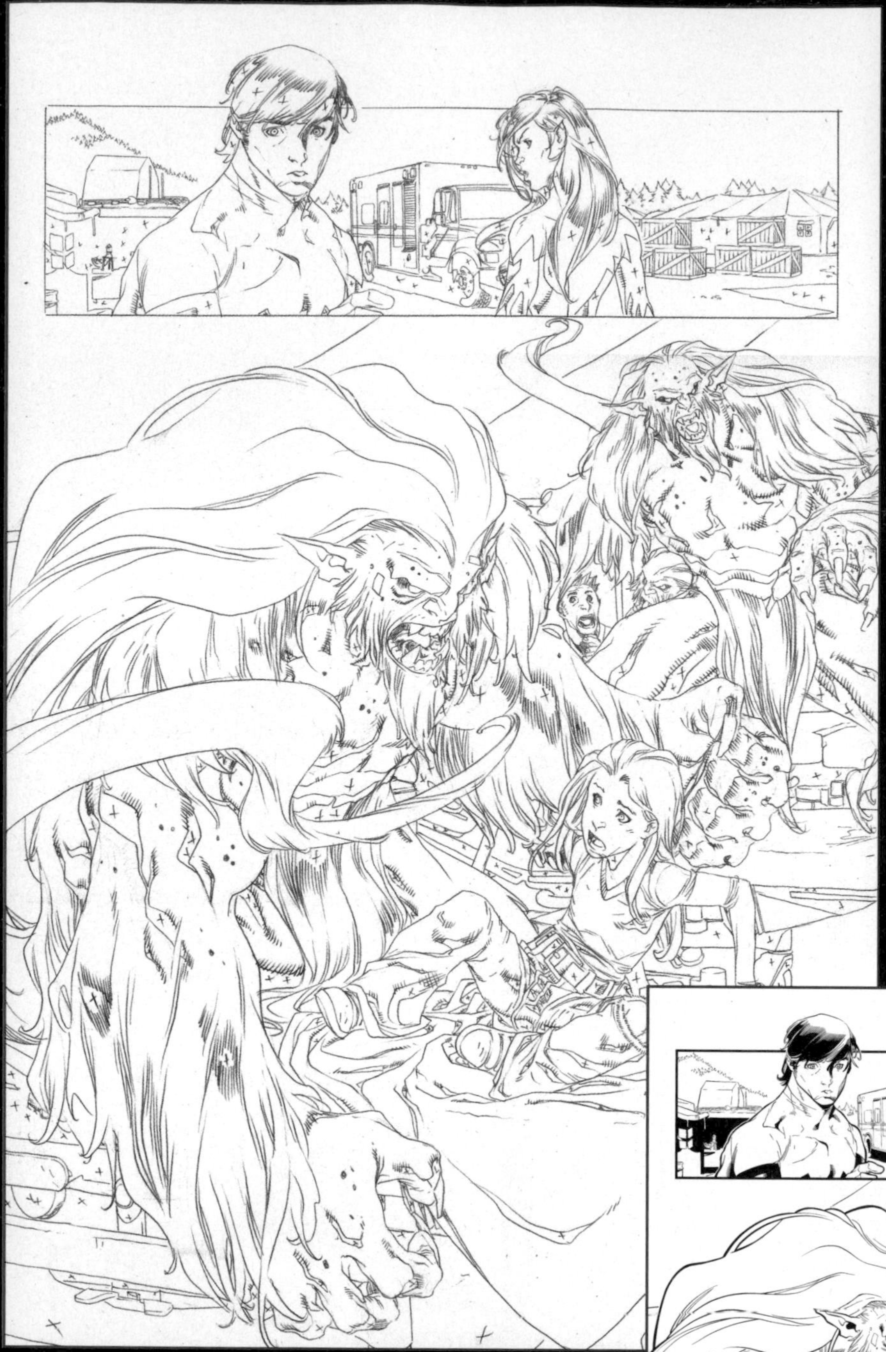

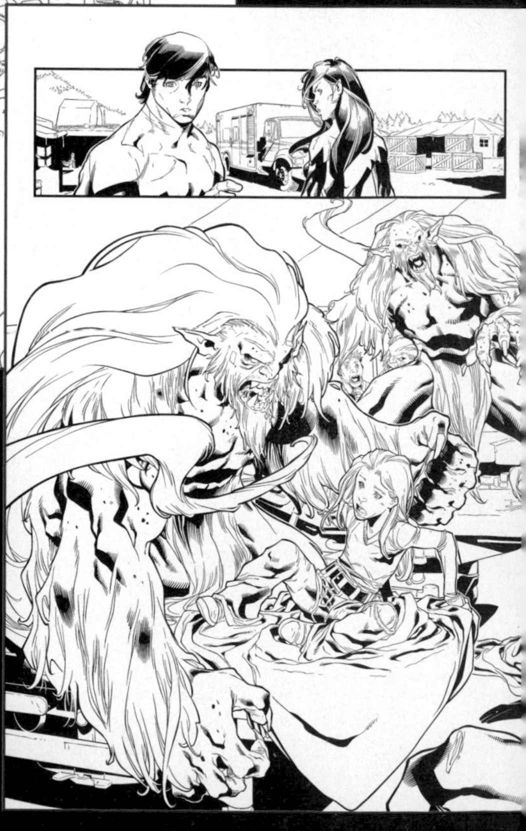

AMAZING X-MEN #11, PAGE 20 PENCILS & INKS
BY CARLO BARBERI & JUAN VLASCO